Critical Issues in Educational Leadership Series
Joseph Murphy, Series Editor

Redesigning Accountability Systems for Education
SUSAN H. FUHRMAN AND RICHARD F. ELMORE, EDS.

Taking Account of Charter Schools:
What's Happened and What's Next?
KATRINA E. BULKLEY AND PRISCILLA WOHLSTETTER, EDS.

Learning Together, Leading Together:
Changing Schools through Professional Learning Communities
SHIRLEY M. HORD, ED.

Who Governs Our Schools?
Changing Roles and Responsibilities
DAVID T. CONLEY

School Districts and Instructional Renewal
AMY M. HIGHTOWER, MICHAEL S. KNAPP,
JULIE A. MARSH, AND MILBREY W. MCLAUGHLIN, EDS.

Effort and Excellence in Urban Classrooms:
Expecting—and Getting—Success with All Students
DICK CORBETT, BRUCE WILSON, AND BELINDA WILLIAMS

Developing Educational Leaders: A Working Model:
The Learning Community in Action
CYNTHIA J. NORRIS, BRUCE G. BARNETT,
MARGARET R. BASOM, AND DIANE M. YERKES

Understanding and Assessing the Charter School Movement
JOSEPH MURPHY AND CATHERINE DUNN SHIFFMAN

School Choice in Urban America:
Magnet Schools and the Pursuit of Equity
CLAIRE SMREKAR AND ELLEN GOLDRING

Lessons from High-Performing Hispanic Schools:
Creating Learning Communities
PEDRO REYES, JAY D. SCRIBNER, AND
ALICIA PAREDES SCRIBNER, EDS.

Schools for Sale: Why Free Market Policies
Won't Improve America's Schools, and What Will
ERNEST R. HOUSE

Reclaiming Educational Administration as a Caring Profession
LYNN G. BECK

Redesigning Accountability Systems for Education

EDITED BY

SUSAN H. FUHRMAN
RICHARD F. ELMORE

Teachers College, Columbia University
New York and London

Published by Teachers College Press, 1234 Amsterdam Avenue, New York, NY 10027

Chapter 2 is a reprint from the *Harvard Educational Review*.
Chapter 9 copyright © Martin Carnoy and Susanna Loeb.

Library of Congress Cataloging-in-Publication Data

Redesigning accountability systems for education / edited by Susan H. Fuhrman, Richard F. Elmore.
    p. cm. — (Critical issues in educational leadership series)
   Includes bibliographical references and index.
   ISBN 0-8077-4425-5 (cloth : alk. paper)
     1. Educational accountability—United States.   2. Competency based education—United States.   3. School improvement programs—United States. I. Fuhrman, Susan.   II. Elmore, Richard F.   III. Series.
   LB2086.22.R433 2004
   379.1'58—dc22   2003059537

ISBN 0-8077-4425-5 (cloth)

Printed on acid-free paper

Manufactured in the United States of America

11 10 09 08 07 06 05 04   8 7 6 5 4 3 2 1

Contents

Part IV   MOVING FORWARD: REFINING ACCOUNTABILITY SYSTEMS

Acknowledgments

Redesigning Accountability Systems for Education is the result of a collaborative effort between the Consortium for Policy Research in Education (CPRE) and the Center for Research on Evaluation, Standards, and Student Testing (CRESST). Both CPRE and CRESST receive key funding from the U.S. Department of Education's Institute of Education Sciences (Grants No. R308A960003 and R305B960002).

CPRE unites five of the nation's leading research institutions to improve elementary and secondary education through research on policy, finance, school reform, and school governance. CPRE studies alternative approaches to education reform in order to determine how state and local policies can promote student learning. Members of CPRE are the University of Pennsylvania, Harvard University, Stanford University, the University of Michigan, and the University of Wisconsin–Madison.

CRESST's mission focuses on the assessment of educational quality, addressing persistent problems in the design and use of assessment systems to serve multiple purposes. CRESST is a partnership of the University of California–Los Angeles, the University of Colorado, Stanford University, RAND, the University of Pittsburgh, the University of Southern California, the Educational Testing Service, and the University of Cambridge–United Kingdom.

In February 2001, CPRE and CRESST co-sponsored a meeting on accountability issues and thereafter commissioned a series of papers. This volume is the result of those efforts.

We gratefully acknowledge Deborah Nelson, who compiled the volume and patiently worked with the authors, the editors, and Teachers College Press. We also would like to thank Robb Sewell who copyedited and proofread each chapter, and Kelly Stanton who handled the logistics for the meeting. We appreciate the support and patience of Brian Ellerbeck and Cheryl DeJong-Lambert of Teachers College Press. Finally, we wish to thank Elizabeth Demarest, formerly of the Office of Educational Research and Improvement, who provided helpful comments on the papers.

Susan H. Fuhrman
Richard F. Elmore

PART I

INTRODUCTION

Chapter 1

Introduction

Susan H. Fuhrman

This book is about understanding and redesigning accountability systems. The accountability systems we write about are those established over the past 5 to 10 years, mostly at the state level, although a number of districts have similar systems. These systems are distinguished by their attention to school-level performance and by their inclusion of consequences for that performance. They are quite different from earlier approaches to accountability that attended primarily to district compliance with state regulations. The new systems grow out of a climate that makes strong parallels between education and business; they intend to focus schools on the bottom line. They also reflect an attempt, strong in rhetoric if not reality, by states to back off from detailed regulations about the process of education. The new systems have an explicit theory of action about improving student achievement that stresses the motivation of teachers, students, and administrators.

In this book we address that theory of action, looking at how these new systems are framed, their technical specifications, their implementation, and their effects. Our purpose is to illustrate the technical, political, and educational challenges these systems pose. It is our hope that understanding these challenges will assist policy makers in their efforts to make mid-course corrections to these systems in ways that address some of the problems we write about.

NEW ACCOUNTABILITY SYSTEMS

All states currently have accountability systems of the type we examine in this book. The systems vary considerably from state to state. For example, 33 states set performance goals for schools, but they differ in the level of performance they set as a goal (e.g., basic or proficient), in the percentage of students required to meet the goal, and in the length of time schools are given to meet the goal. Time periods set by states range from 5 to 20 years (Goertz & Duffy, 2001).

Despite the differences, the systems share a number of characteristics that distinguish them from earlier efforts of states to keep tabs on local districts and schools.

The new systems are centered around student *performance* on state-wide assessments that are specifically developed for states or purchased commercially. Forty-eight states use a state assessment to measure performance; Iowa and Nebraska require districts to test in certain grades but don't specify the assessment (Goertz & Duffy, 2001). Schools are held accountable either for achieving a certain level of performance (e.g., a percentage of students achieving at a "proficient" level) or for increasing performance from assessment period to assessment period. Some states use both status and gain measures. In most states, the assessments are said to be aligned with state standards for student learning, although as a number of authors in this volume point out, alignment is frequently partial and insufficient. Performance measures frequently are combined with other outcome measures, such as graduation rates, and some process measures, such as attendance, into indices that are used as the central features of the system.

The focus on performance, on actual student achievement, is quite a change from the way states previously gauged the health of local schools. Mostly, states were interested in whether localities complied with the input and process standards the states set to ensure that a minimum level of education was being provided across districts. Through district self-reports and occasional visits, they monitored fiscal management, the use of certified teachers, the presence of curricula, the state of facilities, the provision of programs for special-needs students, and the like.

The new systems are focused on *schools and students*. Test scores and other measures incorporated into indices are collected at the school level. In addition, by 2008, 28 states will require that students pass a state-administered test for high school graduation (Goertz & Duffy, 2001). State-required graduation testing dates back to the 1970s when many states developed minimal competency exams. Testing also has been used as a promotion requirement. But the major state focus for accountability in the past was on the district, which was the unit receiving state aid for education. States were interested in whether districts were providing services in compliance with law and regulation. Whether individual schools were functioning well was considered a local matter. In fact, the underlying assumption was that the state role focused mostly on ensuring some minimally equal threshold—through state aid and regulation about minimal inputs. It was considered beyond the state's reach in most states (New York, with its historic Regents system, may be an exception) to ensure that districts used their resources well to promote student learning.

The new systems include *consequences* for poor performance. Forty states produce report cards making school assessment data public; the other 10 states require localities to do the same. Only 13 states, however, use public reporting as the primary mechanism for attaching stakes to assessment results; the others have more serious consequences. Nineteen states have monetary or nonmonetary rewards for exemplary performance. A majority of the states require school improvement planning for low-performing schools. Beyond that, remedies range from technical assistance to intervention. Nineteen states have policies enabling them to reconstitute schools, changing the staff and/or student body (Goertz & Duffy, 2001).

In the past, states might have denied poorly functioning districts accreditation, but the ultimate punishment for noncompliance with state law and regulation was the loss of state aid, which was understood to be conditional on conformance to state policy. However, states were loath to deny aid to students who were the victims rather than the agents of failure, and the ultimate step was rarely a realistic threat, much less actual punishment.

New state systems' emphases on performance, school-level improvement, and consequences are likely to become stronger as the provisions of the newly reauthorized Elementary and Secondary Education Act take hold. The "No Child Left Behind Act" of 2001 requires that states adopt single, statewide accountability systems, whereas in the past many states treated Title I students and other students differently. Annual tests of all students (in reading, mathematics, and eventually science) from grades 3–8 are the cornerstone of the new, unified systems. States must define the yearly progress schools must make on the assessments in a way that gets all students to proficiency in 12 years. Measurable objectives must be set for subgroups, including economically disadvantaged students, students from major economic and racial groups, students with disabilities, and limited English proficiency students. Schools failing to make yearly progress for 2 consecutive years must be identified by districts for improvement. Students have the right to transfer to another public school, and after a year to receive supplemental services, if progress is still not made. The district is to begin technical assistance, which must be supplemented by "corrective action," if progress is not forthcoming. School staff can be replaced, for example. After 2 years of corrective action, the district must restructure the school by, for example, closing it and reopening as a charter school, turning it over to the state, or contracting with a private management company (Education Funding Research Council, 2002).

ROOTS OF THE NEW ACCOUNTABILITY

From where did these ideas come? Why did states shift from focusing on inputs at the district level, with few if any consequences for noncompliance, to focusing on outputs, at the school level, with numerous consequences attached to various levels of performance?

The notion of focusing on *performance*, on outputs, can be traced to the influence of business leaders and ideas in education policy. In the 1980s, American business was unhappily comparing itself with other more productive economies, particularly in Asia. Many of the ideas that corporate leaders used to engineer company turnarounds—such as restructuring and quality benchmarking—were touted as applicable to the public sector as well. Particularly influential were notions about setting explicit goals and then devolving substantial authority to the production line, flattening out management to give maximum flexibility to frontline workers who would be held accountable for results but given considerable independence in figuring out how to reach the results. As states were becoming more and more active in education policy in the wake of *A Nation at Risk*, increasing standards for *both* students and teachers and seeking more accountability for the greater amounts of money they were spending on education, policy makers' strongest allies were business elites who saw improving education as central to improving productivity (McDonnell & Fuhrman, 1985). Since policy makers depended on business support for the large, costly comprehensive reform packages they promoted, it's not surprising that business ideas about accountability were influential.

Policy makers were explicit about their endorsement of the idea of accountability for results in return for less regulation about inputs and process. In 1986, Tennessee Governor Lamar Alexander, speaking for the National Governors Association, proposed a "horse trade," whereby schools would be accountable for results and receive deregulation in return. Many states began experimenting with deregulation and began to plan for accountability systems hinged around performance.

By the end of the 1980s, California and some other leading states began to anchor various previously discrete policies, like assessment and professional development, around standards for student learning. Standards-based reform spread rapidly across the country. Its central feature, the idea of coherent policies tied to student standards, gave more impetus to outcome-based accountability. If standards were to be the primary focus, then achievement of the standards should be what schools were held accountable for, not compliance with regulations that might or might not contribute to greater achievement of the standards.

The notion of *school-level*, as opposed to district-level, accountability reflects significant research identifying schools as the unit of improvement. From the effective schools research of the late 1970s, through the studies of student achievement using large-scale, longitudinal databases in the 1980s, it was clear that some schools, particularly those that were more cohesive and more focused on academics, performed better than others, even within the same district (Edmonds, 1979; Lee & Bryk, 1988; Purkey & Smith, 1983). School-level policies and decisions are therefore critical, and it is the school to which states should look for improving performance. In addition, throughout the 1990s, rapid advances in technology made direct school-to-state reporting and statewide collection much more feasible. It's now commonplace to find data for every school in a state on the web; without the ability to get performance and accompanying data by school rapidly and easily, centering accountability at the school level would be much more difficult.

The notion of increased *consequences* for performance, just like the performance focus itself, reflects business influence. In the 1980s, the term for state takeover of troubled districts was "academic bankruptcy." Districts that were having performance problems were treated as businesses that needed temporary receivership to restructure them and get them on their feet. Generally, the districts that were taken over were those with severe fiscal problems, and reputations for poor management and even corruption, not those that were just low performing. States knew what to do with poorly managed places; they knew how to clean up central offices, but they had much less knowledge and experience when it came to improving instruction. This problem persists; while states are much more actively placing themselves in the role of receiver in cases of low-performing schools, they continue to lack the know-how and staff capacity to effect improvement. But the fact that states are stepping up to the plate and asserting a role for themselves in exacting consequences for low performance reflects an acknowledgment that states are ultimately responsible for performance and grows naturally out of the increasing state role in education. The acceptance of ultimate responsibility—whether or not policy makers understand how to or are able to place instructional improvement at the core of a remedy—comes after decades of continually increasing financial responsibility and policy activity. Just as courts pressing states to live up to their constitutional responsibility when it comes to financing education have argued, states are finally on the line for education, so the notion of state-imposed consequences for low performance seems appropriate.

THE THEORY OF ACTION UNDERLYING
NEW ACCOUNTABILITY SYSTEMS

The assumptions underlying new accountability systems indicate how the new systems are supposed to work; they comprise a general "theory of action" (Argyris & Schön, 1978).

The new systems assume that, when they are operating as intended,

Performance, or student achievement, is the key value or goal of schooling, and constructing accountability around performance focuses attention on it. Since the indices that are used to measure school status and progress are composed primarily of achievement measures, the systems are intended to maximize focus on those measures. Once school-level progress in meeting standards of achievement is public, and, in most states, rewarded and/or sanctioned, it becomes the most important concern of school personnel. They will devote energy and resources, in a concerted fashion, toward improving student performance.

Performance is accurately and authentically measured by the assessment instruments in use. Assessments are aligned with student standards and gauge achievement of those standards in reliable and valid ways. If accountability is to hinge on performance, then the key measures used by the accountability system must correctly assess performance. Further, the new systems generally assume that school performance can be fairly assessed through testing; in only a few states do accountability systems include provisions for visiting and reviewing schools by observing teaching and learning.

Consequences, or stakes, motivate school personnel and students. Not only do those subject to stakes focus more on performance, but they work harder, because both positive inducements (such as bonuses) and negative sanctions (such as school takeover or reconstitution, or denial of promotion or graduation) are meaningful and real.

Improved instruction and higher levels of performance will result. Teachers working harder to teach and students working harder to learn will connect to mean better interaction around content. The assessments also will help promote good instruction by providing feedback on student performance. Following this assumption, the provision of information and enhanced motivation, rather than educator knowledge or skill, are the key levers for improving instruction. If teachers don't have the capacity necessary to respond to the accountability system incentives, it is assumed that the incentives are strong enough to motivate them to find it somehow; by seeking additional professional development, for example. Also, attaching consequences at the school level assumes that schools collectively will be able to fashion a response and, therefore, that they have, or will be motivated to form, some sort of internal coherence.

Unfortunate unintended consequences are minimal. If the systems work as intended, the goal of higher performance will not be undermined by perverse incentives or other negative developments. For example, instruction will improve, not become narrowly focused around test-taking skills, higher hurdles for high school graduation will not increase dropout rates, and holding schools accountable will not cause them to exclude special-needs students from testing or retain students in non-tested grades.

Whether these assumptions bear out in practice is the subject of this book. Now that new systems have been operating for a number of years, we can bring empirical evidence to bear. Are the new systems functioning as intended? Do they accurately assess performance and increases in performance? Is instruction improving? Do stakes motivate as intended and what about the problem of capacity? What are the side effects of these systems? And, most important, what are the implications of experience with these systems for improving accountability? Should adjustments be made and how might they be made?

OVERVIEW OF CHAPTERS

In the next chapter, which joins this one in the introductory section, Jennifer O'Day examines the effect of accountability policies on the ability of schools to improve over time. The chapter begins with the premise that accountability measures will be successful only to the extent that they contribute to the development of educational organizations and systems that foster improvement of student learning. Viewing schools as complex adaptive systems, the chapter focuses on the role of information, interaction, and learning in change processes. To foster systemic improvement, accountability systems must generate and focus attention on information relevant to teaching and learning, motivate educators (and others) to attend to relevant information and expend effort to augment or change strategies in response to this information, develop the knowledge and skills to promote valid interpretation of information and appropriate attribution of causality, and allocate resources where they are most needed. To understand whether new accountability systems meet these criteria, O'Day examines the example of the Chicago accountability system. Data from Chicago suggest that, while school accountability policies may successfully focus attention on student outcomes and target resources where they are needed, they are unlikely to bring about the deep changes necessary for long-term improvement. The chapter concludes with a discussion of how school accountability models based on a combination of bureaucratic and professional accountability mechanisms may be more likely to foster conditions of sustained improvement. It also suggests specific principles that should be considered in the design of such systems.

The next part, on "Issues in Designing Accountability Systems," starts off with a set of chapters on the technical functioning of new systems. In "Validity Issues for Accountability Systems," Eva Baker and Robert Linn focus on the validity of the measures that are used to make accountability decisions. They describe a general theory of action that underlies accountability systems and focus, in particular, on the critical role of testing within that theory of action. Specifically, Baker and Linn look at how the accuracy of information and validity of interpretation of assessment results affect the ability of accountability systems to accomplish their broader goals. The authors discuss issues related to the design and use of assessment measures, including the alignment of assessments with content standards and classroom instruction, and the use of scores for high-stakes decisions about students and schools. They demonstrate how inattention to these issues may result in a number of unintended consequences, such as the narrowing of instruction or misclassification of students and schools. Following this discussion, the authors suggest standards to guide the design and fine-tuning of accountability systems.

Robert Linn, in "Accountability Models," reviews the variety of accountability models that have been introduced by states. The analysis focuses on the methods by which state accountability systems use assessment data to determine stakes for schools and the relative advantages and disadvantages of these methods for system reliability, transparency to the public, and power to guide instructional improvement. The chapter pays special attention to three different models of assessment reporting—successive groups, longitudinal, and quasi-longitudinal—demonstrating the strengths and weaknesses as well as the substantially different effects of each model. Linn concludes with recommendations about how states can improve the accuracy of their reporting methods.

In "Benchmarking and Alignment of State Standards and Assessments," Robert Rothman argues that the success of standards-based reform depends more than anything else on two elements: strong standards, and assessments that measure what the standards expect. Nearly all states have embarked on the standards strategy. However, there is little evidence about the quality of both of these elements. This chapter describes two studies sponsored by Achieve that examined both the quality of standards and alignment between assessments and standards in a number of states. The findings suggest that the state systems have a number of important strengths that could help lead to improvements in student performance. The analyses also indicate a significant need for improvement in both the quality of standards and tests, and the alignment between the two.

"Biting the Bullet: Including Special-Needs Students in Accountability Systems" examines the technical and political issues that states are confronting as they move to include students with disabilities and students with limited English proficiency in their accountability systems. Author Martha Thurlow reviews research on the unintended effects of exclusion, federal policies regarding inclusion, the technical challenges of including students who need accommodations, the effects of various accommodations on scores, and the political and legal battles over accommodations. The chapter presents an analysis of the various approaches currently being taken by states, including development of alternative assessments, testing accommodation policies, and different approaches to including special-needs students in accountability systems. Early indications suggest that states have made much progress on their inclusion of special-needs students in assessments, but have been slower to incorporate these students into accountability systems. The author concludes that designing accountability systems that raise expectations and improving instruction for special-needs students will require continued study and careful balancing of technical and political issues.

In the next part, "Effects of Accountability Systems," we turn to what research is saying about the effects of accountability systems. First, Joan Herman addresses "The Effects of Testing on Instruction." The chapter reviews research on the effects of accountability measures on instructional practices in elementary schools and makes recommendations for the future use of assessments for instructional improvement. While there is some evidence that accountability for assessments has stimulated reform, many have raised concerns about the quality of assessment-driven instructional change, specifically whether the nature of instructional change reflects all of the learning goals set forth by standards. Based on research reviewed in this chapter, policy makers can take a number of specific steps to improve the use of assessments to inform instruction. Recommendations include using multiple measures and test forms; coordinating external assessments with locally developed assessments that provide timely and relevant feedback for improving instruction; providing sustained and high-quality professional development that builds teachers' capacity to use information provided by assessments, in conjunction with other resources, to improve instruction; and continuing evaluation of assessments and reporting procedures to ensure that reported gains actually signal increased student learning.

Leslie Siskin writes about "The Challenge of the High Schools." This chapter discusses the distinct characteristics of high schools and the way they shape the variability, within as well as between schools, of the instructional effects of high-stakes testing. These characteristics include the size of schools, the unique academic and social needs of adolescents, the variety of course offerings, the separation of students into academic tracks, and the departmentalized structure of school administration. Instructional effects also vary among high schools serving different functions and student populations.

In "Does External Accountability Affect Student Outcomes?" Martin Carnoy and Susanna Loeb look at the relationship between the strength of states' accountability systems and student outcomes, as measured by achievement data, high school retention rates, and high school survival rates. Analyses are performed for entire student populations, as well as for racial and ethnic groups. Results indicate a positive association between strength of accountability systems and gains in eighth-grade basic skills proficiency rates in mathematics; there is, however, considerable variation between states with similar levels of accountability, indicating that variables other than accountability are important in explaining gains. Results indicate little effect of stronger accountability on the retention rate of students in the first year of high school or the survival rate of students through high school.

"High-Stakes Testing in a Changing Environment" examines empirical, policy, and legal issues associated with high-stakes graduation and promotion tests. Jay Heubert explores empirical evidence on whether current high-stakes tests have a disproportionate impact on minority students, students with disabilities, and English-language learners; and whether all students (and these groups in particular) are already being taught the kinds of knowledge and skills that current tests measure. The chapter then considers how civil-rights claims and due-process claims would likely be resolved under current federal legal standards. Concluding that many such claims would not succeed, Heubert explores whether legal standards could be refined and applied more appropriately in light of such important developments as the shift from minimum competencies to world-class standards, substantially higher failure rates on many current high-stakes assessments, the challenges of ensuring alignment and opportunity to learn in a high-standards environment, the obligation to include students with disabilities and English-language learners in large-scale assessments, improved understanding of the consequences of promotion testing and grade retention, and greater clarity in the norms of the measurement profession. The author suggests steps that judges, educators, and policy makers can take to help ensure that large-scale assessments enhance rather than diminish the life chances of students who historically have been underserved by U.S. schools.

The final part, "Moving Forward: Refining Accountability Systems," turns to the future, to remedying systems to account for some of the problems that the previous chapters highlighted. In "Slow Down, You Move Too Fast," Susan Fuhrman, Margaret Goertz, and Mark Duffy examine a mounting backlash from parents and educators, distressed about poor results on assessments and the consequences of high stakes for students. As a result, many states are making or considering mid-course corrections in their design of stakes for students. This chapter presents case studies of the political resistance and system responses in four such states: Arizona, California, Maryland, and Massachusetts. It explores the issues and themes that are common across these states, including public attention to high failure rates and opportunity-to-learn issues. It also discusses how states are finding the political space to change their systems.

In the concluding chapter, Richard Elmore asserts that the role of stakes is critical in understanding the theories of action and implementation issues associated with performance-based accountability systems. State accountability systems vary considerably in the way they allocate stakes among students, schools, and school systems, yet little is understood about the behavioral effects of these stakes. At the same time, the allocation of stakes could be the source of some of the most troubling legal and political problems confronting standards-based reforms in the near future. These questions are discussed in the analysis of different types of state accountability systems. The chapter also summarizes the volume, providing principles for accountability policy design that draw on the work of the various authors.

State policy makers now must redesign their accountability systems to conform to the No Child Left Behind Act of 2001. Although the act has a number of provisions that will restrict states' options, it is our hope that, as they go about making refinements, policy makers will take into account the emerging research, such as that presented in this volume. Accountability systems appear to be having some positive effects, but much could be done to improve their validity, reliability, fairness, and effectiveness.

REFERENCES

Argyris, C., & Schön, D. (1978). *Organizational learning: A theory of action perspective*. Reading, MA: Addison Wesley.

Edmonds, R. (1979). Effective schools for the urban poor. *Education Leadership*, *37*, 15–24.

Education Funding Research Council. (2002). *Title I monitor*. Washington, DC: Author.

Goertz, M. E., & Duffy, M. C., with Le Floch, K. C. (2001). *Assessment and accountability systems in the 50 states: 1999-2000* (Research Report No. RR-046). Philadelphia: Consortium for Policy Research in Education, University of Pennsylvania.

Lee, V. E., & Bryk, A. S. (1988). Curriculum tracking as mediating the social distribution of high school achievement. *Sociology of Education, 61*, 78-94.

McDonnell, L., & Fuhrman, S. H. (1985). The political context of education reform. In V. D. Mueller & M. P. McKeown (Eds.), *The fiscal, legal, and political aspects of state reform of elementary and secondary education* (pp. 43-64). Cambridge, MA: Ballinger.

Purkey, S. C., & Smith, M. S. (1983). Effective schools: A review. *Elementary School Journal, 83*(4), 427-452.

Chapter 2

Complexity, Accountability, and School Improvement

Jennifer A. O'Day

INTRODUCTION AND FRAMEWORK

This book, like much of the conversation among reformers and policy makers today, is about accountability. Everywhere you turn—from Congress to the Statehouse to local communities and parent groups—some people are trying to make other people more accountable for some thing in education. However deafening at times, these cries for accountability should not surprise us. After all, public education consumes over $400 billion in public revenue. It is reasonable for the public and its representatives to want to know where the money is going and what it is producing. Are educators doing what they are being paid to do? Are administrators being responsible in how they are spending money? Are children engaged and learning what they need to know to be responsible and productive citizens?

Such questions are hardly new. In the early days of the common school, for example, teachers were closely scrutinized by the membership of their communities and called to task even for such personal habits as demeanor and dress as well as for their duties in the classroom. Meanwhile, student accountability—in the form of grades and report cards—has been around for even longer, while fiscal accountability for districts really came to the fore with the rise of federal programs like Title I in the 1960s and 1970s. Yet, as many observers have noted, the current emphasis and efforts toward educational accountability represent a departure—or evolution—from pre-

Redesigning Accountability Systems for Education. ISBN 0-8077-4425-5 (cloth). Prior to photocopying items for classroom use, please contact the Copyright Clearance Center, Customer Service, 222 Rosewood Drive, Danvers, MA, 01923, USA, telephone (978) 750-8400.

vious practice. Consortium for Policy Research in Education (CPRE) researchers have labeled this evolution the "new accountability" in education and have analyzed its various components or manifestations. Central among these are the emphasis on student outcomes as the measure of adult and system performance, a focus on the school as a basic unit of accountability, public reporting of student achievement, and the attachment of consequences to performance levels (Elmore, Abelmann, & Fuhrman, 1996; Fuhrman, 1999). Other analysts have delineated typologies of educational accountability (Adams & Kirst, 1999; Darling-Hammond & Ascher, 1991; O'Day & Smith, 1993; O'Reilly, 1996), noting differences among administrative/bureaucratic accountability and legal, professional, or market accountability systems with respect to who is holding whom accountable for what. In each case, reformers and observers assume that the goal of current accountability-based interventions is (or should be) the improvement of instruction and student learning. Indeed, the policy rhetoric from both parties is replete with such assumptions.

This chapter focuses on one class of the current accountability mechanisms—those that take the school as the unit of accountability and thus seek to improve student learning through improving the functioning of the school organization. (It is important to note that while this chapter focuses on the explicit organizational improvement goals of school accountability, these policies have symbolic and political purposes as well. For a fuller discussion of some of the politics underlying Chicago's school probation policies, see Bennett, 2001.) In the discussion that follows, I place the current trends and typologies of school accountability policies into a theoretical framework that focuses on the central role of information in organizational learning and adaptation. Using the Chicago school accountability model as an example, I discuss the promise and limitations of administrative (bureaucratic) approaches to school accountability in light of this framework. I highlight problems common to all accountability policies that take the school as the basic unit of intervention, and argue that a combination of administrative and professional accountability is the most promising approach for fostering organizational learning and improvement in schools. The final section of the chapter draws out several implications of the discussion for the refinement of accountability policies.

SCHOOL-BASED ACCOUNTABILITY: TENSIONS AND PROBLEMS

This discussion starts from the premise that school accountability mechanisms, by their very nature, seek to increase student performance by improving the functioning of the school organization. Mechanisms of school accountability vary from jurisdiction to jurisdiction, but generally include the establishment of some target level of performance (aggregated across the school, although targets may include disaggregated benchmarks as well), with consequences (and sometimes assistance) meted out to the school unit for achieving or not achieving the target performance. Whatever their differences in terms of the targets or the consequences, policies that take the school as the basic unit of accountability must contend with a number of inherent problems if they are to effect organizational change. I raise three such problems here and return to them at the conclusion of this chapter.

Problem 1: The school is the unit of intervention, yet the individual is the unit of action. The first of these problems concerns the relationship between collective accountability and individual action. School accountability by definition targets the school unit for monitoring, intervention, and change. But schools are collections of individuals, and to the extent that the needed change involves the behavior of the members of the organization, it must occur ultimately at the individual level. That is, individual teachers, administrators, and parents must in some way change what they are doing in the hope that this will change what students do (individually and in interaction with teachers) in such a way as to increase or deepen student learning. School-level accountability approaches bank on school members' identification and interaction with their organizational environment to motivate and direct individual action. In other words, such policies assume that targeting the school unit will generate the necessary and desired changes in the behavior of individuals within that unit. This assumption leads to two questions: How will school accountability mechanisms reach beyond the collective level to mobilize such changes among individuals? What conditions need to be in place for this connection to occur?

Problem 2: External control mechanisms seek to influence internal operations. Just as individuals operate within schools, schools are nested within larger systems and environments. New accountability approaches, by their very nature, seek to influence from the outside what goes on inside schools. Moreover, such policies assume that external forces can play a determining role in changing the internal workings of schools. The limitations of such assumptions, however, have provided grist for the vast literature on policy implementation in education. (For a range of implementation discussions over the past 3 decades, see, for example, Berman & McLaughlin, 1977; Goertz, Floden, & O'Day, 1995; McLaughlin, 1987; Spillane, 2000; and Weatherly & Lipsky, 1977.)

The heart of the issue is the problematic relationship between external and internal sources of control and the implications of this relationship for organizational learning and improvement. Organizational systems have several mechanisms at their disposal to control the behavior of individuals and subunits. Two such mechanisms are formal rules and normative structures. Large systems—like public education—tend toward bureaucracy and reliance on rules. Teachers work a certain number of hours a day, teach their classes in a prescribed order, and follow a variety of district, state, and federal mandates. But rules decreed from on high often have little impact, especially when it comes to the core technology of teaching and learning (Elmore, 1996; Marion, 1999). One reason is that externally generated rules may come up against the power of an organization's internal norms of behavior. Normative structures inside schools, such as the privacy of classroom practice, are often the determining factor not only in the implementation of policy, but more important, in the school's overall effectiveness in fostering student learning. (See, for example, DeBray, Parson, & Woodworth, 2001; Elmore, 2001; McLaughlin & Talbert, 1993; or Newmann & Wehlage, 1995, for a discussion of the power of internal norms.) The resulting questions for school accountability policies are profound. What is the appropriate and most effective balance between external and internal control? What are the mechanisms for achieving this balance? Can external accountability measures influence the development of internal norms that are more conducive to improving student learning?

Problem 3: Information is both problematic in schools and essential to school improvement. The third problem in school accountability concerns the nature and role of information in school improvement. Indeed, information is the lifeblood of all accountability mechanisms: One accounts to someone for something, and this accounting gets done by conveying information. Current school accountability policies, such as public reporting of student test scores, assume that, armed with accurate information about the achievement of students in the school, stakeholders and participants in the instructional process will take whatever action is necessary to improve learning outcomes. But again, this simple assumption raises a host of questions, the answers to which are anything but straightforward. What are the most effective forms and uses of information in the school improvement process? What is the potential for the external accountability system to generate and disseminate the information needed to accomplish the accountability goals? What are the motivational and learning links between information on the one hand and individual and collective action or the other?

SCHOOLS AS COMPLEX ORGANIZATIONS

The three problems discussed above—collective accountability versus individual action, internal versus external sources of control, and the nature and uses of information for school improvement—undergird this chapter on school accountability. In this section, I present an analytic framework developed from the extensive literature on complexity and organizational learning to illuminate the interrelationships among these problems and their influence on accountability effects. The full version of the article from which this chapter is excerpted (O'Day, 2002) explores the theoretical underpinnings of that framework in some depth. While space limitations do not permit the inclusion of that more extensive discussion in this chapter, two of its premises are important to note before proceeding to the framework itself.

The first of these is that like other complex adaptive systems, schools are places "in which many players are all adapting to each other and where the emerging future is very hard to predict" (Axelrod & Cohen, 2000, p. xi). It is the *interaction* among the members of the system and between them and their environment that gives the organization its form and meaning. If teachers did not interact with students, with one another, and with various administrators in the school and district in the way that they do, schools would not look like schools. (Indeed, some reforms fail precisely because they so fundamentally change patterns of interaction that schools become unrecognizable to the public and support for the reform erodes.) While we generally assume that these interactions have the purpose of student learning, individuals in fact have a multitude of purposes and are adapting to one another's goals as much as to variations in strategies and outcomes. What is critical to understand is that the patterns and nature of interactions in complex systems are central to any discussion of organizational learning and improvement, for it is through these interactions that members of the organization encounter new information, the source of all learning. As Huber (1991) explains: "An entity learns if, through its processing of information, the range of its potential behaviors is changed. This definition holds whether the entity is a human or other animal, a group, an organization, an industry, or a society" (p. 89). A teacher thus learns—that is, alters her potential range of behaviors—both by discarding those that appear to be ineffective and by taking on those that appear more effective. Unfortunately, appearances, as we all know, can be deceiving.

This brings us to the second major premise of the framework: For learning to take place, information must be *interpreted*, and interpretations are often wrong. When they are, "mislearning" takes place and improvement falters. The ability of an individual or group to learn in a way that actually improves desired outcomes is constrained by several factors in complex systems—by limitations in the individual or collective knowledge base, by socially constructed belief systems, and by the very complexity of the interactions that define the organization. The end result is that valid attributions of cause and effect are extremely difficult. Consider just one educational example: Fourth grader Jane is not understanding a lesson on probability. Is it because of a problem in curriculum? Because students her age simply can't grasp probability? Or because the teacher has a weak mathematical background and cannot respond adequately to Jane's confusion? Or perhaps it is something unconnected with the lesson itself. Perhaps Jane is distracted by a fight she had with another student on her way to school, has a visual or hearing problem, or is worried about her parents' impending divorce. The list of possibilities goes on and on. How is Jane's teacher to acquire sufficient information on Jane's situation (or her own) to determine the nature of the problem and how to address it effectively? Multiply this problem by 30 students in a class, 1,000 students and 50 teachers in a school, and then add in administrators, political pressures, and multiple subjects, and the difficulty is nearly overwhelming.

The bottom line here is that successful school improvement (adaptation) is dependent on two related factors—*interaction* (through which actors obtain information) and *interpretation* (through which they make meaning of that information and are able to act on it). Of course, other factors also are involved, but understanding the vital role of information for organizational learning and improvement, and its dependency on interaction and interpretation, lies at the core of the framework presented below. (See O'Day, 2002, for a complete discussion of the theory underlying this framework.)

A FRAMEWORK FOR UNDERSTANDING SCHOOL ACCOUNTABILITY

Starting from the assumption that schools are complex adaptive systems challenges traditional, linear views of reform and suggests alternative criteria for evaluating the potential impact of accountability-based interventions on school improvement. School accountability mechanisms will be successful in improving the functioning of school organizations to the extent that those interventions are able to:

- *Generate and focus attention on information relevant to teaching and learning* and to changes in that information as it is continually fed back into and through the system. Note that to alter what happens in classrooms, this focus must occur not only at the school level, but at the level of individual teachers as well. Interaction patterns are likely to be very important in the generation and spread of such information.
- *Motivate educators (and others) not only to attend to relevant information but to expend effort to augment or change strategies in response to this information.* Central here is the problematic relationship of collective accountability and individual action, discussed earlier. Motivation

ultimately must occur at the individual level, but it is likely to be dependent in part on the normative structures of the school as well as on individual characteristics of educators and students.

- *Develop the knowledge and skills to promote valid interpretation of information* (at both the individual and system levels). Learning takes place through the interpretation of information, whether that information is data from a student assessment, research on reading instruction, or observation of a colleague's lesson. Interpretation is dependent on and constrained by prior learning. Data often remain unused because educators lack the knowledge base for interpretation and incorporation of the new information. Further, the complexity of interaction patterns inside and outside a school organization and of the learning process itself makes attribution of cause and effect difficult and unreliable. If accountability systems are to be successful, they will need not only to build knowledge and skills for interpretation in the short run but also to establish mechanisms for continued learning through use of information generated by the system.

- *Allocate resources where they are most needed.* Information at all levels can promote the allocation of resources—human and material—to where they are most needed. At the classroom level, this occurs when a teacher allocates more time and attention to a student who is having trouble understanding a new concept. It also occurs when a district allocates resources to a low-performing school or one taking on a new challenge. To what degree does the accountability system encourage allocation (or reallocation) of resources to foster student learning based on information generated?

BUREAUCRATIC ACCOUNTABILITY AND SCHOOL IMPROVEMENT

How do current school accountability policies fare with respect to the framework above? To answer this question requires that we first define what is meant by "current school accountability policies." Here I turn to the earlier mentioned analyses of the "new accountability" in education (Elmore, Ablemann, & Fuhrman, 1996) as well as the more expansive typologies of educational accountability (Adams & Kirst, 1999; Darling-Hammond & Ascher, 1991; O'Reilly, 1996).

Accountability systems, according to these and other observers, differ in large part by the way they respond to four central questions: *Who* is accountable? *To whom* are they accountable? *For what* are they accountable? And *with what consequences*? Fuhrman notes that one of the distinguishing characteristics of the "new accountability" in standards-based reform is that the *who* in this formulation is generally the school unit—-and as previously indicated, this chapter focuses exclusively on school-level accountability. In addition, while school accountability policies differ in their particulars from jurisdiction to jurisdiction, the *to whom* designation almost universally refers to the district and/or state agencies. That is, schools as collective entities are accountable to the higher levels of the educational system. In this respect, such policies represent a form of administrative (O'Day & Smith, 1993) or *bureaucratic accountability* (Adams & Kirst, 1999; Darling-Hammond & Ascher, 1991). They differ from traditional forms of bureaucratic accountability in one very important respect, however: They hold schools and school personnel accountable not for delivering designated educational *inputs and processes* but for producing specific levels or improvements in student learning *outcomes*. They are thus examples of what might best be termed "outcome-based bureaucratic accountability." (In this chapter, the terms "bureaucratic accountability," "outcome-based accountability," and "outcome-based bureaucratic accountability" will be used interchangeably with "school accountability" to denote these systems. Note also that this discussion excludes choice systems in which schools are held accountable directly to parents through the market. Application of the framework to such systems remains for a future analysis.) In this section, I will use Chicago as an exemplar of this form of school accountability.

ACCOUNTABILITY CHICAGO STYLE

Chicago Public Schools (CPS) provide a particularly useful model for this illustration, since in 1995 the Illinois legislature amended the Chicago School Reform Act to include specific provisions for school accountability. Following those provisions, the Chicago School Board designated school-level targets for student performance and instituted sanctions (probation and reconstitution) for schools falling below those targets. The district has now accumulated 6 years experience with school accountability. Several colleagues and I have had the opportunity to follow the design, practice, and results of this system over the past several of those years. Our investigation has included in-depth interviews with business, political, education, and community stakeholders; analyses of school improvement plans and the planning process; interviews and shadowing of support providers; school case studies; and multilevel analyses of survey and achievement data on all CPS elementary schools since 1994 (2 years prior to the implementation of sanctions). Our data are thus both rich and varied. They provide an inroad into understanding the linkages between similar forms of accountability and school improvement.

Outcome-based school accountability: Addressing the framework

What do these data suggest about Chicago's system in light of the above framework? At first blush, CPS and similar school accountability systems seem to address well the criteria laid out in the framework above.

Attention. On the most basic level, these systems call attention to information on student outcomes by designating not only a particular indicator (or indicators) of those outcomes but by defining specific performance targets as well. In Chicago's case, the focus is sharpened by the district's use of a *single* indicator—the Iowa Test of Basic Skills (ITBS)—in only two subject areas, reading and mathematics. Moreover, the targeted performance benchmark is simple, measurable, and clear: Schools must have at least 20% of their students in grades 3–8 or 9–11 reading at or above national grade-level norms in the spring administration of the ITBS or be declared "on probation." Attention to the outcomes is further enhanced through school planning and reporting mechanisms that single out reading and math scores and require all schools to provide information on how they will increase student performance in these areas. Such mechanisms establish attention priorities in the organization and thus should help school personnel sift through the usual information overload to focus on that most directly related to the improvement goals.

Motivation. The policy provides motivation for this sifting process and related improvement efforts by attaching consequences to the outcome targets. For all schools, these consequences come in the form of public and administrative scrutiny of reported school outcome data. For schools falling below the target, sanctions include the stigma of the "probation" label; decreased autonomy (as local school councils lose authority to select their principals); additional requirements for planning, monitoring, and assistance; and potentially even reconstitution or re-engineering (both of which entail involuntary changes in personnel). Policy designers believe that even the threat of such sanctions will increase educator motivation and efforts to improve student learning.

Knowledge Development. Attending to outcome information is of little value, of course, if school personnel don't know how to interpret it, and motivation to act will produce nothing if educators don't know what actions they should take. Recognizing the need for site-based knowledge and skill development, CPS administrators instituted an elaborate program of assistance for schools that includes mentoring for principals, help with business and school improvement plans, and professional and organizational development provided by "external partners." A particularly interesting feature of the CPS design of external assistance is the district's response to the tension between internal and external sources of control, discussed earlier. In an effort to balance these sources of control and enhance normative buy-in among school personnel, CPS allows probation schools to select their own partners from an approved list. Policy designers hoped that this selection process would both enhance motivation and ensure attention to the particular conditions in each school.

Resource Allocation. Finally, funding for this assistance demonstrates a major way in which the district has used information generated by the accountability system to allocate resources. Low test scores trigger the targeting of discretionary monies—initially from the district surplus and then from federal programs like the Comprehensive School Reform Demonstration Program and class-size reduction—to probation schools. The district covers 100% of the cost of the first year of assistance and 50% of the second year, and in subsequent years the school picks up the cost. In the first 2 years of the probation policy, CPS spent $29 million for external support alone. (This doesn't count the resources allocated for remedial summer or after-school classes or for practice and testing materials. See Finnigan & O'Day, 2003, for a fuller discussion of the assistance program.)

Chicago is not alone in its approach to school accountability. Other jurisdictions have set in place similar systems—in part in response to the accountability requirements incorporated into Title I of the Elementary and Secondary Education Act in 1994. Of course, jurisdictions vary considerably in the specifics of their policies. One important dimension of this variation is in the definition of targets. Some jurisdictions have set improvement targets for all schools and rewards for those meeting or exceeding targets. The intent is to focus and motivate improvement in higher-performing schools as well as in lower-performing ones. Jurisdictions also vary in the forms of assistance provided and in the consequences attached to either high or low performance relative to the targets. Despite these variations, the general school accountability model is the same.

Impact of school-based accountability

Although experience and research on school accountability are still in the early stages, some evidence of its impact is beginning to accumulate. Our data from Chicago (Finnigan & Gross, 2001) and CPRE research in Kentucky and Charlotte-Mecklenburg (Kelley, Odden, Milanowski, & Heneman, 2000) indicate that teachers are working harder in response to the accountability measures and are more focused on externally set student learning goals. In addition, many systems (e.g., Boston, San Diego, Tennessee, California) are using school-level data on student outcomes to allocate additional discretionary resources where they appear to be most needed. Some jurisdictions, such as New York City and Baltimore, have even put in place special monetary incentives to attract highly skilled teachers and principals to the lowest-performing schools and to encourage them to stay there.

There is also evidence of an impact on achievement. In the first 4 years after instituting its school accountability policy, Chicago posted increasing scores in both reading and mathematics, although reading scores began to level off in 2000. Similarly, Kentucky, California, Texas, Tennessee, and other jurisdictions claim that their accountability policies have resulted in higher student achievement. However, some observers question whether increases in test scores really indicate higher levels of student learning or whether later scores have been artificially inflated by concentrated "teaching to the test" and increased familiarity with test questions and format. In the case of Texas and Tennessee, rising scores on the National Assessment of Educational Progress seem to validate similar increases on the state assessments, but in these and in all other cases it is difficult to attribute such increases to school accountability mechanisms. For varying perspectives of the impact of these accountability systems, see Grissmer, Flanagan, Kawata, and Williamson (2000); Haney (2000); Klein, Hamilton, McCaffrey, and Stecher (2000); and Koretz and Barron (1998).

What is perhaps most relevant to this discussion is the mounting evidence that schools respond unevenly to outcome-based accountability policies and that this unevenness may be directly tied to internal conditions in the schools that make them more or less able to use the information generated by the accountability systems. The CPRE research team led by Richard Elmore and Leslie Siskin, for example, has found that schools that are "better situated" in terms of their socioeconomic composition and their prior academic performance respond more readily and coherently to the demands of external performance-based accountability systems than those schools less well situated (DeBray, Parson, & Woodworth, 2001; Elmore, 2001; Siskin, this volume). Their research suggests that initially lower-performing schools actually lose ground relative to well-situated schools once an external accountability system is instituted.

Our own research on the lowest-performing schools in Chicago extends the CPRE analysis to variations in response even among those schools that might be considered less well situated—that is, among those at similarly low socioeconomic and achievement levels. The first indication of this variation is a rapid bifurcation in the graph of achievement trends for all elementary schools placed on probation in 1996, despite comparable initial achievement. More specifically, one group of schools—those that came off the probation list by the spring of 1998—posts a significantly sharper increase in scores than those schools that remained on probation after 1998. Multilevel analysis of survey data for this rapidly improving group suggests that they differed significantly from other probation schools along several dimensions of initial school capacity: peer collaboration, teacher–teacher trust, and collective responsibility for student learning (Gwynne & Easton, 2001). Referring to the earlier discussion of organizational complexity, one might surmise that the first two of these dimensions—peer collaboration and teacher–teacher trust—reflect stronger patterns of interaction among the organizational agents (teachers, in this case). The third dimension—collective responsibility for student learning—suggests that attention and effort in these schools were already directed to a higher degree to student learning and bolstered by the normative structure of the school—what Elmore and his colleagues call "internal accountability" (Abelmann & Elmore, 1999).

That schools with such characteristics would be more successful at adaptation makes sense in light of the earlier discussion of complexity, information, and learning. Meanwhile, the failure of other schools to show similar improvement and their propensity to stay on probation for as long as 5 years or more suggest something about the limitations of bureaucratic accountability for catalyzing school improvement in low-capacity schools. Indeed, our qualitative data on policy, assistance, and individual school response point to significant limitations of bureaucratic outcome-based accountability for fostering school improvement.

LIMITATIONS OF BUREAUCRATIC SCHOOL ACCOUNTABILITY

The discussion of complexity suggests that adaptation (improvement) is based on the feedback (information) that agents receive from one another and from the environment; the interpretations, and dispersal of this information through patterns of interaction in the organization; and then the invention, selection, and recombination of strategies to produce improvement along some measure of performance. Our data from Chicago indicate several ways in which bureaucratic outcome-based accountability may inhibit—or at least fail to promote—widespread organizational adaptation.

Nature and quality of information

A central limitation of school accountability in Chicago and elsewhere is that the nature and quality of the information produced and dispensed by the system are simply inadequate for effective organizational adaptation and learning. Three aspects of this inadequacy stand out.

Validity. The first concerns the validity of the outcome measure on which improvement is to be based. Much of the criticism of Chicago's model of school accountability has centered on the use of a norm-referenced basic skills test that is not fully aligned with either the district or the state standards, that emphasizes fragmented and discrete skill acquisition, and that lacks validation for the types of decisions (e.g., probation and grade retention) made on the basis of its results. Validity with respect to measurement of the goals (e.g., standards) is a critical aspect of an assessment's quality: If the assessment does not measure what it purports to measure, it actually could draw attention away from the goals of the system rather than toward them. This potential problem is compounded in a situation like that of Chicago, where the use of a *single* measure and the attachment of consequences to that measure (see below) intensify attention to the measure rather than to the larger goal. In this regard, it is important to note that the ITBS has not been validated for the purpose of either school or student accountability.

Specificity. A second limitation of Chicago's—and most—school accountability systems concerns the periodicity and specificity (grain size) of the information provided by the outcome measure. On the one hand, a test given once a year that reports a general indication of the content and skills that students have—and have not—mastered can be extremely valuable for identifying schools and subject areas that may need additional attention, resources, or possibly changes in strategies. An important contribution of school accountability systems in places like Chicago and Maryland, for example, is that they have directed the spotlight at failing parts of the system that then can be given additional assistance. However, while such information is useful at these higher levels of aggregation, its potential for directly improving strategies in the classroom is limited. Usually, such assessments are administered in the spring to capture student learning during the academic year, but the results are not available in time for the relevant teacher to alter instruction in response to the test. Even if the scores were available earlier in the year, the infrequency and lack of specificity of results are still a problem. In short, the measure of outcomes through such a test is simply too distant from the complexities of instructional inputs for the teacher to make reasonable attributions of causality. Superstitious learning is common in such circumstances—that is, attributing increases or decreases in student performance to spurious "causes." For this reason, some schools supplement the annual testing with more regular and focused assessments aligned with the ITBS. These periodic tests can give teachers more information on outcomes, although they also may underscore concerns about teaching to the test.

Processes. A third problem with the quality of the information is an extension of the second. Attribution is a process of assigning credit or blame to a strategy or set of strategies for producing a given outcome. The implication is that the actor—whether an individual or an organization—must have valid and reliable information on both outcomes and processes. Yet, school accountability systems focus almost exclusively on outcomes, producing little in the way of reliable information on instruction or organizational practices. Indeed, some authors have argued persuasively that the production of such information at aggregated levels would introduce further measurement problems and unduly constrain practice. (See, for example, *The Debate on Opportunity-to-Learn Standards: Supporting Works* [National Governors Association, 1993] or the report of the National Academy of Education Panel on Standards-Based Reform [McLaughlin, Shepard, & O'Day, 1995].) The lack of data on practice generated by the accountability system might not be a problem if such information were available at the school level. Indeed, substantial research suggests that when teachers share information about instruction as well as student learning, they are better able to adapt their practice to the needs and progress of their students. (See, for example, the literature on the role of professional community [e.g., McLaughlin & Talbert, 1993, 2001; Newmann & Wehlage, 1995] and on information sharing in high-performing schools [Darling-Hammond, 1996; Mohrman & Lawler, 1996].) However, the egg-crate structure of American schools means that information on instructional strategies and processes is held privately by teachers and only rarely shared across the school as the basis for future learning. Research demonstrating the lack of such sharing of information in most schools is plentiful (Lortie, 1975; McLaughlin & Talbert, 2001). While some teachers regularly reflect on their practice in light of observed student learning, this is rare and usually occurs on an individual basis. Teachers in most schools, but especially in low-capacity schools, lack the patterns of interaction (internal networks, professional community) to generate and use information on practice that would enable effective attribution. Our research suggests that bureaucratic school accountability policies are insufficient to establish those patterns.

Patterns of interaction

Indeed, if CPS is any indication, bureaucratic school accountability mechanisms serve to maintain interaction patterns that foster compliance and hierarchy rather than system learning. We observed two main manifestations of this phenomenon. First, our data reveal a fairly unidirectional (top-down) flow of information throughout the system. For example, rather than opportunities for collective sharing of information and knowledge, meetings of assistance providers with central office staff and of principals with district liaison personnel were reportedly occasions in which schools and those working with them were simply the *recipients* of information and mandates rather than sources of valuable information in their own right. When information did flow the other way, it focused on whether people were carrying out prescribed tasks—that is, whether external partners were providing agreed-upon services, whether schools were implementing specifics of school plans, and whether teachers were understanding and using the tools and techniques disseminated by the external partners (Finnigan & O'Day, 2003).

Even those instances where one might expect more collective problem solving—such as in the school improvement planning process—more often than not became symbolic exercises in responding to formulaic requirements of the district office rather than thoughtful and inclusive learning experiences for the staff. The planning template was handed down from the Office of Accountability; schools complied—with emphasis on compliance instead of self-reflection being noticeably stronger in the least improving, lowest-capacity schools. What was perhaps most distressing was that this transmission model of information flow also characterized the professional development provided by the external partners, the bulk of which consisted of traditional short workshops rather than intensive inquiry-based explorations of either content or instructional practice (Finnigan & O'Day, 2003).

The end result is that much of the response we saw in schools involved their reacting to directions imposed from above and outside the school rather than reflecting internal practices. That such would be the case is perhaps unsurprising. Hierarchical control and information dissemination are characteristic of large bureaucracies like CPS, and well-established and internalized organizational codes are difficult to change (March, 1991). Moreover, the "get tough" theory of action and the urban politics underlying the school probation policy could be expected to exacerbate these tendencies. By defining the problem as low expectations and lack of effort on the part of school staff, forces from higher in the system and outside schools seek to push those inside to work harder. The accompanying incentives only reinforce control and enforcement at the expense of system learning.

Maladaptive incentive structures

While much of the benefit of current school accountability schemes is supposed to be their provision of incentives for motivating improvement, we found the incentive structures in Chicago actually exacerbated the problems in low-performing, low-capacity schools.

Negative Effects of Negative Incentives. The emphasis on negative incentives (stigma of probation, threat of reconstitution) tied to a single measure (ITBS) appears to have resulted in two tendencies that work against long-term improvement. First, attention in these schools became focused not so much on student learning per se, as on getting off (or staying off) probation. This goal essentially places adult desires (to remove the professional stigma and avoid administrative scrutiny) over the needs of students (Evans & Wei, 2001). Second, to achieve this goal, probation schools exhibited an emphasis on strategies to produce immediate increases in test scores, often to the neglect of longer-term success. The combination of these tendencies produced a number of dysfunctional practices. Most common was the emphasis on test preparation in the form of intensive drill and practice to raise student scores. Some schools even redesigned their curriculum not only to reflect the general skills on the ITBS but to align the proportion of time allotted in the curriculum to a given discrete skill with the proportion of test items measuring that skill. In such cases, the test specs became the curriculum specs as well. Another common practice was to triage assistance (mostly test prep) to students scoring near grade-level cutoffs (stanines 4–5) in the hope that by raising these students' scores slightly, the school could escape probation. These and similar practices suggest the allocation of resources to achieve adult ends (getting off probation) rather than to meet the greatest student needs.

Such patterns, which have been noted in prior research on high-stakes testing in education (see, for example, Firestone & Mayrowetz, 2000; Nolen, Haladyna, & Haas, 1992; Smith & Rottenberg, 1991), are not uncommon in organizations undergoing crisis. A focused search for short-term strategies to satisfy a specific target is typical when an organization's performance falls below its aspirations or goals (March, 1994; Simon, 1986). When low performance is combined with a threat to the organization's position or survival (as is the case in school probation), the potential for dysfunctional or maladaptive response increases. These responses include: (1) restricting information processing in favor of previous patterns of thought and action, and (2) centralization of authority and bureaucratic control (see Staw, Sanderlands, & Dutton, 1981, for a comprehensive review of research on organizational response to threat). Both patterns were observed in low-performing schools in Chicago. We can expect individual and system learning to be constrained under these conditions, as will be innovation and examination of existing practice and assumptions. These tendencies might be mitigated if the policy included positive incentives (rewards) for learning and for improvements in instructional practice. While some systems do include re-wards, those rewards are tied to improvements in outcomes rather than in practice or learning. Observers often note the need for interim indicators of organizational practice and of capacity to be included in the accountability structures, but which they rarely are.

Unbalanced Reliance on Collective Incentives. A second limitation of the incentive structures concerns the problem raised at the beginning of this chapter regarding the relationship between individual action and collec-tive accountability. With a focus on schoolwide consequences, the policy offers few incentives for individuals to improve their practice. Individual teacher evaluation is not well aligned either with outcome measures or with standards of practice likely to produce those outcomes. In many schools, there is little accountability for individual teachers, and in others, teachers receive little recognition for improvement of practice. These policies thus rely on the principal (or others in the school community) to motivate the individuals on the school's staff. Where the principal is weak (often the case in low-performing schools), the effect of the policy on individual teachers is likely to be weak—or even negative. Alternatively, where the principal is strong or where the connections among individuals are mutually reinforc-ing, the lack of individual incentives may be mitigated by the strong identifi-cation of individuals with the group. This may help to explain why schools with higher levels of teacher–teacher trust, peer collaboration, and collec-tive responsibility improved more rapidly than did others. Perhaps in these schools, other incentives are at work to motivate individual behavior. (For a discussion of these other incentives, see, for example, Darling-Hammond, 1996, and Mohrman & Lawler, 1996.)

Weak resource allocation and knowledge development strategies

One of the most promising aspects of outcome-based school accountability is the use of information to direct attention and resources where they are most needed. In Chicago, this reallocation mainly took the form of provid-ing funds for external assistance to low-performing schools. Unfortunately, the potential impact of this substantial reallocation was mitigated by the low intensity and lack of focus of most of the support actually provided. In part, the limitations of the assistance may be attributed to problems of implementation, such as weak quality control in the selection of support provider candidates. In addition, the policy was only vaguely specified with regard to the desired goals or content of assistance, thus providing little guidance to either the schools or the support providers about where to concentrate their energies. Such weak specification is common in school accountability policies in other jurisdictions as well. It derives on the one hand from a desire to respond flexibly to variations in internal school context and on the other from the policy's emphasis on student outcomes to the neglect of information—or a theory of action—about instruction. The resulting diffuseness of the assistance does little to solve the problems of attribution in schools, discussed earlier. Moreover, the policy neglect of other inputs—such as reallocation of human or other resources—also weakens the potential impact.

SUMMARY

What does this discussion of the CPS experience add up to in light of the framework and central problems of school accountability outlined earlier? On the one hand, school accountability policies like those in Chicago, Maryland, California, and elsewhere clearly have helped focus attention throughout the system on student outcomes and have provided data that can be used for targeting resources and assistance where they are most needed—particularly in low-performing schools. On the other hand, school accountability approaches suffer from a number of inherent weaknesses that make them, as they are currently construed, unlikely to effect deep changes necessary for long-term improvement, particularly in the low-performing, low-capacity schools targeted by the systems. Four such weaknesses stand out.

1. The problems of validity, periodicity, and specificity in the outcome measures, coupled with inattention to information on instructional practice, make attribution and thus learning at the school or individual teacher level difficult.
2. Most school accountability systems still operate from a bureaucratic control model and thus fail to create the interaction patterns and normative structures within schools that encourage sustained learning and adaptation. Most low-performing schools lack those patterns and structures on their own.
3. Reliance on negative incentives undermines innovation and risk taking in threatened schools and diverts attention to organizational survival rather than student learning. Moreover, most current incentive structures fail to foster individual motivation or to reward learning and changes in practice that might lead to sustained improvement.
4. Finally, the reallocation of assistance and resources for increasing the capacity of low-performing schools is generally inadequate and weakly specified. Unfocused assistance based on transmission mod-

els of learning does little to build the knowledge base needed for valid interpretation of information produced by the system.

While some of these shortcomings are exacerbated by poor implementation, they derive from fundamental assumptions inherent in the design of current school accountability systems. Current approaches have not solved any of the three problems outlined at the beginning of this chapter: the relationship between collective accountability and individual action; the tension between external and internal sources of control; and the production, spread, and use of information that can help solve problems of attributions caused by the complexity of school organizations. Thus, reliance on bureaucratic forms of accountability, even with better implementation, is unlikely to lead to the kind of improvement desired.

Is there an alternative?

PROFESSIONAL ACCOUNTABILITY: ALTERNATIVE OR ADDITION?

Perhaps the most commonly posed alternative to bureaucratic or administrative accountability in education is that of professional accountability (Adams & Kirst, 1999; Darling-Hammond & Ascher, 1991; O'Reilly, 1996). Professional accountability is rooted in the assumption that teaching is too complex an activity to be governed by bureaucratically defined rules and routines. Rather, like other professions, effective teaching rests on professionals acquiring specialized knowledge and skills and being able to apply that knowledge and those skills to the specific contexts in which they work. In mature professions, the requisite knowledge is articulated in professionally determined standards of practice, and professional accountability involves members of the professions assuming responsibility for the definition and enforcement of those standards.

In education, the focus of professional accountability might be described as threefold. First, it is centered on the process of instruction—that is, on the work of teachers as they interact with students around instructional content (Cohen & Ball, 1999; McLaughlin & Talbert, 2001). Professional accountability thus concerns the performance of adults in the system at least as much as the performance of students. (See Campbell, McCloy, Oppler, & Sager, 1993, for the importance of the distinction between performance and outcomes.) Second, much of the focus of professional accountability concerns ensuring that educators acquire and apply the knowledge and skills needed for effective practice. Knowledge development is thus front and center. And third, professional accountability involves the norms of professional interchange. These norms include placing the needs of the client (students) at the center of professional work, collaborating with other professionals to address those needs and ensure the maintenance of standards of practice, and commitment to the improvement of practice as part and parcel of professional responsibility.

At the system level, mechanisms of professional accountability center on teacher preparation, teacher licensure, and peer review. At the school level, professional accountability rests both on individual educators assuming responsibility for following standards of practice and on their professional interaction with colleagues and clients. Mentoring, collaboration, and collective problem solving in response to student needs, and some form of peer review to ensure quality of practice, are all aspects of school-site professional accountability. Advocates for professionally based forms of accountability argue that this approach holds the most promise for the improvement of teaching and, by extension, for the improvement of student learning.

THE PROMISE AND LIMITATIONS OF PROFESSIONAL ACCOUNTABILITY

Our earlier discussion of complexity and organizational adaptations lends some theoretical support for the claims of advocates of professionalism. In particular, professional accountability at the school site would seem to address problems of attribution and of motivation more productively than what we have seen from bureaucratically based models.

With respect to the use of information for effective attribution, three aspects of professional accountability seem most pertinent. First is the fact that professionalism draws attention both to instructional practice (agents' strategies) and to teachers' collective responsibility for student learning (outcomes). Second, norms of collaboration around instruction enhance patterns of interaction at the school site that allow for the generation and spread of information about both practice and outcomes, and the dissemination of effective strategies based on analysis of that information (i.e., data-driven change). This information is naturally more fine-grained and immediate than that accumulated at higher levels of aggregation, and thus the linkages between specific strategies and their effects are more easily discerned. In part, this is because the articulation of both outcome targets and standards of practice allows for the testing of hypotheses about those linkages, particularly where experience/results run contrary to expectations (Axelrod & Cohen, 2000; Sitkin, 1992). Finally, more valid attribution also is likely to come about because of the emphasis on professional knowledge and skills, which lay the groundwork for meaningful interpretations of the information available (and more meaningful sharing of information with others).

Standards of practice, constructed generally across the profession and more particularly within the professional community of the school, provide the cognitive maps (Huber, 1991) for this process of meaning creation.

In addition to addressing problems of attribution, professional accountability expands the incentives for improvement, with particular emphasis on the intrinsic motivators that bring teachers into teaching in the first place — commitment to students (clients) and identity as educators. Scott (1998) has delineated three types of incentives commonly at work in organizations: material incentives (monetary rewards, job promotion, or loss), community/solidarity incentives (based on individuals' identity as a member of a community or profession and desire to maintain or gain position in that community), and purposive incentives (satisfaction from achieving a valued goal such as learning objectives for students). Our work in probation schools in Chicago suggests that school accountability policies often fail to tap into solidarity and intrinsic purposive incentives, focusing instead on the threat of material sanctions (reassignment or job loss) or reward (Finnigan & Gross, 2001). By contrast, research on professional communities of practice notes the motivational aspects of membership in those communities and of normative structures that focus on student learning (goal attainment) and professional identity (Darling-Hammond, 1996; McLaughlin & Talbert, 2001).

Beyond its theoretical appeal, there is a growing body of empirical evidence that points to aspects of professionalism as important components of school improvement. Lee and Smith (1996), for example, find a significant positive relationship between student achievement gains and teachers' collective responsibility for students' academic success in high school. Similarly, one of the most consistent findings from the work of the Institute for Research on Teaching at Michigan State University was the impact on achievement of teachers' acceptance of appropriate responsibility for student learning. (For a discussion of this work, see Porter and Brophy, 1988.) Meanwhile, various researchers have pointed to the positive impact of teacher interaction and collaboration in school-based professional communities (Little, 1990; McLaughlin & Talbert, 1993, 2001; Newmann & Wehlage, 1995), and Community School District 2 in New York City provides proof of the deep impact of professional culture and professional development as a strategy for improvement and system management (Elmore, 1996). Finally, as mentioned previously, there is some recent evidence that professionally based aspects of internal school accountability and capacity are essential for a school's ability to respond effectively to outcome-based accountability (DeBray, Parson, & Woodworth, 2001; Elmore, 2001) and can help explain the differential gains among schools that are targets of accountability policies (Gwynne & Easton, 2001).

LIMITATIONS OF PROFESSIONAL ACCOUNTABILITY

Despite its promise, however, reliance on professional accountability alone cannot ensure that the needs of all students in today's schools are addressed. The most obvious limitation of such a strategy is the overall weakness of professionalism and professional accountability throughout U.S. education. Most American schools are atomized structures where responsibility rests with the individual educator rather than with the collective staff or with the profession as a whole (Abelmann & Elmore, 1999; Lortie, 1975). Mentoring and collaboration are simply too rare to ensure the information sharing necessary for ongoing organizational learning. In addition, teachers' knowledge and skills are not what they need to be (especially in light of more challenging goals for *all* students), and professional standards of practice are only beginning to be defined and enforced. (The work of the National Board for Professional Teaching Standards, the Interstate New Teacher Assessment and Support Consortium, and the National Council for Accreditation of Teacher Education are promising but still beginning efforts in this regard.) Given this situation, U.S. educational systems may well need external incentives and administrative assistance to stimulate the development of professional accountability and attention to learning objectives for all students.

A second limitation of this approach concerns the problem of equity. Failures of professionalism are most notable in schools serving disenfranchised groups, especially schools in inner cities with large proportions of poor students and students of color. Many of these schools have been allowed to languish for years, during which time the profession has not stepped forth to fight for the needs of these "clients." External administrative accountability is needed to address these failures of professionalism and help ensure equal opportunity.

Tied to the equity limitations of professionalism is the fact that outcome-based school accountability is able to address some system purposes and needs more readily than is professional accountability alone. For example, at more aggregated levels of the system, performance reporting and other outcome-based accountability tools provide a useful mechanism for managing the resources necessary for instruction and school improvement. Low performance can be a trigger indicating areas of greatest need. In addition, monitoring and reporting of outcomes are important avenues for informing the public about the status of the system and the degree to which it is addressing the needs of, and providing opportunities to, all students. This is particularly important in the United States, where neither the public nor its representatives are ready to fully trust professional educators.

A BETTER WAY: COMBINING BUREAUCRATIC
AND PROFESSIONAL ACCOUNTABILITY

What this discussion suggests is that a combination of professional and administrative/bureaucratic school accountability may be most useful for establishing the conditions to foster long-term school improvement. Such combinations are common in other professions. In medicine, for example, physicians establish and enforce standards of medical practice, but hospitals, insurance companies, and sometimes governments pay attention to outcome (as well as process) data to identify and respond to breakdowns and problems in the distribution and management of medical resources.

Similarly, some educational jurisdictions are experimenting with combinations of outcome-based administrative accountability (to identify areas of low performance) and professionally based interventions and accountability (to foster school adaptation to address these problems). One such example is the recently formed CEO District in Baltimore, Maryland. In this case, the state has established the outcome targets, based on the Maryland Student Performance Assessment Program, and identified schools that are the farthest from (and declining in relation to) those targets. Those schools are deemed "reconstitution eligible." The preponderance of reconstitution-eligible schools in Baltimore City was one factor contributing to a change in governance for the district (a district–state partnership) and additional funding being directed to the district (reallocation of resources based on outcomes). Once in place, the new leadership of the district collected a group of the lowest-performing schools into a special configuration, the "CEO District," and turned to the local education fund to assist these schools in becoming "effective learning organizations."

The resulting intervention incorporates many of the aspects of teacher professionalism discussed above as well as the challenges to organizational learning discussed earlier. These include a focus on literacy for teacher and student work and on the generation and sharing of information about that work; ongoing assessments through Running Records and regular evaluation of student work to provide frequent, fine-grained information about learning outcomes; team structures like regular grade-level meetings to foster teacher interaction, sharing of strategies, and collective responsibility; and ongoing professional development designed to build a "culture of shared learning." Professional development, which is central to the intervention, is site-based, focuses on standards in literacy, and incorporates teachers' professional interchange through collective study, inter-class visitations, and common planning. A client-centered focus (also central to notions of professionalism) is manifested throughout these endeavors, but most especially in the identification of, targeted assistance to, and monitoring of all students reading below grade level. Finally, the intervention fosters a full range of incentives, from material rewards for taking on the challenge of and showing progress in these schools, to solidarity incentives derived from membership in a professional community, to the intrinsic purposive rewards of success with students.

An interesting characteristic of this and several similar approaches (e.g., the Chancellor's District in New York City, SURR schools in District 2, and Boston's school cohort approach) is the apparent division of labor between the generation and use of information at the state level (following a more administrative/bureaucratic model) and that at the local level (with strong infusion of professionalism). This division of labor may be suggestive of a necessary distinction in the balance of accountability approaches depending on the level of aggregation—and thus on the distance from or closeness to the point of instruction and school change. What seems critical here is that the bureaucratic accountability mechanisms from the more aggregated levels of the system not get in the way of the development of professional norms, structures, and standards at the school site.

Of course, the Baltimore CEO District and similar models represent only one approach to combining professional and bureaucratic accountability. Many others are possible and undoubtedly are being designed and implemented in varying ways and contexts. What is important to note is the synergistic interplay of professional and bureaucratic accountability. On the one hand, outcome-based targets for schools and performance reporting are critical for identifying problem areas, for the allocation of resources to address those problems, and for the monitoring of progress. But the real action at the school site—and across identified school sites—is on developing professional knowledge (through focused assistance with instruction), professional norms, and professional patterns of interaction necessary for establishing the basis for ongoing organizational adaptation. This combination allows for a more thorough and balanced incorporation of all aspects of the accountability framework discussed earlier: It generates and draws attention to information relevant to teaching and learning (both student and adult performance), motivates individuals and units by way of intrinsic as well as extrinsic incentives to attend to and to use that information, builds the knowledge base for valid interpretations of information, and allocates resources where they are most needed.

The combination also addresses the three underlying problems and tensions in school accountability introduced earlier. The first of these problems concerned the interplay between collective accountability for the school unit and the requisite change in behavior of the individuals within that unit. The addition of professional accountability at the school site strengthens the linkages between individual teachers and their schools by fostering interaction around common work, a sense of shared purpose, and identity as members of the school community. These ties increase individual motivation to act in accordance with the community's collectively defined endeavor. Moreover, the deprivatization of practice through sharing of student work and teacher strategies, as well as inter-class visitations, provides a mechanism for developing and enforcing common standards of practice.

This latter point has implications for the second problem identified earlier—the relationship between external and internal mechanisms of control. Attempts to control individual and group behavior by means of external rules and policies are notorious for their inevitable failure, especially in situations where tasks and environments are complex and ambiguous. Resistance and superficial compliance are the common responses. In the case of education, compliance with externally produced rules can even be counterproductive, as it does not allow for the flexible application of professional knowledge to specific contexts and students. By contrast, the strong professional norms generated by the infusion of professional accountability (especially collective responsibility for student learning) become potential resources and mechanisms for orienting the entire school community toward the higher levels of student performance sought by reformers and the general public.

Finally, with respect to the third problem—the generation, flow, and use of information for organizational learning and adaptation—the combination of professional and outcome-based school accountability holds considerable promise. Drawing on the discussion of complexity and the examples described above, we might posit a number of principles of information generation and use for accountability purposes. The first of these, which is the subject of several chapters in this volume, is that information on performance must be valid and accurate and must reflect the goals of teaching and learning. This principle applies to all forms of accountability, regardless of target or mechanism.

With respect to school accountability and improvement, four additional principles follow from our discussion. First, for individuals and systems to evaluate performance, make appropriate attributions, and adapt their strategies, information must be available both on student performance (achievement) and on adult performance (instructional and other relevant strategies). Second, the grain size and periodicity of the information feedback should match the level and purposes of its use. For the improvement of instructional practice at the school and classroom level, fine-grained and frequent information (including instructionally integrated diagnostic assessments of student learning and feedback on instructional practice tied to that learning) provides the basis for professional reflection. Meanwhile, at higher levels of the system, more aggregate and less frequent information feedback provides sufficient basis for allocation of resources and for evaluating and refining policies. Third, because information in complex systems derives from interaction, accountability systems should foster connections within and across units to enable access to and reflection on information relevant to teaching and learning. And finally, accountability systems must pay particular attention to developing the knowledge base necessary for valid interpretation of the information generated.

A thoughtful combination of outcome-based school accountability and professional accountability provides the means for addressing all these information needs and thus for fostering the "data-driven" improvement sought by the accountability policies described in this volume and promoted in jurisdictions across the country. Whether such a thoughtful combination is likely to come about, however, particularly in light of the testing and accountability provisions of the newly reauthorized Title I, is another matter.

ACKNOWLEDGMENTS

Work for this chapter was supported in part by a grant from the Office of Educational Research and Improvement (Grant No. R308A960003) to the Consortium for Policy Research in Education and by two grants from the Spencer Foundation (one to the Wisconsin Center for Education Research for the study of school probation in Chicago elementary schools and the other to Marshall S. Smith to explore implementation issues in standards-based reform). All findings, opinions, and conclusions expressed in this chapter, however, are those of the author and do not necessarily reflect the views of any of the funders.

REFERENCES

Abelmann, C., & Elmore, R. F., with Even, J., Kenyon, S., & Marshall, J. (1999). *When accountability knocks, will anyone answer?* (CPRE Research Report No. RR-42). Philadelphia: Consortium for Policy Research in Education, University of Pennsylvania.

Adams, J. E., & Kirst, M. W. (1999). New demands for educational accountability: Striving for results in an era of excellence. In J. Murphy & K. S. Louis (Eds.), *Handbook of research in educational administration* (pp. 463–489). Washington, DC: American Educational Research Association.

Axelrod, R., & Cohen, M. D. (2000). *Harnessing complexity: Organizational implications of a scientific frontier.* New York: Free Press.

Bennett, A. (2001, April). *The history, politics, and theory of action of the Chicago probation policy*. Paper presented at the annual meeting of the American Educational Research Association, Seattle.

Berman, P., & McLaughlin, M. (1977). *Federal programs supporting educational change: Vol. VII. Factors affecting implementation and continuation.* Santa Monica, CA: RAND.

Campbell, J. P., McCloy, R. A., Oppler, S. H., & Sager, C. E. (1993). A theory of performance. In N. Schmitt, W. C. Borman, & Associates (Eds.), *Personnel selection in organizations* (pp. 35–70). San Francisco: Jossey-Bass.

Cohen, D. K., & Ball, D. L. (1999). *Instruction, capacity, and improvement* (CPRE Research Report No. RR-43). Philadelphia: Consortium for Policy Research in Education, University of Pennsylvania.

Darling-Hammond, L. (1996). Restructuring schools for high performance. In S. H. Fuhrman & J. A. O'Day (Eds.), *Rewards and reform: Creating educational incentives that work* (pp. 144–192). San Francisco: Jossey-Bass.

Darling-Hammond, L., & Ascher, C. (1991). *Creating accountability in big city school systems*. New York: ERIC Clearinghouse on Urban Education.

DeBray, E., Parson, G., & Woodworth, K. (2001). Patterns of response in four high schools under state accountability policies in Vermont and New York. In S. H. Fuhrman (Ed.), *From the capitol to the classroom: Standards-based reform in the states* (pp. 170–192). Chicago: University of Chicago Press.

Elmore, R. F. (1996). *Staff development and instructional improvement: Community District 2, New York City*. New York and Philadelphia: National Commission on Teaching and America's Future, and Consortium for Policy Research in Education, University of Pennsylvania.

Elmore, R. F. (2001, April). *Psychiatrists and light bulbs: Educational accountability and the problem of capacity*. Paper presented at the annual meeting of the American Educational Research Association, Seattle.

Elmore R. F., Abelmann, C. H., & Fuhrman, S. H. (1996). The new accountability in state education reform: From process to performance. In H. F. Ladd (Ed.), *Holding schools accountable: Performance-based reform in education* (pp. 65–98). Washington, DC: Brookings Institution.

Evans, L. E., & Wei, H. H. (2001, April). *Focusing the work of teachers and schools: The Chicago Public Schools probation policy*. Paper prepared for the annual meeting of the American Educational Research Association, Seattle.

Finnigan, K. S., & Gross, B. M. (2001, April). *Teacher motivation and the Chicago probation policy*. Paper presented at the annual meeting of the American Educational Research Association, Seattle.

Finnigan, K., & O'Day, J. A. (2003). *External support to schools on probation: Getting a leg up?* Philadelphia: Consortium for Policy Research in Education, University of Pennsylvania, & Chicago: Consortium on Chicago School Research.

Firestone, W. A., & Mayrowetz, D. (2000). Rethinking "high stakes": Lessons from the United States and England and Wales. *Teachers College Record, 102*(4), 724–749.

Fuhrman, S. H. (1999). *The new accountability* (CPRE Policy Brief No. RB-27). Philadelphia: Consortium for Policy Research in Education, University of Pennsylvania.

Goertz, M. E., Floden, R., & O'Day, J. A. (1995). *Studies of education reform: Systemic reform: Vol. 1. Findings and conclusions.* New Brunswick, NJ: Consortium for Policy Research in Education, Rutgers University.

Grissmer, D., Flanagan, A., Kawata, J., & Williamson, S. (2000). *Improving student achievement: What state NAEP test scores tell us* (MR-924-EDU). Santa Monica, CA: RAND.

Gwynne, J., & Easton, J. Q. (2001, April). *Probation, organizational capacity, and student achievement in Chicago elementary schools.* Paper presented at the annual meeting of the American Educational Research Association, Seattle.

Haney, W. (2000). The myth of the Texas miracle in education. *Education Policy Analysis Archives, 8*(41).

Huber, G. P. (1991). Organizational learning: The contributing processes and the literatures. *Organizational Science, 2*(1), 88–115.

Kelley, C., Odden, A. R., Milanowski, A., & Heneman, H. (2000). *The motivational effects of school-based performance awards* (CPRE Policy Brief No. RB-29). Philadelphia: Consortium for Policy Research in Education, University of Pennsylvania.

Klein, S. P., Hamilton, L. S., McCaffrey, D. F., & Stecher, B. M. (2000). *What do test scores in Texas tell us?* Washington, DC: RAND.

Koretz, D., & Barron, S. (1998). *The validity of gains on the Kentucky Instructional Results Information System* (MR-1014-EDU). Santa Monica, CA: RAND.

Lee, V., & Smith, J. (1996). Collective responsibility for learning and its effects on gains in achievement for early secondary school students. *American Journal of Education, 104*, 103–147.

Little, J. W. (1990). The persistence of privacy: Autonomy and initiative in teachers' professional relations. *Teachers College Record, 91*, 509–536.

Lortie, D. C. (1975). *Schoolteacher: A sociological study.* Chicago: University of Chicago Press.

March, J. G. (1991). Exploration and exploitation in organizational learning. *Organizational Science, 2*(1), 71–87.

March, J. G. (1994). *A primer on decision making: How decisions happen.* New York: Free Press.

Marion, R. (1999). *The edge of organization: Chaos and complexity theories of formal social systems.* Thousand Oaks, CA: Sage.

McLaughlin, M. (1987). Learning from experience: Lessons from policy implementation. *Educational Evaluation and Policy Analysis, 9*(2), 171–178.

McLaughlin, M. W., Shepard, L. A., & O'Day, J. A. (1995). *Improving education through standards-based reform: A report by the National Academy of Education Panel on Standards-Based Reform.* Stanford: National Academy of Education.

McLaughlin, M. W., & Talbert, J. E. (1993). *Contexts that matter for teaching and learning.* Stanford: Center for Research on the Context of Teaching, Stanford University.

McLaughlin, M. W., & Talbert, J. E. (2001). *Professional communities and the work of high school teaching*. Chicago: University of Chicago Press.

Mohrman, S. A., & Lawler, E. E. (1996). Motivation for school reform. In S. H. Fuhrman & J. A. O'Day (Eds.), *Rewards and reform: Creating educational incentives that work* (pp. 115–143). San Francisco: Jossey-Bass.

National Governors Association. (1993). *The debate on opportunity-to-learn standards: Supporting works*. Washington, DC: Author.

Newmann, F. M., & Wehlage, G. G. (1995). *Successful school restructuring: A report to the public and educators by the Center on Organization and Restructuring of Schools*. Madison: Center on Organization and Restructuring of Schools, University of Wisconsin–Madison.

Nolen, S. B., Haladyna, T. M., & Haas, N. (1992). Uses and abuses of achievement test scores. *Educational Measurement: Issues and Practice, 11*(2), 9–15.

O'Day, J. A. (2002). Complexity, accountability, and school improvement. *Harvard Educational Review, 72*(3), 293–329.

O'Day, J. A., & Smith, M. S. (1993). Systemic reform and educational opportunity. In S. H. Fuhrman (Ed.), *Designing coherent education policy: Improving the system* (pp. 313–322). San Francisco: Jossey Bass.

O'Reilly, F. E. (1996). *Educational accountability: Current practices and theories in use*. Cambridge, MA: Consortium for Policy Research in Education, Harvard University.

Porter, A., & Brophy, J. (1988). Good teaching: Insights from the work of the Institute for Research on Teaching. *Educational Leadership, 45*(8), 75–84.

Scott, W. R. (1998). *Organizations: Rational, natural, and open systems* (4th ed.). Upper Saddle River, NJ: Prentice Hall.

Simon, H. A. (1986). Theories of bounded rationality. In C. B. McGuire & R. Radner (Eds.), *Decision and organization* (Vol. 2, pp. 161–176). Minneapolis: University of Minnesota Press.

Sitkin, S. B. (1992). Learning through failure: The strategy of small losses. *Research in Organizational Behavior, 14*, 231–266.

Smith, M. L., & Rottenberg, C. (1991). Unintended consequences of external testing in elementary schools. *Educational Measurement: Issues and Practice, 10*(11), 7–11.

Spillane, J. (2000). Cognition and policy implementation: District policymakers and the reform of mathematics education. *Cognition and Instruction, 18*(2), 141–179.

Staw, B. M., Sanderlands, L. E., & Dutton, J. E. (1981). Threat-rigidity effects in organizational behavior: A multilevel analysis. *Administration Science Quarterly, 26*, 501–524.

Weatherly, R., & Lipsky, M. (1977). Street-level bureaucrats and institutional innovation: Implementing special-education reform. *Harvard Educational Review, 47*, 171–197.

PART II

ISSUES IN DESIGNING ACCOUNTABILITY SYSTEMS

Chapter 3

Validity Issues for Accountability Systems

Eva L. Baker
Robert L. Linn

The purpose of this chapter is to provide an analysis of the validity issues that arise in the context of educational accountability systems. We will address validity from three interlocking perspectives. The first explores the theory of action underlying accountability provisions. Here, we will consider problems ensuing from the distance between aspirations for accountability in education reform and the actual strength of the research base supporting sets of policies and procedures. A second component of our analysis will concentrate on the role of testing in accountability systems, as it defines the characteristics and potential of many systems. This discussion is grounded strongly in the *Standards for Educational and Psychological Testing* (American Educational Research Association, American Psychological Association, & National Council on Measurement in Education [AERA, APA, & NCME], 1999). The third set of issues will offer suggestions about an approach to improve the validity of accountability systems.

THEORY OF ACTION FOR ACCOUNTABILITY SYSTEMS

The theory of action underlying the adoption of accountability systems derives from the adage "knowledge is power." It assumes that when people (or institutions) are given results of an endeavor, they will act to build on strengths and remedy or ameliorate weaknesses. Such positive actions depend on at least seven enabling conditions.

1. the results reported are accurate;
2. the results are validly interpreted;
3. cognizant individuals are willing to act and can motivate action by team members;
4. alternative actions to improve the situation are known and available;
5. cognizant individuals and team members possess the requisite knowledge to apply alternative methods;
6. the selected action is adequately implemented; and
7. the action(s) selected will improve subsequent results.

The theory also assumes that barriers to improvement have lower strength than the desire to achieve goals and that there are clear and powerful incentives for positive actions.

Parsing education reform in this framework raises numerous questions. In this chapter we focus primarily on issues related to the first two enabling conditions, accurate and validly interpreted results. It is, however, important to recognize that those aspects derive their importance within the broader theory of action just outlined. Additional chapters in this volume address other aspects of this theory of action.

The first two conditions, accurately reported and validly interpreted results, depend on the quality of measures available and the capacity of users to understand and interpret information. The first of these concerns is extensively treated in the section on assessment. In summary, it may be that some assessments are not sensitive to instructional remedies and therefore are unsuitable for the accountability purposes to which they have been put.

The second concern, the ability of individuals to use systematically derived information, is a known problem in education. Research at the National Center for Research on Evaluation, Standards, and Student Testing on the development of the Quality School Portfolio (Baker, Bewley, Herman, Lee, & Mitchell, 2001) has documented a lack of sophistication in data interpretation on the part of many members of the school community, from school board members to teachers. However, it also has suggested that there is a real appetite for learning about how results can lead to improvement. Such experience leads us to believe that the third condition—willingness to act—may be a reality, despite commentary to the contrary about cleaving to the status quo and exerting low energy.

The fourth condition, knowledge of powerful alternatives, is undermined by the general failure of educational systems to document rigorously the effects of such alternatives and make them available to teachers. In the absence of these alternatives, it is far more likely that teachers or instructional leadership teams draw on a palette of limited value, one largely composed by happenstance. In part, this limitation relates to the woeful lack of systematic curriculum designed to help students achieve the knowledge and skills required by standards-based assessments used in accountability systems.

Further, many practitioners may lack the knowledge or skills necessary to apply alternative methods. Educational literature is replete with discussions of the lack of background—sometimes, for instance, particular content knowledge—on which pedagogical knowledge hinges. There is some motion to replace teacher-generated instruction with more lock-step, scripted formats; however, teacher knowledge of the to-be-learned standards, of pedagogical strategies, and of the students themselves is required if any productive extemporizing is to occur.

The sixth condition has led to a particular focus in the evaluation world on implementation—that is, the need to verify that any alternative has been implemented as intended. In fact, results from many experimental studies have been discounted because the treatment variations were not implemented as planned, resulting in great within-group differences in process by teachers.

Finally, it is difficult to know *a priori* whether an instructional treatment, even if all previous conditions have been met, will be effective for the particular student group, standard, and context for which it has been implemented.

It should be clear that failure to meet any one of the conditions enumerated above could substantially undermine the success of the theory of action that underlies accountability systems. This raises serious questions about the likelihood that these components will link together effectively across teacher background, subject matter, student population, and educational setting.

While incentives and sanctions may focus attention on desired system results, they will not necessarily enable the people in classrooms and schools to do now what they have been unwilling or unable to do before—that is, systematically to improve learning for students who have done poorly in the past. Of concern to us as observers is that the rewards and sanctions indeed may focus attention on the bottom line, but not on needed steps or processes to get there. A lack of capacity (whether through selection, turnover, or inadequate professional development and resources) cannot be directly remedied by increased motivation to do well, especially over a short period.

The central notion of the validity of accountability systems resides in their ability to build system-wide capacity to achieve desired results. Accountability systems intending to promote real learning and improved effectiveness of educational services must themselves be analyzed to ensure that changes in performance (the proverbial bottom line) are real, are due to quality instruction plus motivation, are sustainable, and can be attributed to the system itself. Before we further address how such accountability information could be obtained, let us turn our attention to the core of all educational accountability systems, the measures of student achievement.

EDUCATIONAL TESTING AND ASSESSMENT

Since testing is the key feature of systems currently under consideration at the federal level, as well as those that have been implemented by states in the past decade, a substantial portion of this chapter deals with the validity of uses and interpretations of tests. There are, however, broader validity issues for accountability systems, which go beyond those normally thought of in connection with tests, and we also will address some of those issues.

Our discussion will make frequent reference to the *Standards for Educational and Psychological Testing* (AERA, APA, & NCME, 1999), which we hereafter will refer to as the Test Standards. The Test Standards are widely recognized as the most authoritative statement of professional consensus regarding expectations for tests on matters of validity, fairness, and other technical characteristics. The Test Standards define validity as follows: "Validity refers to the degree to which evidence and theory support the interpretations of test scores entailed by proposed uses of tests" (p. 9). The Test Standards go on to say that "validity is, therefore, the most fundamental consideration in developing and evaluating tests" (p. 9).

As is clearly indicated in the Test Standards, validity is not a property of a test, but rather a property of the specific uses and interpretations that are made of test scores. Hence, it is not appropriate to make an unqualified statement that an assessment is valid. Rather, an assessment that has a high degree of validity for a particular use may have little or no validity if used in a quite different manner. For this reason, the Test Standards admonish developers and users of assessments to start by providing a rationale "for each recommended interpretation and use" (AERA, APA, & NCME, 1999, p. 17).

INTENDED USES AND INTERPRETATIONS OF TESTS

Tests are used for a wide array of purposes, ranging from low-stakes diagnosis for instructional purposes to high-stakes uses such as the award of high school diplomas. At the institutional level, high stakes may mean the identification of schools that are failing or of schools where teachers are given a substantial monetary reward for progress shown in students' test results. Although the uses of tests by teachers for day-to-day instructional purposes are among the most significant uses that are made of tests for improving instruction (Black & Wiliam, 1998a, 1998b), our focus is limited to the uses of tests for externally mandated accountability purposes; however, we expect that in the future such differences in purpose may blur. For example, in the Los Angeles Unified School District, classroom-administered assessments are intended to both guide instructional practice and provide information about effectiveness. Common models are used to guide the design of tests so that standards, cognitive demands, apt content, and criteria are common to all purposes (Baker, 1997). In order to create assessments that provide a common framework for teacher practice, the design of authoring systems for teachers to use to measure standards is in process. Such systems may very well allow the use of teacher-developed tests to be aggregated to supplement externally mandated examinations (Baker & Niemi, 2001).

The utility of a coherent system—where assessments are used at all levels, for internal purposes such as on-the-spot improvement of learning, for teacher planning, and for accountability—is obvious. One such vision in science has been proposed by Pellegrino, Chudowsky, and Glaser (2001). Even so, there will remain many variations in uses and interpretations of test results that deserve attention within the context of accountability systems, and those variations can have important implications for the evaluation of the validity of specific inferences drawn from test results and the decisions that are based on those results.

The following examples provide some indication of the range of uses and interpretations of test scores that are made within the context of accountability systems.

- Students who do not obtain a passing score on a test must attend summer school and pass an alternative form of the test to be promoted to the next grade.
- Students must score at the proficient level or higher on tests in four subject areas in order to receive a high school diploma.
- Teachers in schools that rank in the top 10% in terms of gains on the state's school accountability assessment will receive a bonus of $25,000.
- Parents of students attending schools found to be failing, as defined by the test performance of their students, may transfer their children to another public school.
- Schools with schoolwide Title I programs that fail to make adequate yearly progress in student test performance will be declared unsatisfactory and targeted for assistance.

- To be accredited by the state, schools must either have overall student achievement at or above a specified goal on the state assessment or meet targets for gains in student achievement.

Each of these examples of test use, as well as others that could be specified, has a number of validity questions associated with it. Each demands the identification of the most salient of those questions and the accumulation of evidence relevant to answering those salient questions. We will illustrate some of the issues that are linked most closely to specific uses and interpretations. There are, however, some issues that are general across the variety of uses of tests in accountability systems. We will begin with a discussion of those general issues. That discussion will be followed by a discussion of validity issues that are most relevant to three broad uses, beginning with the use of test scores for making high-stakes decisions about individual students. We next will consider uses of test results for making high-stakes decisions about schools. We then will turn to a discussion of the impact of accountability systems on instruction and learning. We will end with a brief summary and conclusion.

TEST SPECIFICATIONS

Educational achievement tests focus on content domains such as reading, mathematics, or science. Such tests are intended to provide evidence of what a student knows and is able to do in a content domain without regard to an external criterion measure, such as subsequent performance in college or in the workplace. Hence, the content of an educational achievement test is an appropriate starting place for the validation process. The content of a test is critical to the creation of scores that support valid inferences about student achievement.

Two questions are central in the evaluation of content aspects of validity. Is the definition of the content domain to be assessed adequate and appropriate? Does the test provide an adequate representation of the content domain it is intended to measure? The first of these questions focuses on the content standards that states have developed to specify the content that teachers are expected to teach and students are expected to learn. The content standards also specify the domain that a state test is expected to measure. The adequacy of the content standards for specifying the domain the test is intended to measure generally depends on the specificity and concreteness of the content standards. Given the breadth of most content standards, there is usually a need to create a table of test specifications that serves to map content standards into detailed prescriptions for the makeup of tests. Tables of specifications usually provide the basis for mapping test items according to specific content (e.g., addition, subtraction, multiplication) and process (e.g., factual knowledge, conceptual understanding, problem solving) categories, represented in different item formats (e.g., multiple choice or short answer). Additional levels of specificity might well be desirable in order to create a full descriptive system of test content (Baker, 2000), including a finer-grained analysis of cognitive demands (see, for example, Anderson & Krathwohl, 2000) and linguistic characteristics of items (Abedi, 2001; Bailey, 2000; Butler, Stevens, & Castellon-Wellington, 1999; Stevens, Butler, & Castellon-Wellington, 2000). The adequacy of content aspects of validity is judged in terms of the definition of the content domain identified by the test specifications and the representativeness of the coverage of that domain by the test.

Whatever the breadth and depth of coverage or emphases of the content standards, it is generally intended that the assessment will be well-enough aligned with the content standards so that student performance on the assessment can be used as the basis for making inferences about the degree to which a student has mastered the domain of content defined by the standards. Detailed analyses of the relationship between the content domain of the content standards and the specific content of the assessment are needed to support such inferences. Confirmation of alignment of the test items and content standards by independent judges provides one type of evidence. This may be accomplished by having judges assign assessment tasks to the content standards they believe the tasks measure and comparing those assignments with the assignments of the developers of the assessment tasks. The Test Standards are explicit about the need to relate the content of the test to that of the content standards (Standard 13.3, AERA, APA, & NCME, 1999, p. 145).

Most tests are unlikely to cover the full domain of content covered by content standards. Hence, it is important to make it clear which aspects of the content standards are left uncovered by the test, which are covered only lightly, and which receive the greatest emphasis. Such an analysis provides a basis for judging the degree to which generalizations from the assessment to the broader domain of the content standards are defensible. Messick (1989) referred to the threat to validity of inadequate coverage of the domain as "construct under-representation." Construct under-representation is a major concern in large-scale assessment because of the potential effect that only aspects of the domain that are relatively easy to measure will be assessed, which, in turn, can lead to a narrowing and distortion of instructional priorities.

In addition to identifying the content that students are expected to learn, content standards adopted by states generally specify the cognitive processes that students are expected to be able to use (e.g., reasoning, conceptual understanding, problem solving). Hence, judgments of the alignment of the test with content standards need to attend to cognitive processes that students need to use to answer test items, as well as the content (Standard 1.8, AERA, APA, & NCME, 1999, p. 19).

USE OF TESTS TO MAKE HIGH-STAKES DECISIONS ABOUT INDIVIDUAL STUDENTS

Evaluating the adequacy and appropriateness of test content, and of the cognitive demands of a test, provides only one link in a validity argument. Other links depend on evidence that can be used to judge the adequacy and appropriateness of the uses that are made of test results and the interpretations of the scores. The latter considerations clearly depend on the specific uses and interpretations that are made of test scores. Our discussion of the validity demands associated with specific uses is divided into three broad categories of use. We begin with uses for high-stakes decisions about individual students and then turn to uses for high-stakes decisions about schools.

ESTABLISHING PERFORMANCE STANDARDS

Using tests to make high-stakes decisions, such as for grade-to-grade promotion or high school graduation, involves the use of a passing score on the test. Performance standards are set, and cut scores on the test are identified that yield interpretations—for example, performance above the cut score implies that the student is proficient (passing), and performance below the cut score indicates that the student is not proficient (failing). The validity of these standards-based interpretations, also called criterion-referenced interpretations, depends on the appropriateness of the cut score. At a minimum, the interpretation needs to be supported by a rationale, as required by the Test Standards (Standard 4.9, AERA, APA, & NCME, 1999, p. 56).

The rationale for a cut score to be used to define performance that is called "proficient," for example, might include a description of the basis for the adoption of content standards and a description of the process used to identify judges and to obtain judgments, the definition of "proficient" used by the judges, and the process used to elicit judgments of performance on the test that was considered proficient. The rationale for a cut score used to determine grade-to-grade promotion might be similar to that for determining proficient performance, but also might include an analysis of the performance in the next grade for students whose scores are above and below the cut score.

CLASSIFICATION ERRORS

The use of performance standards to determine whether a student is proficient or not (passes or fails) reduces test scores to a dichotomy. Measurement error that is associated with any test score results in classification errors. That is, a student whose true level of achievement should lead to a passing score earns a score that is below the passing standard, and vice versa. Valid inferences about student proficiency are undermined by measurement errors that result in misclassification of students. Hence, it is critical that the probability of misclassification be evaluated and the information be provided to users of the performance standards results (Standard 13.14, AERA, APA,& NCME, 1999, p. 148).

The precision of test scores can be enhanced by increasing test length. As Rogosa (1999a) has shown, however, even tests that have reliability coefficients that normally are considered to be quite high (e.g., .90) result in substantial probabilities of misclassification. For example, if the passing standard is set at the 50th percentile for a test with a reliability of .90, the probability is .22 that a student whose true percentile rank is 60, and who therefore should pass, would score below the cut score and therefore fail on a given administration of the test. Even a student whose true percentile rank is 70, a full 20 points above the cut score, would have a .06 probability of failing (Rogosa, 1999a).

MULTIPLE OPPORTUNITIES TO TAKE ALTERNATE FORMS OF THE TEST

Students also should be provided with a reasonable number of chances to take equivalent versions of the test before being retained in grade or denied a diploma, and with additional opportunity to learn between test administrations (Standard 13.6, AERA, APA, & NCME, 1999, p. 146).

The importance of providing multiple opportunities to pass a test using alternate forms of the test when failure has high-stakes consequences can be illustrated by a simple example. Assume that the cut score has been set at a level corresponding to the 10th percentile. Rogosa's (1999a) analyses show that if the test has a reliability of .90, a student whose true performance was at the 20th percentile would have a probability of .0633 of scoring below the cut score due to errors of measurement. If given an opportunity to take an equivalent form of the test, however, the probability that the student would score below the cut score a second time would drop to .0040. Thus, while there would still be a nonzero probability that the 20th percentile student would fail twice due to errors of measurement, the probability is substantially reduced by providing the second opportunity and would, of course, be reduced still further by a third testing opportunity.

MULTIPLE WAYS OF DEMONSTRATING SPECIFIED COMPETENCIES

Since no test can provide a perfectly accurate or valid assessment of a student's mastery of a content domain, the Test Standards caution against overreliance on a single test score when making high-stakes decisions about students. The Test Standards indicate that multiple sources of information should be considered when the addition of information other than a test score would enhance the validity of the decision (Standard 13.7, AERA, APA, & NCME, 1999, p. 148).

This recommendation is consistent with conclusions reached in a National Academy of Sciences report prepared by a committee formed in response to a congressional mandate to review the use of tests for purposes of tracking, grade-to-grade promotion, and graduation (Heubert & Hauser, 1999). According to a recent decision by the U.S. District Court for the Western District of Texas (*G.I. Forum* v. *Texas Education Agency*, 2000), the inclusion of other information in a decision that may have a major impact on students need not be done in a compensatory manner. The court ruled that Texas could require students to exceed a specified score on the Texas Assessment of Academic Skills test as well as pass certain required courses, thus allowing a conjunctive use of a test requirement.

In addition to using alternative indicators of student achievement to supplement test score information when making high-stakes decisions about students, it is often desirable to permit the substitution of alternative measures for test scores. Alternative indicators of achievement can be especially important in cases where student performance on a test is likely to give a misleadingly low indication of the student's knowledge and understanding of the material because of debilitating test anxiety or student disabilities that call the validity of standardized test results into question. Alternative measures have been shown to generate high levels of dependability when the conditions of administration and training of scorers are controlled. It is also possible, as has been done for years with the New York Regents examinations, to check on scoring adequacy through audits of a sample of papers.

OPPORTUNITY TO LEARN MATERIAL TESTED

For tests used to determine grade-to-grade promotion or high school graduation, the Test Standards call for evidence regarding the opportunity students have to learn the material for which they are being held responsible (Standard 13.5, AERA, APA, & NCME, 1999, p. 148).

There are legal as well as moral and educational reasons for ensuring that students are provided with an adequate opportunity to learn the material on tests used for high-stakes decisions such as determining the award of high school diplomas (see Heubert, this volume). In *Debra P.* v. *Turlington* (1981), the court ruled that the graduation test must be a fair measure "of that which was taught" (p. 406).

REMEDIATION FOR STUDENTS WITH REPEATED FAILURES

Accountability is most effective when it encourages shared responsibility for results. When individual students are held accountable for meeting established performance standards on a test, it is critical that teachers and the educational system also be held accountable for providing adequate opportunity for students to meet the established standards. Where students continue to fail to meet the standards on the test after repeated attempts, it is critical that the educational system be held responsible for providing continued remediation.

USE OF TEST RESULTS FOR HIGH-STAKES DECISIONS ABOUT SCHOOLS

Many of the Test Standards are easily extrapolated to inferences drawn about schools. However, there are particular issues that might be considered for institutions. Consequences for poor performance may mean additional assistance, public identification, and consequent transfer of leadership or staff, either voluntarily or directed.

SUBJECTS AND GRADES TESTED

Accountability systems differ in who is tested and on what content (see Linn, this volume, for extended discussion of differences between assessments used in accountability systems). Some systems test every student in adjacent grades, allowing for an apparently longitudinal picture of growth. However, because the tests given at grade 4 and at grade 5 will be different, interpretation of results may be confusing. For example, students scoring at the 50th percentile in fourth grade who, in the following year, score at the 50th percentile in fifth grade did not stand still; they learned a considerable amount of new material. But often such results are used as evidence that the educational system is not making progress.

Consistent with law (Improving America's Schools Act, 1994), many systems focus only on particular grade levels (e.g., fourth-grade students) and only on a subset of subject matters (e.g., reading and mathematics). These emphases can have predictable results. The first, focusing on successive cohorts of students, assumes that changes from year to year in fourth-grade performance can be attributed to improvement, or lack thereof, in the instructional program. In fact, sources of error in the inference are many.

Changes in the student population from year to year account for one source of error. For example, in one California district, performance in mathematics and reading greatly improved in a single year. Although attributions to a talented principal generally were made, the finding actually was attributable to a business closing in a nearby wealthier county and the influx of a well-prepared student group to the target school (L. Burstein, personal communication, 1988).

The second source of error is the idea that the school itself is a unit that is stable enough to be credited for changes in student performance. We know, for example, that turnover rates of teachers in urban schools are high and that schools change internally even if they keep the same name; there is no evidence (and no request for it) to support the implication that a certain teacher, principal, or team accounts for performance year to year.

A third source of error stems from the assumption that scores in tested subjects reflect the overall quality of instruction in schools. Warnings about "narrowed" curriculum, or glowing reports of "focused instruction," may amount to the same thing—overemphasis on assessed subjects at the expense of others. If schools are to be responsible for services such as the arts, sciences, or community service, then such efforts must find their way into accountability systems.

CHARACTERISTICS OF STUDENTS ATTENDING SCHOOLS

Testing results are notoriously sensitive to student background characteristics. These characteristics include the economic and educational levels of parents, parents' expectations for student success, students' language backgrounds, the average length of time students attend a school, and the regularity with which students come to school. Even though notable variations in performance can be found within these factors, it is clear that accountability systems must address these differences. We also know that students with at-risk backgrounds often attend schools with fewer credentialed teachers and fewer resources, and in less well-maintained facilities.

One approach is to focus on the absolute status of the school—how its students at targeted grade levels are doing in a cross-sectional view. In addition, some systems report growth, the change from year to year. Thus, the inferences about student growth, or the targets set for individual schools, need to recognize these differences. Far different actions may be inferred, however. Schools with children far behind may in fact need to have high growth targets if they are to catch up to more affluent students.

Yet, such catching up is likely to be difficult for students who may not have acquired desired prerequisite knowledge, skills, and cognitions, or attitudes that support school achievement.

INCLUSION OF STUDENTS WITH LIMITED ENGLISH PROFICIENCY

When we think of census testing, that is, testing all students in a school, we normally believe that every child will be included in test results. However, there are numerous examples in the past of testing programs that have tested all students, but systematically excluded results of a subset. To remedy this problem, many accountability systems require that the percentage of students tested in the school be published. Further, some, such as the current California system, require that a stated percentage must be tested if the school is to receive a special monetary award.

How best to handle the inclusion of students with emerging English proficiency is not straightforward. Language experts and parent advocates argue that students should be tested in their native language until they have demonstrated a sufficient level of English-language proficiency. Some states have prohibitions against testing in translated languages, or translate only one or two languages when students may represent 50 or 100 languages and dialects. Other systems provide various linguistic accommodations to assist students in testing. Common accommodations include longer testing periods, glossaries, or oral support. It is true that many of these accommodated test conditions are not subjected to validity studies to determine whether the construct or domain tested has been significantly altered. In part, this lack of empirical data results from restricted resources. Nonetheless, the major threat to accurate interpretation is that of construct-irrelevant variance (Messick, 1989), where inferences drawn about the domain under examination may be contaminated by difficulty experienced by students in deciphering the meaning of the language in which the test question(s) are embedded. Standard 9.1 deals with this concern. The Test Standards recommend that tests be "designed to reduce threats to the reliability and validity of test score inferences that may arise from language differences" (AERA, APA, & NCME, 1999, p. 97).

INCLUSION OF STUDENTS WITH DISABILITIES

Students with disabilities also are required to participate in accountability-focused testing programs. Depending on the nature of the disability, students may be given accommodations involving more time, or sensory support, or may, in fact, be given an alternative assessment intended to address the particular goals identified for the learner. Such modifications or alternative assessments should be, although often are not, subject to empirical study (Standard 10.3, AERA, APA, & NCME, 1999, p. 148).

ACCOUNTING FOR PERFORMANCE OF IDENTIFIABLE SUBGROUPS OF STUDENTS

Many accountability systems and the 2001 Elementary and Secondary Education Act legislation require that student performance be disaggregated by identifiable subgroups. The logic is that schools should not try to meet their accountability targets by focusing on one or more groups to the exclusion of others. Many such systems require that progress by each subgroup must reach a particular threshold (e.g., 80% of the projected target). In some cases, even where the school as a whole has met a growth target, rewards are withheld if one or more subgroups had subpar performance.

CLASSIFICATION OF SCHOOLS

Accountability systems typically array schools into categories intended to reflect their level of performance and rate of progress in meeting explicit standards. These classifications may be wholly based on weighted averages of test score performance in some or all grades tested. There is a growing literature that addresses the problem of reliably classifying schools in categories such as advanced, adequate, or needs improvement (Kane & Staiger, 2002; Linn, this volume; Linn & Haug, 2002; Rogosa, 1999b). The probability of misclassifying a school based on student test scores depends on a number of factors, including the number of categories used, the number of students that enter into the calculation of the school's scores used in the classification, whether current performance or change in student performance is used, and whether subgroup performance as well as total group performance is used to determine classification.

The research investigating the dependability of school-level results and classification error rates has shown that the probability of misclassification is substantial. Error rates increase as the number of students decreases. Thus the probability that a small school will be misclassified is greater than the probability of misclassification of a large school. Because of the relationship of misclassification probability to school size, it is common for the set of schools identified as the best performers and the ones classified as the worst performers to be disproportionately made up of small schools. Also, as a consequence of the effects of size on misclassification probabilities, it is common to find that the schools that look best (or worst) based on their gains from year 1 to year 2 generally will not show up in the same category based on their gains from year 2 to year 3. As Linn and Haug (2002) have shown, there is a negative correlation between the gains schools make from year 1 to year 2 and the gains they make from year 2 to year 3.

Accountability systems that demand gains for schools not only for the total student population, but for all subgroups of students defined by the socioeconomic background or racial/ethnic group to which students belong, also will have higher rates of misclassification. As Kane and Staiger (2002) have shown, disaggregating scores by racial/ethnic group reduces sample size and therefore exacerbates the problems of volatility of school-level results.

Uncertainty is also greater when change scores are used than when status measures are used. It is well known that difference scores are less reliable than the scores that are used to compute the difference. This general result for individual student scores also applies to scores for schools.

The limited precision in estimates of school improvement based on comparisons of successive groups of students presents a major challenge for school accountability systems that rely on annual improvements in the performance of successive cohorts of students. There are several approaches that can be used to help ameliorate the problems of imprecision and the resulting high probabilities of misclassification errors. Accuracy can be improved by combining data across multiple grades, multiple subject areas, and/or multiple years. Combining across either grades or years increases the precision of results by increasing the number of students used to estimate school results. Combining across grades has the added advantage of increasing the number of teachers who are teaching students whose performance directly contributes to the accountability results for the school, and thereby may increase the sense of shared responsibility of results. Combining across several years lengthens the accountability cycle, but produces results that are more trustworthy and therefore more likely to lead to real long-term improvements and to the identification of exemplary practices.

Whatever the level of precision of school-level results, the results for schools should be accompanied by information about the dependability of those results as required by the Test Standards. This might best be done where schools are placed into graded performance categories by reporting information about the accuracy of classifications. Procedures for evaluating school-building misclassification probabilities are described by Rogosa (1999b) and by Hoffman and Wise (2000).

IMPACT OF ACCOUNTABILITY SYSTEM ON INSTRUCTION AND LEARNING

The Test Standards require that validation of test use for high-stakes decisions about students include attention to empirical evidence of the intended and unintended consequences of those uses. Test requirements for promotion or graduation clearly are intended to ensure that students have mastered specified content before they are allowed to move on to the next grade or graduate. There is also the implicit intent that students will learn more in the long run if they are held accountable for achieving at a specified level for the promotion or graduation decision. The Test Standards require that evidence be provided so that a reasonable evaluation can be made of the degree to which these intentions are realized by the promotion or graduation policy (Standard 1.23, AERA, APA, & NCME, 1999, p. 148).

In addition to providing evidence that the intended effects of the test requirements are met to a reasonable degree, the Test Standards require that attention also be given to the collection of evidence relevant to plausible unintended negative consequences of the test use and whether those consequences may be related to the test's failure to represent the intended construct or its sensitivity to characteristics it did not intend to assess (Standard 1.24, AERA, APA, & NCME, 1999, p. 148).

IMPROVING ACCOUNTABILITY SYSTEMS

We have embarked on a great national experiment, with various states attempting to meet desirable performance goals using their own systems of tests and accountability. How do we support the good intentions of policy makers in improving schools and simultaneously correct processes that potentially may mislead us? Furthermore, how can we create systems that will motivate students and educators to focus on high standards without sacrificing quality instruction and breadth of learning? The real answer is that no one knows for sure. Our proposal, however, is to promote a set of accountability standards to assist policy makers, the public, and the education community in understanding the quality of accountability systems in place. Standards for products, systems, and services give users and managers criteria to use to improve the quality of their efforts and outcomes. In education, standards have been promulgated for instructional products, for interoperability of software, for tests, for evaluations, and for desired goals and competencies of teachers and students.

In this era of educational accountability, standards for accountability system design, operation, and interpretation can assist educational policy makers, managers, teachers, the media, and parents to develop reasonable expectations and to draw appropriate conclusions from test results or other systematically collected educational information. The standards may help such systems to avoid inadvertent negative effects and, instead, to promote the interests of students and educational personnel who participate in accountability systems.

The standards offered below (Baker, Linn, Herman, Koretz, & Elmore,

2001) represent models of practice derived from three perspectives: (1) research knowledge, (2) practical experience, and (3) ethical considerations. The standards are intended to guide those interested in improving the validity and utility of accountability information. Because experience with accountability systems is still developing, the standards we propose are intended to help evaluate existing systems and to guide the design of improved procedures. They should be conceived of as targets for systems. It is not possible at this stage of development of accountability systems to know in advance how every element of an accountability system actually will operate in practice or what effects it will produce, so we also suggest standards for the evaluation of impact.

To accommodate the differing maturity levels of accountability systems, we have devised standards that fall into two general categories: (1) those that should be applied to existing systems, and (2) those that specify necessary evaluation requirements for new systems. It should be understood that tests included in an accountability system should meet the Test Standards. What we have highlighted here are criteria that apply especially to accountability systems. It is likely also that additional standards will be developed subsequently based on evaluations of accountability system effects.

STANDARDS ON SYSTEM COMPONENTS

1. Accountability systems should employ different types of data from multiple sources.
   Comment: Although measures of student achievement may be of primary interest for accountability purposes, it is important also to obtain information about student and teacher characteristics to provide context for interpreting student achievement. It also is important to consider other student outcome data, such as attendance, mobility, rates of retention in grade, dropout, and graduation. Moreover, it is important to obtain data on instructional resources and curriculum materials, and about the degree to which students are provided with adequate opportunity to learn the content specified in content standards and curriculum materials.
2. The weighting of elements in the system, different test content, and different information sources should be made explicit.
   Comment: Making sense of overall accountability indices requires an understanding not only of the elements that go into the indices, but of the weights that are assigned to each element. It is informative to provide not only the weights that are assigned to the different elements by policy, but also information about how each element relates to the overall index. The relationship of an element to a weighted accountabil-

ity index depends on the variability of the element across institutions as well as the weight assigned to the element according to policy.

3. Accountability systems should include data elements that allow for interpretations of student, institution, and administrative performance.
   Comment: Students, teachers, administrators, and policy makers have a shared responsibility for achieving the results expected by accountability systems. The system needs to provide the information for each of these parties to know what actions need to be taken.

4. Accountability expectations should be made public and understandable for all participants in the system.
   Comment: Explicit information about expectations is a prerequisite for participants to perceive the accountability system as fair. It also is needed for participants to act in ways that will allow them to meet expectations and to monitor their progress.

5. Accountability systems should include the performance of all students, including subgroups that historically have been difficult to assess.
   Comment: Previous practices that excluded many students from testing, due to absence on the day of test administration, or because of limited English proficiency, or because of student disabilities, gave a distorted and usually exaggerated view of overall performance. It also meant that there was no accountability for the performance of excluded students. Legal requirements as well as ethical considerations demand that all students be included in the accountability system. Many students who would have been excluded in the past can be included without any alterations in the test or administration conditions. Some accommodations in administration conditions will be required for other students, and for some students the test will need to be modified, or alternative assessments used, in order for the students to be included in the accountability system. No student should be left out of the system, however.

TESTING STANDARDS

6. Decisions about individual students should not be made on the basis of a single test.
   Comment: No test is perfectly valid or perfectly reliable. There is always a degree of uncertainty associated with any test score. That uncertainty needs to be taken into account when making decisions about individual students. This can be done by looking for other information that will either support or disconfirm the information provided by a single test score. The importance of obtaining other information to confirm or disconfirm the information provided by a single test score in-

creases as the importance of the decision and the stakes associated with it increase.

7. Multiple test forms should be used when there are repeated administrations of an assessment.

   Comment: The items contained on a test form are only a sample of the domain that the test is intended to measure. Learning the answers to the items on a single form by focusing exclusively on those items is not the same as learning the material for the domain of content the test is intended to measure. Consequently, it is important to evaluate the generalizability of performance by administering a different form when a test is administered for a second or third time.

8. The validity of measures that have been administered as part of an accountability system should be documented for the various purposes of the system.

   Comment: Validity is dependent on the specific uses and interpretations of test scores. It is inappropriate to assume that a test that is valid when used for one purpose also will be valid for other uses or interpretations. Hence, validity needs to be specifically evaluated and documented for each purpose.

9. If tests are to help improve system performance, data should be provided illustrating that the results are modifiable by quality instruction and student effort.

   Comment: Tests need to be sensitive to differences in instructional quality and student effort in order to be useful as tools in improving system performance. Sensitivity to instruction and to student effort is also a prerequisite for fairness if educators and students are to be held accountable for results.

10. If test data are used as a basis of rewards or sanctions, evidence of technical quality of the measures and error rates associated with misclassification of individuals or institutions should be published.

    Comment: Because tests are fallible measures, classification errors are inevitable when tests are used to classify students or institutions into categories associated with rewards or sanctions. In order to judge whether the risk of errors is acceptably low, it is essential that information be provided about the probability of misclassifications of various kinds.

11. Evidence of test validity for students with different language backgrounds should be made publicly available.

    Comment: Validity needs to be assessed separately for students with different language backgrounds. Whether a test is administered in English or in a student's primary language, validity of the test for students of different language backgrounds cannot be assumed from evidence based only on test results of students whose first language is English. Testing students in their primary language may be required for some students. However, translation and adaptation of tests to different languages is a complex undertaking. There are many threats to validity of tests administered in different languages. Lack of consistency between the language of the test and the language of instruction is one of the major threats to validity that needs to be evaluated.

12. Evidence of test validity for children with disabilities should be made publicly available.

Comment: Accommodations may be needed for some students with disabilities to be able to participate in testing in a meaningful way. The goal of accommodations is to remove sources of difficulty that are irrelevant to the intent of the measurement. That is, an accommodation should make it possible for a student with disabilities to demonstrate her knowledge and skills in the content domain being tested so that the score reflects the knowledge and skills rather than the student's disability. The accommodation should level the playing field, but it is not intended to give the student with a disability an unfair advantage over other students. The validation task is to provide evidence that the test reflects the student's knowledge and skills and not her specific disability. For students with severe disabilities, assessments may need to be modified, or alternative assessments may need to be selected or developed, possibly designed to assess different learning goals than those of the assessments used for the majority of students. Evidence regarding the validity of interpretations made from modified or alternative assessments should be provided to the extent feasible.

13. If tests are claimed to measure content and performance standards, evidence of the relationship to particular standards or sets of standards should be provided.

Comment: The degree of alignment of a test with content standards may be evaluated, for example, by providing a mapping of the test specifications to the content standards. Such a mapping can reveal areas of the content standards that are not included in the test specifications as well as areas that are lightly or heavily sampled in the test specifications. The mapping also may reveal areas tested that are not part of the content standards. Performance standards generally provide verbal descriptions of levels of performance that are considered satisfactory or exemplary. The degree to which the descriptions map directly to the test items and the correspondence of the performance standards to the cut scores on the test need to be documented and evaluated.

STAKES

14. Stakes for accountability systems should apply to adults and students.
    Comment: Asymmetry in stakes may have undesirable consequences, both perceived and real. For example, if teachers and administrators are held accountable for student achievement but students are not, then there are likely to be concerns about the degree to which students put forth their best effort in taking the tests. Conversely, it may be unfair to hold students accountable for performance on a test without having some assurance that teachers and other adults are being held accountable for providing students with adequate opportunity to learn the material that is tested.

15. Incentives and sanctions should be coordinated for adults and students to support system goals.
    Comment: Incentives and sanctions that push in opposite directions for adults and for students can be counterproductive. They need to be consistent with one another and with the goals of the system.

16. Appeal procedures should be available to contest rewards and sanctions.
    Comment: Extenuating circumstances may call the validity of results into question. For example, a disturbance during test administration may invalidate the results. Individuals also may have information that leads to conflicting conclusions about performance. Appeal procedures allow for such additional information to be brought to bear on the decision and thereby enhance its validity.

17. Stakes for results and their phase-in schedule should be made explicit at the outset of the implementation of the system.
    Comment: Making plans for phasing in stakes for results is part of making accountability expectations explicit to participants. Explication of plans allows participants to make informed decisions about how best to achieve the ends expected by the accountability system.

18. Accountability systems should begin with broad, diffuse stakes and move to specific consequences for individuals and institutions as the system aligns.
    Comment: Starting with broad, diffuse stakes (e.g., public reporting of aggregate achievement results for schools) allows participants time to make the changes needed to meet expectations before being confronted with specific rewards or sanctions for performance (e.g., monetary rewards to schools or teachers, graduation requirements for students). Advance warning and phasing in of stakes enhance both the perception of fairness and the actual fairness of the accountability system.

PUBLIC REPORTING FORMATS

19. System results should be made broadly available to the media, with sufficient time for reasonable analysis and with clear explanations of legitimate and potential illegitimate interpretations of results.
    Comment: The media plays an important role in the interpretation of the results produced by accountability systems. Legitimate interpretations of results require an understanding of what goes into them and some of their technical characteristics. Those responsible for the accountability system also have a responsibility to help ensure proper interpretation of the results and to minimize inappropriate interpretations to the extent possible. Efforts to assist the media in understanding the results, their strengths and limitations, and their legitimate and illegitimate interpretations, can pay considerable dividends in improved coverage by the media and better understanding by the public.

20. Reports to districts and schools should promote appropriate interpretation and use of results by including multiple indicators of performance, error estimates, and performance by subgroup.
    Comment: Interpretations of results can be enriched by the reporting of consistencies and inconsistencies provided by multiple indicators of performance. Performance by subgroups needs to be considered to ensure that overall results do not conceal great disparities in subgroup performance. Understanding the degree of uncertainty in results can reduce the likelihood of misinterpretation and enhance the likelihood of appropriate use of results.

EVALUATION

21. Longitudinal studies should be planned, implemented, and reported, evaluating effects of the accountability program. Minimally, questions should determine the degree to which the system:
    a. builds capacity of staff;
    b. affects resource allocation;
    c. supports high-quality instruction;
    d. promotes student equity access to education;
    e. minimizes corruption;
    f. affects teacher quality, recruitment, and retention; and
    g. produces unanticipated outcomes.
       Comment: The primary purpose of educational accountability systems is to improve instruction and student learning. The overarching evaluation question is the degree to which the intended benefits are realized and the costs in terms of unintended negative consequences

are minimized. Listed items (a) through (d) reflect intended positive consequences, the realization of which is the focus of evaluation. Items (e) and (g) emphasize the needed evaluation of plausible unintended negative consequences. Item (f) requires the evaluation of both intended positive and unintended negative influences of the accountability system.

22. The validity of test-based inferences should be subject to ongoing evaluation. In particular, evaluation should address:

   a. aggregate gains in performance over time; and

   b. impact on identifiable student and personnel groups.

   Comment: Gains in performance may be spurious or real. Evaluation of the gains may be aided by investigations of the degree to which gains on the measures used by the accountability system are reflected in changes on alternative indicators of performance obtained from other tests or more general indicators such as performance beyond school in college or the workplace. Differential effects on identifiable student or personnel groups may lead to different conclusions than those that are supported by the overall aggregate performance.

APPLICATION OF THE ACCOUNTABILITY STANDARDS

Standards abound in education—to guide content for students, to express expectations for performance, even to standardize software protocols. In the area of testing, the AERA–APA–NCME (1999) standards follow in a tradition of professional consensus and guide graduate training, testing practices, and legal interpretations. They are augmented by other efforts to summarize and highlight key concerns, including the *Code of Fair Testing Practices in Education* (Joint Committee on Testing Practices, 1994), *Responsible Test Use: Case Studies for Assessing Human Behavior* (Eyde et al., 1993), *High Stakes: Testing for Tracking, Promotion, and Graduation* (Heubert & Hauser, 1999), and *Testing, Teaching, and Learning: A Guide for States and School Districts* (Elmore & Rothman, 1999).

SUMMARY AND CONCLUSION

Educational accountability systems may not, by themselves, achieve the many goals held by their supporters. Through the adoption of these standards as achievable goals, however, state accountability systems themselves can become what they espouse—systems that learn from experience. To improve their quality and, as a result, the validity of inferences derived from their data, we suggest the following cycle. First, we need to understand the theories of action that support the development of one or another model, and address the implications of particular approaches. Second, without fail, the measures used to assess student and school performance should be grounded in and exemplify the best of the considerable research base associated with the technical quality of tests. Third, the public, parents, politicians, and educators should hold accountability systems to high technical standards. We must find a way to support states and districts that attempt to reach accountability standards, and to encourage the collection of evaluation data on them to assess the extent to which accountability systems or components help, are indifferent to, or undermine the goal of educational excellence.

REFERENCES

Abedi, J. (2001). *Standardized achievement tests and English language learners: Psychometrics and linguistics issues.* Submitted for publication.

American Educational Research Association, American Psychological Association, & National Council on Measurement in Education. (1999). *Standards for educational and psychological testing.* Washington, DC: Authors.

Anderson, L. W., & Krathwohl, D. R. (2000). *A taxonomy for learning, teaching, and assessing: A revision of Bloom's taxonomy of educational objectives.* New York: Longman.

Bailey, A. (2000). Language analysis of standardized achievement tests: Consideration in the assessment of English language learners. In *The validity of administering large-scale content assessments to English language learners: An investigation from three perspectives* (Final deliverable to OERI/OBEMLA, Contract No. R305B60002; pp. 85–105). Los Angeles: National Center for Research on Evaluation, Standards, and Student Testing, University of California.

Baker, E. L. (1997). Model-based performance assessment. *Theory Into Practice*, *36*(4), 247–254.

Baker, E. L. (2000). *Understanding educational quality: Where validity meets technology.* Princeton, NJ: Educational Testing Service.

Baker, E. L., Bewley, W. L., Herman, J. L., Lee, J. J., & Mitchell, D. S. (2001). *Upgrading America's use of information to improve student performance* (Proposal to the U.S. Secretary of Education). Los Angeles: National Center for Research on Evaluation, Standards, and Student Testing, University of California.

Baker, E. L., Linn, R. L., Herman, J. L., Koretz, D., & Elmore, R. (2001, April). *Holding accountability systems accountable: Research-based standards.* Symposium presented at the annual meeting of the American Educational Research Association, Seattle.

Baker, E. L., & Niemi, D. (2001). *Assessments to support the transition to complex learning in science* (Proposal submitted to the Interagency Education Research

Initiative [IERI], Program Solicitation NSF-01-92). Los Angeles: National Center for Research on Evaluation, Standards, and Student Testing, University of California.

Black, P., & Wiliam, D. (1998a). Assessment and classroom learning. *Assessment in Education, 5*(1), 7-74.

Black, P., & Wiliam, D. (1998b). *Inside the black box: Raising standards through classroom assessment.* London: King's College London, School of Education. (See also article with the same title, 1998, in *Phi Delta Kappan, 80*, 139-148.)

Butler, F. A., Stevens, R., & Castellon-Wellington, M. (1999). *Academic language proficiency task development process* (Final deliverable to OERI, Contract No. R305B60002). Los Angeles: National Center for Research on Evaluation, Standards, and Student Testing, University of California.

Debra P. v. *Turlington,* 644 F.2d 397, 6775 (5th Cir. 1981).

Elmore, R. F., & Rothman, R. (Eds.). (1999). *Testing, teaching, and learning: A guide for states and school districts.* Washington, DC: National Research Council.

Eyde, L. G., Robertson, G. J., Krug, S. E., Moreland, K. L., Robertson, A. G., Shewan, C. M., Harrison, P. L., Porch, B. E., Hammer, A. L., & Primoff, E. S. (1993). *Responsible test use: Case studies for assessing human behavior.* Washington, DC: American Psychological Association.

G.I. Forum v. *Texas Education Agency,* 887 F. Supp. 2d 667, 675 n. 7 (W.D. Tex. 2000).

Heubert, J. P., & Hauser, R. M. (Eds.). (1999). *High stakes: Testing for tracking, promotion, and graduation.* Washington, DC: National Academy Press.

Hoffman, R. G., & Wise, L. L. (2000). *School classification accuracy final analysis plan for the Commonwealth accountability and testing system.* Alexandria, VA: HumRRO.

Improving America's Schools Act of 1994, Pub. L. No. 103-382, 108 Stat. 3518 (1994).

Joint Committee on Testing Practices. (1994). *Code of fair testing practices in education.* Washington, DC: American Psychological Association.

Kane, T. J., & Staiger, D. O. (2002). Volatility in school test scores: Implications for test-based accountability systems. In D. Ravitch (Ed.), *Brookings papers on education policy, 2002* (pp. 235-283). Washington, DC: Brookings Institution.

Linn, R. L., & Haug, C. (2002). *Stability of school building accountability scores and gains* (CSE Report). Los Angeles: National Center for Research on Evaluation, Standards, and Student Testing, University of California.

Messick, S. (1989). Validity. In R. L. Linn (Ed.), *Educational measurement* (3rd ed.; pp. 13-103). New York: Macmillan.

Pellegrino, J. P., Chudowsky, N., & Glaser, R. (Eds.). (2001). *Knowing what students know: The science and design of educational assessment.* Washington, DC: National Academy Press.

Rogosa, D. (1999a). *Accuracy of individual scores expressed in percentile ranks: Classical test theory calculations* (CSE Tech. Rep. No. 509). Los Angeles: Center for Research on Evaluation, Standards, and Student Testing, University of California.

Rogosa, D. (1999b). *Reporting group summary scores in educational assessments: Properties of proportion at or above cut-off (PAC) constructed from instruments with continuous scoring.* Los Angeles: National Center for Research on Evaluation, Standards, and Student Testing, University of California.

Stevens, R. A., Butler, F. A., & Castellon-Wellington, M. (2000). *Academic language and content assessment: Measuring the progress of ELLs* (Final deliverable to OERI/OBEMLA, Contract No. R305B60002). Los Angeles: National Center for Research on Evaluation, Standards, and Student Testing, University of California.

Chapter 4

Accountability Models

Robert L. Linn

By making accountability the centerpiece of his education agenda, President George W. Bush (The White House, 2001) reinforced what was already a central theme of state policies aimed at improving education. In the past few years, states throughout the country have introduced accountability systems based on student testing linked to state content standards. Those systems are intended to lead to improvements in student learning by clarifying expectations and motivating greater effort on the part of students and teachers, using student achievement as a primary mechanism of accountability.

The current landscape of testing and accountability systems, however, is quite varied. At last count, every state except Iowa had adopted content standards, and most states have put in place tests that arguably align, to varying degrees, with the adopted content standards. The state systems that are in place differ along many dimensions, including, but not limited to, those described here. They differ in terms of the uses that are made of test scores; the stakes that are attached to results for teachers, other educators, and students; the ways in which results are reported; the emphasis given to performance standards; and the level at which performance standards are set. The systems vary in relative emphasis given to current status and to improvement; the grade levels and the subject areas tested; the use, if any, of performance-based assessment tasks; whether normative comparisons are made; the weight given to performance of students belonging to different racial/ethnic groups; whether student socioeconomic status is taken into account; and whether students are tracked longitudinally. Additional differences can be found among states in their inclusion of students with disabilities and English-language learners, and the types of accommodations that are provided for those groups of students. The states also vary a good deal with regard to the length of time that the tests and accountability systems have been in place, the stability of the systems, and whether there are plans for phasing in new testing and accountability requirements over the next several years. Each of these dimensions has important implications for the design and evaluation of assessment and accountability systems.

The purpose of this chapter is to review the variety of accountability models that have been introduced by states. Emphasis will be given to features of the models that distinguish one model from another and that have an impact on the determination of which schools are deemed to be successful and which are found wanting. Although some brief discussion of the use of test results for student or teacher accountability is included, the emphasis is on systems that focus on school accountability.

FOCUS OF ACCOUNTABILITY

When a group of educators was asked to definite accountability, they focused on shared responsibility among students, teachers, school administrators, and policy makers. They stressed students' and teachers' responsibilities to put forth effort, and administrators' and policy makers' responsibilities to provide support, in the form of instructional resources and professional development, for students and teachers to meet the goals set by accountability systems (T. Bergeson, personal communication, April 9, 2001). Porter and Chester (2001) refer to this general concept of shared responsibility of students, teachers, administrators, and policy makers as symmetric accountability programs. Despite these broader definitions of accountability, the reality is that most accountability systems now in place focus primarily on educators and/or students.

STUDENT ACCOUNTABILITY

Student accountability generally takes one of two forms: passing one or more tests to earn a high school diploma or test-based, grade-to-grade promotion requirements. There are variations on high school diplomas, such as endorsed diplomas based on test performance and the Certificate of Initial Mastery requirement in Oregon. There are variations on retention-in-grade standards, such as mandatory summer school or extended school days. Other variations may involve external end-of-course exams, or external course-based tests that are a required part of teacher-assigned grades.

But high school exit tests and grade-to-grade promotion tests are the two most common ways of implementing student-level accountability in state or district systems.

TEACHER ACCOUNTABILITY

With a few notable exceptions, the use of student test results as a means of holding teachers accountable for the performance of their students generally is found only at a collective level as part of school accountability models. Perhaps the best-known example of a system that links student performance on tests to individual teachers is the Tennessee Value-Added Assessment System (TVAAS) developed by William Sanders (see, for example, Sanders & Horn, 1994; Sanders, Saxton, & Horn, 1997). TVAAS uses a sophisticated data analysis methodology that allows the estimation of gains in student achievement from one year to another in ways that can be linked to individual teachers as well as to individual schools. Student achievement data from several previous years are used as the basis for estimating gains in a particular year. School-level and teacher-level contributions to student gains are estimated. Each of these contributions is interpreted as the value added by a teacher or a school. Estimates of individual teacher contributions to student gains in test scores are not publicly reported, but instead are reported to individual teachers for formative evaluation purposes.

SCHOOL ACCOUNTABILITY

Perhaps the most widespread use of state-mandated tests is for purposes of school accountability. Once it has been decided to create a school accountability system, the question arises: How much emphasis should be given to current performance and how much to improvement? The most common way of reporting school assessment results is in terms of current status. This may be done by reporting the school mean or median score for students in the grade assessed using a scale score or percentile rank metric, or, as has become more popular in recent years, the percentage of students who meet or exceed a performance standard (e.g., "proficient") or the percentage of students in each of several performance categories (e.g., advanced, proficient, basic).

Meyers (2000) recently provided a critique of aggregate school indicators based on current status on a student assessment. He argued that such indicators, whether mean or median test scores, or a proficiency-level indicator, are "contaminated by factors other than school performance, in particular, the average level of achievement prior to entering first grade—and the average effects of student, family, and community characteristics on student achievement growth from first grade through the grade in which students are tested" (Meyers, 2000, p. 2). Meyers's critique of current-status school indicators discusses three additional shortcomings, but his first criticism alone is enough to raise serious reservations concerning the exclusive reliance on current-status school indicators to evaluate school performance, because, if used in isolation, they are unfair and will lead to invalid judgments regarding school quality.

Proponents of current-status indicators note that it is important to have the same high expectations for all children. The standards movement gives high priority to setting high standards of achievement for all students. Even the strongest proponents of the standards movement recognized, however, that one cannot expect all students to meet standards overnight, and, therefore, one cannot expect all schools to achieve at desired levels on a current-status indicator at this time. Universal achievement of high standards nevertheless remains an important future goal.

Current-status reports are considered important because they reveal where students and schools stand at any given point in time, and, when compared with desired performance targets, how far there is to go. The Florida school accountability system, for example, grades schools from A to F based on current performance of students on the Florida Comprehensive Assessment Test. The purpose of the reports is described as follows: "The School Accountability Report groups schools with similar performance characteristics. It identifies critically low schools, stimulates academic improvement, and summarizes information about school achievement, learning environment, and student characteristics" (Florida Department of Education, 1999, p. 1).

Most state accountability systems that report school current status based on aggregate student assessment results also include some basis for rating improvement in achievement. This may be by comparing grade-level cohorts in the school in a given year (or years) with a cohort at the same grade for a previous year (or years). It may involve comparing the performance of this year's fifth graders with that of students in the school who were in fourth grade the previous year. Or, it may involve comparisons of performance of students to the performance of those same students at an earlier point in time using matched longitudinal student records. Carlson (2000) referred to these approaches as the successive groups, the quasi-longitudinal, and the longitudinal approaches, respectively. He has presented analyses showing that they do not give the same answers to the question of which schools have shown the most improvement. More detailed comparisons of these three approaches are made later in this chapter.

A number of states report a target performance level that all schools are expected to attain by some specified date in the future. Colorado, for example, reports the percentage of students in a school who score at the proficient or advanced levels on their assessments and has set a target of 80% for schools to be accredited. There is also a provision, however, for schools with percentages below that level to be accredited if there is a 25% increase over the baseline percentage in a 3-year period. California summarizes student performance using a scale, called the Academic Performance Index (API), that ranges from a low of 200 to a high of 1,000. A target of 800 on the API has been set by the state as a common goal that schools are expected to work toward. Annual growth targets on the API also have been set for schools.

MEASURES

Some states make use of a variety of other indicators, but student achievement tests are at the heart of state accountability systems. The number of tested subjects, the grades tested, and the nature of the tests varies widely from state to state. These testing variations have important implications for the types of accountability models that are feasible, for the influences the tests have on teaching and learning, and for the validity of results that are produced by the system.

ACHIEVEMENT TESTS

Some would argue that because various tests of, say, mathematics designed for a given grade level will be substantially correlated with each other, especially when the focus is on the aggregate level of schools, differences among the features of tests are of little practical importance. That view, however, is misguided. The specific content of a test tells teachers and students what is considered to be important for students to learn. When there is a discrepancy between content standards and the test or between the curriculum and the test, it is the test that is most likely to determine what will be emphasized in instruction. Content standards that stress problem solving and deep understanding of mathematical principles will be undermined by a test that stresses memorization of facts and routine computation. Ambitious content standards that specify high levels of accomplishment will not succeed in ratcheting up instruction in the face of a test that is aimed at determining minimum competency. If tests are to reinforce the learning outcomes intended in content standards, they need to be closely aligned with those standards. (For further discussion of the importance of alignment of tests with content standards, see Baker and Linn, and Rothman, this volume.)

The reasoning that close alignment between the test and the curriculum is desirable if the intended goals of content standards are to be supported rather than undermined, has implications that are broader than the construction of a test in a single subject area. It implies that it is also important to choose the subjects to be tested in a way that attends to the range of content standards that states have developed. Systems that test only reading and mathematics, for example, send the message that these are the highest-priority subjects, and this message may lead to a reduced emphasis on writing, history, science, and other content areas. Systems that include direct assessment of student writing, on the other hand, result in greater emphasis on having students write than systems that do not have tests that require students to write. Similarly, systems that include tests of science or history send the message that these subject areas also are valued.

Choice of subject areas to be tested and alignment of tests in each tested area with the curriculum are key considerations, but there are other considerations that also require attention if tests used for school accountability are to support the goals of content standards. One such consideration is the frequency with which new forms of the tests are introduced. The position statement of the American Educational Research Association (2000) on high-stakes tests includes the following argument on this issue:

> Because high-stakes testing inevitably creates incentives for inappropriate methods of test preparation, multiple forms should be used or new test forms should be introduced on a regular basis, to avoid narrowing of the curriculum toward just the content sampled on a particular form. (pp. 2–3)

A single form of a test, no matter how well aligned it is with the curriculum and content standards, cannot possibly cover the whole domain of content of the curriculum. It can only sample from the whole domain, and thus it is critical that the sample tested not become confused with the whole domain.

The grade levels that are selected for testing also matter. President Bush's proposal that states test every year in grades 3–8 is based on the premise that test results are needed for students on an annual basis. Testing in every grade over a specified span of grades provides the basis for pursuing models that track student achievement longitudinally. Although it would be possible in principle to track students longitudinally in a system that administered tests only in, say, grades 3 and 6, the lag time would exacerbate problems of attrition and matching of student records.

There are trade-offs between annual testing in every grade and testing only in a few selected grades. For a fixed amount of money, it is possible to develop tests that are better reflections of the aspirations of content standards when fewer grades are tested than when every grade is tested. It is also possible to test more subjects when fewer grades are tested than when all grade levels are. Another trade-off is between the frequency with which new forms of the tests can be developed and used. When every grade must be tested, there is greater pressure to reuse forms of the tests that have been administered previously than when only a few grades are tested.

INDICATORS OTHER THAN STUDENT ACHIEVEMENT

A number of states include some subset of indicators, such as attendance rates of students and/or teachers, dropout rates, and rates of retention in grade, in addition to student test results in computing indices used for school accountability. Generally the nontest indicators are given less weight than student test results in overall accountability indices. The effective weights are usually even less than those officially assigned for nontest data, because the effective weight of a component of an accountability index depends on the variability of the component from school to school, and indicators such as average daily attendance tend to be less variable across schools than test results are. Nonetheless, inclusion of nontest indicators can send the message that characteristics such as on-time promotion in grade, graduation rates, and attendance of both teachers and students are valued.

REPORTING METRICS

Achievement tests unfortunately do not have a natural metric that is useful for reporting in ways that convey meaning. Intuitive approaches, such as number- or percent-correct scores that are familiar to most people through their experience with classroom tests, are not viable for state tests because they depend so heavily on the particular items included on the test. Since two forms of a test differ in the items they contain, there are bound to be some differences in relative difficulty that would make number- or percent-correct score noncomparable. Unless someone knows a lot about a test, there is no way of telling whether a number-correct score of 40 or a percent-correct score of 68 represents good or poor performance.

Many approaches have been used to address this problem. These include the creation of scales with arbitrary units, such as setting the mean to 500 and the standard deviation to 100 for a particular group of test takers, as has been done for the College Board's SAT I scores used for college admissions. Once the scale has been established, new forms of the test are statistically equated to the base form, and the scale gradually gains meaning through experience.

Similar scaling procedures have been used with norm-referenced achievement tests provided by test publishers for use in elementary and secondary schools. In addition, test publishers provide translations of the underlying scale to other metrics in the hope of making the reported results more readily interpretable. For a good many years, the most common metrics used for reporting norm-referenced test results were grade-equivalent (GE) scores and national percentile ranks (NPR). A GE is determined by setting the median score obtained by students in the norming sample to the grade level of the students at the time they take the test. Thus, if the median scale score for students taking the test in the eighth month of fourth grade was, say, 357, a scale score of 357 would be converted to a GE of 4.8. An NPR score is simply the percentage of students in the norming sample for a given grade and test administration date that scored lower than a designated score. Thus, if 70% of the students in the norming sample had a scale score of less than, say, 374, a student at that grade who earned a scale of 374 would get an NPR of 70.

PERFORMANCE STANDARDS

Although GE and NPR scores provide a basis for interpreting test performance in comparison to the performance of students around the nation, they do not provide an indication of whether that level of performance is as good as would be desired. In the past decade, there has been a push to move away from norm-referenced scores through the introduction of performance standards. Content standards specify the content that teachers are expected to teach and students are expected to learn. Performance standards specify the level of performance that students are expected to achieve. That is, they specify "how good is good enough." Many states have set performance standards for their tests by defining the knowledge and level of skills that a student who is "proficient" should achieve in the content domain specified in the content standards. The performance standards are then translated into cut scores on the test by having judges review test items and/or student performance on the test. A variety of standard-setting methods have been used to translate performance standards into cut scores on the tests (see, for example, Mehrens, 1995; Zieky, 1995).

Performance standards and associated cut scores on a test usually have been set at more than one level. Typically, they are set at three or four levels. With three levels and three associated cut scores, the test score distribution is divided into four regions. The regions commonly are labeled, for example, advanced, proficient, partially proficient, and unsatisfactory; or distinguished, proficient, apprentice, and novice. Not all states name the levels. Some simply refer to them by number.

Standards-based reporting generally is done in two ways: (1) by reporting the percentage of students scoring in each score region defined by the cut scores, and (2) by reporting the percentage of students who score at or above the cut score corresponding to "proficient" or "meets the standard." In some states, an index score also is reported based on the distribution of student scores in the various performance categories. For example, the Kentucky Instructional Results Information Systems that was in place from 1994 through 1998 computed an index score for a school in a given area of achievement by assigning 140 points for each student scoring in the distinguished category, 100 for a student in the proficient category, 40 for a student in the apprentice category, and 0 for a student in the novice category. The target that schools were expected to meet within 20 years was set at 100. The new system that was introduced in Kentucky, called the Commonwealth Accountability Testing System, uses a similar system but awards points differentially to students scoring in the high, medium, or low regions of the two lowest performance levels.

NORMATIVE COMPARISONS

Although norm-referenced scores were in considerable disfavor and rejected as a basis for reporting by a number of states that implemented testing systems with standards-based reporting in the mid-1990s, in the past few years there has been a trend toward reintroducing normative comparisons. Norm-referenced reporting of results has not replaced standards-based reporting, but, in a number of states, has been used as an additional basis of providing information about performance.

One of the reasons for the addition of normative comparisons is that many states set their performance standards and associated cut scores at such high levels that less than half of the students were meeting the proficient standard. In cases where the proficient cut score corresponded to the 60th or 70th percentile, it was found that reporting that information helped to communicate that the standards were set relatively high and to explain that a student performing above the national average might still fall short of the expectations for proficient performance.

THE ROLE OF SOCIOECONOMIC BACKGROUND

Should socioeconomic factors be taken into account? It is well known that socioeconomic background is substantially related to student achievement.

But the existence of a relationship does not lead to an obvious decision about whether socioeconomic factors should be taken into account before passing out rewards and sanctions to schools based on student achievement. Elmore, Abelmann, and Fuhrman (1996) characterized the issue as follows: "One side of this issue . . . argues that schools can fairly be held accountable only for factors that they control, and therefore that performance accountability systems should control for or equalize student socioeconomic status before they dispense rewards and penalties. . . . The other side of the issue argues that controlling for student background or prior achievement institutionalizes low expectations for poor, minority, low-achieving students" (pp. 93–94).

Different states come out on different sides of the issue of making adjustments for socioeconomic status (SES). Pennsylvania, for example, uses a number of community-type and SES variables to identify similar schools (10 schools scoring immediately below and 10 schools scoring above the target school) (Pennsylvania Department of Education, n.d., p. 24), and then reports the interquartile range for reading and mathematics scores for the set of similar schools called the "Similar Schools Score Band." The Pennsylvania Department of Education (n.d.) explains the reasons for using similar school bands to report results as follows:

> It is well established that academic achievement is influenced primarily by two factors: the quality of the educational services provided and the socioeconomic backgrounds of the students themselves. These factors might be classified as "school" and "non-school" factors. Similar school information permits a school to compare its results with those of the same community type and socioeconomic background. The Similar Schools Score Band, therefore, supplements the comparison of school score with the overall state average. (p. 24)

The use of comparisons to other schools with similar SES characteristics is not unique to Pennsylvania. California is one of several other states that use similar schools defined by SES factors as one basis of comparison within an overall system of school accountability. In most cases, the bands of similar school results are a secondary consideration that provides another basis for judging results in addition to the main accountability results that do not take SES into account. Even if the state does not make adjustments for socioeconomic status, others will in secondary analyses. *The Saint Louis Post-Dispatch*, for example, reported results from the Missouri Assessment Program (MAP), along with ratings of plus, equal, or minus based on deviations from a regression of MAP scores on the percentage of students in the school receiving free or reduced-price lunch (Hacker, 2001; "Gateway Guide to Schools," 2001). Schools scoring within one standard error of the regression received an equal rating, those more than a standard error above the regression line received a plus rating, and those more than a standard deviation below received a minus rating in the *Post-Dispatch* report.

PERFORMANCE OF SUBGROUPS OF STUDENTS

Several states use disaggregated results for racial/ethnic subgroups of students in their school accountability systems. Texas, for example, requires that gains be made in test scores for African American, Hispanic, and White subgroups of students, not just for the student body as a whole, for the school to qualify for recognition. California requires that "numerically significant" groups (at least 15% of the student body and at least 30 students) be reported separately, together with results for the overall student body. Potential groups are African American, Native American (or Alaska Native), Asian American, Filipino, Hispanic, Pacific Islander, White non-Hispanic, and socioeconomically disadvantaged students. Disaggregated reporting also is required by Title I (Improving America's Schools Act of 1994) as well as by the 2001 reauthorization of the Elementary and Secondary Education Act.

Disaggregated reporting is part of the strategy of using accountability results to monitor the size of the gap in performance between traditionally low-scoring minority groups and poor students, and White students, and to motivate efforts to close the gap in achievement. This goal is widely supported, and Texas has received a good deal of favorable attention for showing a closing of the gap on the trend lines for African American, Hispanic, and White students on the Texas Assessment of Academic Skills. Although the generalizability of the closing of the gap has been called into question by results reported by Klein, Hamilton, McCaffrey, and Stecher (2000) that show that trends on the National Assessment of Educational Progress do not show a similar closing of the gap in Texas, there is still a widely held belief that disaggregated reporting will help achieve a closing of the gap in achievement by making schools accountable for improved achievement of all subgroups of students.

It should be emphasized, however, that disaggregation for purposes of accountability poses a substantial technical challenge because of the small number of students within various subgroups in schools. The small sample problem for subgroups of students exacerbates the volatility problem that Kane and Staiger (2002) demonstrate is substantial even without disaggregation. As a consequence of the increased volatility, integrated schools that have enough students in each of two or more racial/ethnic groups so that the results can be separately reported, are less likely to be recognized as exemplary or as in need of assistance than schools with only a single racial/ethnic group. This difference due to student body composition raises issues of fairness.

MODELS

Regardless of the model used, school accountability systems report status of performance based on test scores of cohorts of students. In addition, states use some indicators of improvement in judging schools. As indicated previously, there are three distinct models that are used by states to judge improvement. These are: (1) changes in the performance of successive groups of students (e.g., percent of grade 4 students scoring proficient or above in 2000 minus the corresponding percent for grade 4 students in 1999), (2) gains in performance from one grade to the next for students who were tested in both years (e.g., the mean test score for students in a school in grade 5 in 2000 minus the mean test score for those same students in grade 4 in 1999), and (3) gains in mean performance for all tested students from one grade to the next (e.g., the mean test score for all grade 5 students in the school in 2000 minus the mean for all grade 4 students in 1999). The three methods are referred to as the successive groups, the longitudinal, and the quasi-longitudinal models, respectively.

Each of the three models may be generalized to include multiple years and/or multiple grade levels. Kentucky, for example, uses a version of the successive groups model that spans 4 years of data. The first 2 years provide the baseline, and change is computed by taking the difference in performance between years 3 and 4 combined and years 1 and 2 combined. Tennessee uses the longitudinal approach, with school gains analyses spanning several grades and several years. Including multiple years and/or multiple grades has the advantage of reducing variability due to measurement and sampling error by increasing the number of students in the analyses. There are important differences among the three models that influence the results, however, regardless of what combination of grades and years enter into the calculations. The bottom-line implication of the differences is that a school that is identified as outstanding by one of the models would not necessarily be so identified by another model.

SUCCESSIVE GROUPS MODEL

A number of states, including California, Colorado, Kentucky, Maryland, and Washington compare the achievement of students at selected grades in a given year or biennium with that of students from previous years at the same grade in the same school. The school-level changes that are found provide a means of recognizing that schools serve students who start at different places. These comparisons of student performance at a grade level in different years rests on the implicit assumption that the characteristics of the students that affect achievement levels are relatively stable from year to year for the students attending a given school. This assumption is questionable for schools serving neighborhoods whose demographic characteristics are changing rapidly, but is a reasonable approximation for most schools.

Changes in scores for the students tested at a given grade from one year to the next can be quite unreliable. There are several sources of the unreliability. First, the school summary scores for each year are subject to measurement and sampling error. Second, because the results in year 1 have a strong positive correlation with the results in year 2, the change scores are less reliable than the scores used to compute change. Third, it is commonly observed that the between-school variability of change scores is considerably smaller than the between-school variability of the scores for a given year. Fourth, as Kane and Staiger (2002) have shown, a substantial part of the variability found in change scores for schools is due to nonpersistent factors that influence scores in one year but not another. Examples of nonpersistent factors could include a teacher strike, teacher illness, or a traumatic school event such as a student death.

Using data from the state of North Carolina, Kane and Staiger estimated that, for the smallest quintile of schools, 58% of the between-school variability in year-to-year changes in fourth-grade reading plus math scores was due to a combination of sampling variability and other nonpersistent factors. The corresponding percentage for the largest 20% of the schools was only slightly smaller (73%). In other words, only about a fifth to a fourth of the observed between-school variability in school change scores was attributable to persistent factors having to do with the school.

Because so much of the variability in school change scores is attributable to noise, it should not be surprising that schools identified in one change cycle as outstanding for attaining a large change in achievement are unlikely to repeat that performance in the next cycle. The converse is also true. Thus, schools that are identified as needing assistance in one cycle because of falling short of their change target, or even showing a decline, are unlikely to fall in that category the next change cycle. A consequence of this random fluctuation from one change cycle to the next is that the actions taken to assist schools in the latter category may appear to be more effective than they actually are. Moreover, it is likely to be a mistake to assume that the practices of the schools recognized as outstanding are ones that should be adopted by other schools.

LONGITUDINAL MODEL

The longitudinal model obviously requires that student records be maintained so that scores obtained by a student in one year can be linked to scores earned by that same student the previous year, or earlier years if more than 2 years of data are used for each student. Since comparisons of performance are made across grade levels, the longitudinal model also requires that scores be reported on a scale that is comparable across grades. The latter requirement generally will mean that reports in terms of number of students meeting standards cannot be used in the analyses because the performance levels at one grade are not comparable to those at another. Hence, longitudinal analyses generally rely on "vertically equated" scale scores.

North Carolina is an example of a state that uses a longitudinal approach in its "ABC" school accountability system. "The ABCs of Public Education" is a comprehensive plan to recognize public schools in North Carolina. "This plan focuses on (1) strong accountability, (2) emphasis on the basics and on high educational standards, and (3) maximum local control. A key component of the ABCs of Public Education is a new accountability program, which focuses on performance of individual public schools (rather than school systems) in the subjects of reading, writing, and mathematics. Rather than comparing different students from one year to the next, this plan—the School-Based Management and Accountability Program—holds schools accountable for the educational growth of the same groups of students (cohorts) over time. At least a year's worth of growth for a year's school is expected" (North Carolina Department of Public Instruction, 1996, p. 1).

North Carolina used the average rate of growth observed across the state as a whole from one grade in the spring of 1993 to the next grade in the spring of 1994 as a benchmark against which the improvement for students in a given grade in one year to the next grade the following year is judged. The details of how school changes in achievement in, say, third grade in 1999 to fourth grade in 2000 are evaluated, are complicated in that allowances are made both for differential expected rates of growth for students at different points on the scale and for regression to the mean effects, but the basic idea of the system is straightforward. The 1993–1994 state average growth figures set an expectation for school growth for a given pair of grades and a given pair of years of assessment, after adjusting the school results for differential growth rates and differential regression effects. The comparisons to expected growth are then used to classify schools into one of four categories: exemplary schools, schools meeting expected growth, schools having adequate performance, and low-performing schools.

The longitudinal model is appealing on several grounds. It holds schools accountable only for gains made by students who have been in the school for the full year. Taking the prior year's achievement directly into account minimizes concerns about unfair comparisons among schools that serve student bodies with substantially different socioeconomic backgrounds, since most of those differences are accounted for by controlling for prior achievement. This is so because of the strong correlation between achievement and socioeconomic status, particularly when considering data aggregated to the school level.

Sanders and his colleagues suggest that taking prior achievement into account, as is done in the Tennessee Value-Added Assessment System, is all that is necessary to yield a fair basis of comparison. In a document reporting frequently asked questions and answers, for example, Sanders and Horn (1994) give the following question and answer. Question: "My students are mostly from the inner city. Won't that make a difference in their gain scores?" Answer: "The pilot studies revealed no relationship between the racial composition of student body and gain scores. Whether a school was an inner city school or a suburban one was also found to be unrelated to gains made" (p. 5 after title page, although pages of document are unnumbered). This general conclusion was reaffirmed by Sanders and Rivers (1996).

Results reported by Hu (2000), however, call into question the conclusions by Sanders and his colleagues that race/ethnicity and SES of the student body are unrelated to the gains estimated in TVAAS. Hu obtained school data on per-pupil instructional expenditures, the percent of minority students in the student population, and the percent of students eligible for free or reduced-price lunch. He correlated these variables with value-added estimates based on 3-year averages across grades for reading and mathematics. For the 58 elementary schools in his study, Hu found that per-pupil instructional expenditures had correlations of .39 with the average value added in both mathematics and reading. The correlations for percent minority were .42 and .28 for mathematics and reading, respectively. The corresponding correlations for percent free or reduced-price lunch were .49 and .29. The squared multiple correlations of all three school factors with the 3-year averages of value-added estimates from TVAAS were .27 for reading, .19 for mathematics, and .28 for the composite of reading and mathematics. Thus, between a fifth and a bit more than a fourth of the variability in the value-added, 3-year averages was predictable from a combination of per-pupil instructional expenditure, percent minority students in the student body, and percent of students eligible for free or reduced-price lunch.

Hu's findings lend support to the observation by Shepard, Kupermintz, and Linn (2000) that, although TVAAS adjusts for differences in student achievement, it does so imperfectly. Relationships of TVAAS gains with variables such as percent of minority students in the student body and percent of students eligible for free or reduced-price lunch are consistent with the notion that the adjustments are imperfect. Adjustments for differences in student achievement do not preclude the possibility that students from different socioeconomic backgrounds will have different levels of support for learning and differential access to enrichment experiences outside of school during the year in which gains are being estimated. Therefore, they may yield systematic biases in the estimated school and teacher effects. Although the adjustments for differences in student achievement go a long way toward leveling the playing field, they fall short of fully accomplishing that end.

The longitudinal model produces more-dependable estimates of gains for schools than those produced by the successive groups model. Still, there is a substantial degree of uncertainty in the estimated gains due to a combination of sampling variability and other nonpersistent factors that affect the scores in one year but not another. Kane and Staiger (2002) estimated that for the North Carolina data, 29% of the between-school variance in gains from grade 3 to grade 4 for the schools in the largest-school-size quintile was due to a combination of sampling variability and other nonpersistent factors. For schools in the smallest-school-size quintile, however, the corresponding figure was 58%. Although 58% compares favorably with the 80% reported above for changes for the smallest quintile of schools based on the successive groups model, 58% of the variance in between-school gains of small schools is still a substantial percentage attributable to noise in the results. Certainly, one would find a test where 58% of the variance was attributable to measurement error too unreliable to use in making high-stakes decisions about individual students.

Still, the properties of longitudinal gains look good, especially for large schools, compared with those for successive groups changes. On the other hand, there are two other factors that may mitigate how positively those advantages are viewed. First, because of the requirements of annual testing of students in every grade and the need to have a common vertical scale for reporting results, there is a tendency to use publisher-provided standardized tests that are either off-the-shelf or highly similar in their characteristics to off-the-shelf tests. Such tests are almost sure to be less well aligned with state content standards than an assessment that is specifically designed to measure the knowledge and skills emphasized in the content standards. The same test forms also tend to be reused.

Second, the requirement that students have scores in both years (or all years if more than two are used) generally means that mobile students are more likely to be excluded from the accountability calculations. This may be seen as an advantage by teachers who understandably feel that they cannot be responsible for the learning of students who are not present for most of the school year. However, focusing only on students who are stable in the schools they attend distorts the overall accountability results and may paint an overly optimistic picture of the gains that are being made. One way to minimize this problem is to track students who move from school to school so that they can be included in the analyses. Another approach to the problem is to use the quasi-longitudinal model.

QUASI-LONGITUDINAL MODEL

The quasi-longitudinal model accounts for all the students in a school who are tested in either the first or second year, not just those who are there and tested in both years. Like the longitudinal model, the quasi-longitudinal model requires the use of test scores that are vertically equated across grade levels. For schools with little mobility, there is little difference between the longitudinal and quasi-longitudinal models, but the two models can yield quite different results for schools with a high degree of student mobility.

The quasi-longitudinal model has some of the advantages of the longitudinal model. Both models estimate gains in achievement rather than year-to-year changes in the achievement of successive groups. The quasi-longitudinal model includes mobile as well as nonmobile students. Inclusiveness is a plus in terms of the goal of accounting for all students, but a minus from the perspective of making schools accountable only for students who have been enrolled in the school for a substantial period of time.

MODEL COMPARISONS

The three school accountability models have different requirements and make different assumptions. As a consequence, they yield different rankings of schools. These differences are quite evident in results reported by Carlson (2000), who analyzed data for a state where he was able to obtain longitudinal and quasi-longitudinal school data at four grades over 4 years. With those data he could compute changes for the successive groups. Using the longitudinal model results based on data for all four grade levels and all 4 years as the standard, he computed correlations between estimates of school gain scores from the quasi-longitudinal model and estimates of school change scores from the successive groups model, with gain estimates from the longitudinal model. For the successive groups and the quasi-longitudinal models, he considered the case where data from a single grade and 1 year were used, where data from four grade levels in a school and 1 year were used, and where data from four grade levels in a school across all 4 years were used. The resulting correlations for the successive groups model with the 4-year, four-grade-level standard are quite low, ranging from only .14

for one grade and 1 year to a high of only .48 for four grades and 4 years. The correlations for the quasi-longitudinal model were higher. Even in the best case scenario (four grades and 4 years of data), however, the correlation of .76 still is low enough that the rank-order standing of many schools would be substantially different depending on whether the longitudinal or quasi-longitudinal model was used. The choice of accountability model clearly matters. Unfortunately, however, there is no clear best choice on all counts.

The two longitudinal models have the advantage that they provide direct estimates of gains in achievement and do not depend on the comparability of successive groups of students. The longitudinal models also yield results that are more dependable, that is, less influenced by measurement error, sampling variability, and variability due to other nonpersistent factors. As previously indicated, however, they require more frequent testing, which may have a trade-off with the quality of the tests in terms of their alignment with content standards and therefore their adequacy in serving as targets for instruction.

ANALYTICAL IMPROVEMENTS

The lack of precision in the estimates for all three school accountability models presents a major challenge. Several ways of dealing with this challenge seem worthy of consideration. At a minimum, reports of accountability results for schools need to be accompanied by information on the dependability of those results, as required by the *Standards for Educational and Psychological Testing* (American Educational Research Association, American Psychological Association, & National Council on Measurement in Education, 1999). This might best be done where schools are placed into graded performance categories by reporting information about the accuracy of classifications. Procedures for evaluating school misclassification probabilities are described by Rogosa (1999). Consistent with the Kane and Staiger findings discussed above, Rogosa's results show that the probabilities of misclassifying schools are nontrivial. Alternative approaches to evaluating the likelihood that schools will be misclassified are described by Hoffman and Wise (2000). Kentucky has a contract with HumRRO to evaluate the accuracy of the classification of schools for its accountability system using the analytic procedures described by Hoffman and Wise. Such investigations of the accuracy of accountability system classifications of schools need to be a standard part of the evaluation of the technical adequacy of accountability systems.

Second, improvements in the accuracy of results can be achieved by combining data across multiple grades, multiple subjects, and/or multiple years. In Colorado, for example, test results are averaged across subjects and grades. Kentucky goes a step further, not only averaging across grades and subjects within a school but also doing so biannually. Averaging over subjects, over grades, or over years increases the precision of results by increasing the number of students used to estimate school results. Combining across grades or subjects has the added advantage of increasing the number of teachers who are teaching students whose performance directly contributes to the accountability results for the school, and thereby may increase the sense of shared responsibility of results. Combining across several years lengthens the accountability cycle, but produces results that are more trustworthy and therefore more likely to lead to real long-term improvements and to the identification of exemplary practices as well as to enhanced fairness.

Third, the precision of estimates can be improved by the use of more sophisticated analytic techniques. This has been demonstrated, for example, by Kane and Staiger, who used "filtered" estimates of school gains. The filtered estimates, which are based on the application of empirical Bayes procedures, are more complicated, and therefore less transparent, than estimation procedures commonly in use. They are not more complicated or less transparent, however, than the ways in which test scores are scaled and equated in many states using item response theory. Nor are they more complicated or less transparent than the mixed-model analyses used for the longitudinal analyses of the test data in Tennessee. In any event, the loss of transparency seems a good trade-off for the gain in precision that Kane and Staiger have demonstrated.

SUMMARY AND CONCLUSIONS

State testing and accountability systems vary greatly along a number of dimensions, including the subjects that are assessed, the nature of the tests that are used, the stakes that are attached to results, and whether those stakes are for students and/or for educators. They also vary in their reliance on current achievement results versus the emphasis that is placed on improvement and whether the system relies on cross-sectional, quasi-longitudinal, or true longitudinal data where individual students are tracked over time. Regardless of the details of the systems, all state testing and accountability systems have the same global purpose: the improvement of instruction and student learning. There is considerable debate, however, over the degree to which the systems contribute to that goal.

There is widespread agreement that tests play an important role in shaping instruction and thereby influencing student learning. Subjects assessed are given more attention than ones that are not assessed. When well aligned with content standards, tests make the intent of the standards explicit and focus attention on content that is deemed important for teachers to teach and for students to learn. But the flip side of that is also true, that is, when there is poor alignment, tests can distort the intent of the content standards.

Most states make some use of test results for school accountability. Some emphasize current status. Some use measures of the socioeconomic backgrounds of students to provide a frame of reference for making comparisons among schools that serve similar student bodies. The use of socioeconomic measures is controversial, however, because of the implied use of different expectations for students from different backgrounds. Because of the relationship between these measures and racial and ethnic backgrounds of students, the use of socioeconomic measures can have the particularly undesirable result of creating different expectations for White students than for students of color.

A preferable approach for schools that serve students who have low achievement is to place greater emphasis on improvement than on current status. This can be done by comparing the performance of students in a given grade in one year or biennium with that of students in the next year or biennium. Such comparisons of successive groups are reasonable for schools that serve populations that are fairly stable. Comparisons of the performance of students in a given grade with that of students in the preceding grade the year before also can be used as a way of judging improvement. This can be done for all students in the appropriate grade each year or for only students with scores in both years. The former model is known as a quasi-longitudinal analysis in contrast to the true longitudinal model with matched student records. Both models require tests that have scales that can be compared across grade levels. Both require annual testing in every grade used in the accountability system. Such a requirement generally is associated with the use of off-the-shelf tests or tests with similar characteristics, which may suffer from poorer alignment with content standards than assessments that are targeted for just a few selected grades.

The successive groups, quasi-longitudinal, and longitudinal models lead to substantially different rank orderings of schools. Consequently, it is quite likely that a school that is judged outstanding or in need of improvement using one model would not be classified the same way using another model. Unfortunately, there is no clear best model on all accounts. Each has strengths and weaknesses so that the choice of a model involves trade-offs.

The precision of assessment results is less than commonly is assumed by either policy makers or the general public. It is critical that information about the precision of measurement be obtained and provided with reports of results. Given the current emphasis on reporting results for students in terms of whether they meet standards or in terms of a small number of proficiency categories, such as below basic, basic, proficient, and advanced, the reports' misclassification probabilities are particularly useful in conveying the level of imprecision in the assessment results. This is true not only at the individual student level but for accountability categories used to classify schools.

Accountability systems are more fragile and their results are subject to a greater degree of uncertainty than either the general public or policy makers believe. Technical approaches to analysis and the accumulation of results across multiple subjects, multiple grade levels, and multiple years can enhance the validity, fairness, and trustworthiness of the results. This requires greater patience on the part of policy makers to allow time for the accumulation of dependable data. The alternative, however, leads to misleading findings and to high-stakes decisions that are fundamentally unfair and misleading.

ACKNOWLEDGMENTS

The work reported in this chapter was supported under the Educational Research and Development Centers Program, PR Award Number R305B960002, as administered by the Office of Educational Research and Improvement, U.S. Department of Education. The finding and opinions expressed in this chapter do not reflect the positions or policies of the National Institute on Student Achievement, Curriculum, and Assessment; the Office of Educational Research and Improvement; or the U.S. Department of Education.

REFERENCES

American Educational Research Association. (2000). *Position statement on high-stakes testing*. Washington, DC: Author.

American Educational Research Association, American Psychological Association, & National Council on Measurement in Education. (1999). *Standards for educational and psychological testing*. Washington, DC: Authors.

Carlson, D. (2000, June). *All students or the ones we taught?* Paper presented at the annual conference on large-scale assessment, Council of Chief State School Officers, Snowbird, UT.

Elmore, R. F., Abelmann, C. H., & Fuhrman, S. H. (1996). The new accountability in state education reform: From process to performance. In H. F. Ladd (Ed.), *Holding schools accountable: Performance-based reform in education* (pp. 65–98). Washington, DC: Brookings Institution.

Florida Department of Education. (1999). *School accountability report card guide: June 1999.* Tallahassee: Author.

Gateway guide to schools. (2001, May 3). *Saint Louis Post-Dispatch,* Section C.

Hacker, H. K. (2001, May 3). Gauging the effectiveness of area schools. *Saint Louis Post-Dispatch,* p. 2.

Hoffman, R. G., & Wise, L. L. (2000). *School classification accuracy final analysis plan for the Commonwealth accountability and testing system.* Alexandria, VA: HumRRO.

Hu, D. (2000). *The relationship of school spending and student academic achievement when achievement is measured by value-added scores.* Unpublished doctoral dissertation, Vanderbilt University, Nashville.

Kane, T. J., & Staiger, D. O. (2002). Volatility in school test scores: Implications for test-based accountability systems. In D. Ravitch (Ed.), *Brookings papers on education policy, 2002* (pp. 235–283). Washington, DC: Brookings Institution.

Klein, S., Hamilton, L., McCaffrey, D., & Stecher, B. (2000). *What do test scores in Texas tell us?* Santa Monica, CA: RAND.

Mehrens, W. A. (1995). Methodological issues in standard setting for educational exams. *Proceedings of the joint conference on standard setting for large-scale assessments of the National Assessment Governing Board and the National Center for Education Statistics* (Vol. II, pp. 221–263). Washington, DC: National Assessment Governing Board & National Center for Education Statistics.

Meyers, R. H. (2000). Value-added indicators: A powerful tool for evaluating science and mathematics programs and policies. *NISE Brief, 3*(3), 1–8. Madison: National Center for Improving Science Education, University of Wisconsin–Madison.

North Carolina Department of Public Instruction. (1996). Setting annual growth standards: "The formula." *Accountability Brief, 1*(1), 1–4.

Pennsylvania Department of Education. (n.d.). *Supplemental documentation for 1999: Reading, mathematics, and writing assessment reports.* Harrisburg: Author.

Porter, A. C., & Chester, M. (2001, May). *Building a high-quality assessment and accountability program: The Philadelphia example.* Paper presented at meeting of the Brookings Institution.

Rogosa, D. (1999). *Reporting group summary scores in educational assessments: Properties of proportion at or above cut-off (PAC) constructed from instruments with continuous scoring.* Los Angeles: University of California, National Center for Research on Evaluation, Standards, and Student Testing.

Sanders, W. L., & Horn, S. P. (1994). The Tennessee value-added system (TVAAS): Mixed-model methodology in educational assessment. *Journal of Personnel Evaluation in Education, 8,* 299–311.

Sanders, W. L., & Rivers, J. C. (1996). *Cumulative and residual effects of teachers on future student academic achievement.* Knoxville: Value-Added Research and Assessment Center, University of Tennessee.

Sanders, W. L., Saxton, A. M., & Horn, S. P. (1997). The Tennessee value-added system: A quantitative outcomes-based approach to educational assessment. In

J. Millman (Ed.), *Grading teachers, grading schools: Is student achievement a valid measure?* (pp. 137–162). Thousand Oaks, CA: Corwin Press.

Shepard, L., Kupermintz, H., & Linn, R. (2000, February). *Cautions regarding the Sanders value-added assessment system*. Response panel comments presented at the annual conference of the Colorado Staff Development Council, Denver.

The White House. (2001). *Transforming the federal role in education so that no child is left behind*. Retrieved from: www.whitehouse.gov/news/reports/no-child-left-behind.html

Zieky, M. J. (1995). A historical perspective on setting standards. *Proceedings of the joint conference on standard setting for large-scale assessments of the National Assessment Governing Board and the National Center for Education Statistics* (Vol. II, pp. 1–38). Washington, DC: National Assessment Governing Board & National Center for Education Statistics.

Chapter 5

Benchmarking and Alignment of State Standards and Assessments

Robert Rothman

Despite the lack of a national education ministry, the United States in the 1990s embarked on a *de facto* national education strategy of reforming schools around standards for student performance (Schwartz & Robinson, 2000). Virtually every state has adopted standards—statements of expectations for student learning in core subjects—and nearly all have put assessments in place to measure progress against the standards. More than half of the states also have some kind of mechanism for holding students and schools accountable for their performance ("Gaining ground," 2001).

Although the states went about their efforts in a number of ways, the standards-based strategies share a common theory of action. This theory suggests that an aligned system of standards, assessments, and accountability can raise student performance (Elmore & Rothman, 1999). While this theory may have elided over the specific mechanisms that link state policies to improved student performance, the widespread adoption of state policies in this arena suggests that there is a strong acceptance of the idea that the policies can contribute to improved learning.

Specifically, the theory goes, standards can improve learning by providing guidance to students, parents, and teachers about what students are expected to learn at each level. This guidance can provide clear examples of what high-quality work looks like; this enables students to improve their work by understanding the qualities of high performance, and it enables teachers to improve instruction by understanding what they have to do to elicit such work from their students.

At the same time, standards provide guidance to textbook and materials publishers, test developers, and professional development providers. This guidance helps ensure that the system is aligned, and that the materials, tests, and professional development support the classroom instruction aimed at achieving standards (O'Day & Smith, 1993; Ravitch, 1995).

Assessments also contribute to educational improvement, according to the theory of action, by providing coherent information about student attainment of the standards. If the assessments are aligned with the learning expectations spelled out in the standards, the results indicate the extent to which students have mastered the expectations and offer clues about areas where additional work is needed. In addition, aligned assessments themselves provide models of the type of student work that can demonstrate achievement of the standards. These models can help teachers design appropriate instructional activities.

Achieving these goals and contributing to improved teaching and learning imply certain criteria for standards and assessments. Not all standards or tests can inform instructional decisions equally well. Standards need to be clear, so that students, parents, teachers, and policy makers understand the expectations for student learning and respond appropriately. Yet the expectations must be specific enough so that everyone has the same understanding, rather than being vague and inviting widely varying interpretations.

The goals also imply that standards should set rigorous expectations for student learning. Standards that most students can meet rarely challenge anyone or inspire instructional change. If the standards are to contribute to raising student performance, they need to set challenging expectations to encourage students and schools to aspire to reach them. These expectations, moreover, should show a progression of knowledge and skills over time, so that students develop as they move through the grades.

The most significant criterion for assessments that is implied by the theory of standards-based reform is *alignment*. That is, the tests should measure what the standards expect, so that they can provide information on student progress toward the standards. Aligned assessments also help ensure that teaching students to do well on the tests means that students learn what they need to know to meet the standards—not just what they need to know to answer test questions.

True alignment means that the content of the tests reflects that of the standards; it is also important that the tests do not include extraneous content that would send mixed signals to schools about what is important for students to learn. To be aligned, tests should match the *depth* of the standards—that is, the extent of the cognitive abilities the standards expect students to demonstrate—and the *breadth* of the standards—that is, the range of knowledge and skills included in the standards. Achieving true alignment suggests tests that include open-ended items that tap student abilities not well measured by multiple-choice questions.

Nearly all states have embarked on the standards strategy, but there is little evidence about the quality of standards and assessments. Two organizations have reviewed the quality of state standards over time; however, their criteria differ and their results are not always consistent (American Federation of Teachers, 2000; Finn & Petrelli, 2000). And, although most states claim that their assessments are aligned with their standards, there has been little independent confirmation of these claims.

Since 1998, Achieve has worked with more than 20 states to examine both the quality of state standards and the alignment between the standards and the assessments. Achieve has done so by comparing state standards and assessments against national and international exemplar standards, to gauge whether the standards and tests are as good as they can be. The goal of the process is not to aim toward a national curriculum, but rather to use these exemplars as benchmarks for determining whether each state's standards adhere to a common set of criteria.

Two separate methodologies have been used. One stems from the analysis of curriculum expectations in high-performing nations conducted as part of the Third International Mathematics and Science Study (TIMSS), a comprehensive study of performance and instructional practice in 41 nations. The other methodology, developed by Achieve, provides a more in-depth analysis of state standards and tests.

Both analyses have resulted in similar findings. They suggest that the state systems have a number of important strengths that could help lead to improvements in student performance. But the analyses also found significant weaknesses in both the quality of standards and tests, and the alignment between the two. The findings also indicate some additional issues that states need to consider as they continue down the path toward standards-based reform.

METHODOLOGY

THE ACHIEVE TIMSS STUDY

TIMSS was the most extensive cross-national study of student achievement and educational practices ever undertaken (Schmidt et al., 2001; Schmidt, McKnight, & Raizen, 1997; Schmidt, McKnight, Valverde, Houang, & Wiley,

1997). In addition to comprehensive tests of students' knowledge and skills in mathematics and science in grade 4, grade 8, and at the end of high school, researchers conducted an analysis of the curriculum in 50 nations. The analysis looked at both the "intended" curriculum laid out in official documents, and the "enacted" curriculum that teachers actually used.

The purpose of the analysis was twofold: first, to determine the common elements of the curricula in the participating nations in order to develop a cross-national test of achievement; and second, to provide background information to help researchers understand the factors that influence achievement.

In reports issued at the conclusion of the study, TIMSS researchers found that, in contrast to other nations, U.S. textbooks in mathematics and science are overstuffed with topics, none of which is taught in sufficient depth. In the words of the researchers, the standards are "a mile wide and an inch deep" (Schmidt et al., 2001; Schmidt, McKnight, & Raizen, 1997). They also found that the fact that the expectations in other countries are more focused than in the United States contributes to the higher levels of student achievement those countries exhibit.

In the wake of this analysis, Achieve asked TIMSS researchers to study U.S. states in more depth. In 1998, Achieve commissioned William Schmidt, a professor of education at Michigan State University and the national research coordinator for TIMSS, to study how the state standards and tests in various U.S. states compared with those of the top-achieving nations. Schmidt examined the standards in mathematics and science, and tests in those subjects, in 21 states, and compared the documents with those in the nations that performed highest on TIMSS. The analysis considered

- The content areas included in the standards and tests;
- The grades at which the content areas are introduced and expected to be covered; and
- The proportion of test items devoted to the content areas included in the curricula in the best-performing nations.

To conduct the analysis, Schmidt used the framework developed for TIMSS, which broke down the content of the standards and tests into subsets of the subject areas and enabled comparisons between standards and tests and across nations. For example, the eighth-grade mathematics analysis included the following content areas: numbers; measurement; geometry; proportionality; functions, relations, and equations; data representation, probability, and statistics; elementary analysis; and validation and structure. It also covered subsets of each of these topics.

The analysis examined the number of content areas included in standards in each state and nation, a comparison of when topics were introduced into the curriculum in high-performing nations and a majority of the states studied, a comparison of content areas common to standards and tests in the states studied, and an examination of the proportion of test items covering the different content areas.

ACHIEVE'S BENCHMARKING INITIATIVE

In addition to commissioning the Schmidt study, Achieve launched a benchmarking initiative in 1998 to provide an in-depth analysis of standards and tests in participating states (Achieve, 1998, 2000a, 2000b, 2000c, 2000d, 2001). The effort began that year with studies of standards and tests in Michigan and North Carolina. Since then, Achieve has conducted similar analyses for another seven states. In all but one of the states, the tests used were designed to match the state standards (the state that used an off-the-shelf test has not released its report). The Michigan and North Carolina analyses examined standards and tests in four subjects—English/language arts, mathematics, history/social studies, and science. The rest of the analyses examined English/language arts and mathematics only.

The studies consist of two main phases. First, experts convened by Achieve analyze the standards documents by comparing them against "benchmarks" selected by Achieve's experts as the best in the world. In English/language arts, the benchmark standards are California's and Massachusetts's; in mathematics, Arizona's and Japan's. In addition, standards for early literacy are compared with standards from North Carolina and Texas, as well as New Standards' primary literacy standards.

In the analyses, reviewers consider the rigor of the standards, their comprehensiveness and focus, and their clarity. "Side-by-side" comparisons with the benchmark documents enable the reviewers to determine, among other things, whether a state's standards provide an equivalent level of guiding detail, and whether a state expects students to demonstrate the same knowledge and skills as the benchmark states at a similar grade level.

Following the standards analysis, Achieve reviewers examine a state's tests to determine whether they measure what the standards expect—in other words, the alignment of standards with assessments.

Alignment is the degree to which standards and assessments are in agreement and serve in conjunction with one another to guide and support student learning. Alignment is not an attribute of either standards or assessments per se, but rather of the relationship between them. And because it describes the match between standards and assessments, alignment can be legitimately improved by altering either one of them or both (Webb, 1997).

MANAGEMENT OF EXPERT JUDGMENT

The alignment analysis is a process of managing expert judgment. There is no mathematical formula for matching a test to standards. Rather, the process relies on experienced, knowledgeable educators, who bring their experience and knowledge to bear in applying the criteria for gauging alignment.

The process is analogous to the scoring of performance assessments. It begins with training, in which participants go through each stage of the process using "anchor items" that illustrate each of the ratings. They then try to apply the criteria to a previously analyzed test, to measure their understanding of the criteria, before beginning with the "live" analysis.

The raters selected to conduct the analysis represent a diversity of viewpoints and usually consist of classroom teachers, curriculum specialists, and subject-matter experts. They often have experience with large-scale assessments and many have had experience in standards development. The diversity of backgrounds is useful in making judgments about the appropriateness of test items for particular grade levels, among other things. The participants meet in small groups, facilitated by an experienced group leader, to discuss their judgments. The judgments are further structured by the tools developed for the process, including rubrics for judging the various dimensions of alignment.

THE ALIGNMENT PROTOCOL

The protocol reviewers use to analyze alignment considers four dimensions to be central in determining the degree of alignment between an assessment and standards.

- *Content centrality.* This criterion provides a deeper analysis of the match between the content of each test question and the content of the related standard by examining the degree or quality of the match. Reviewers assign each item to one of four categories based on the degree of alignment.
- *Performance centrality.* This criterion focuses on the degree of the match between the type of performance (cognitive demand) presented by each test item and the type of performance described by the related standard. Each item makes a certain type of cognitive demand on a student (e.g., the item requires a certain performance such as "select," "identify," "compare," or "analyze"). Reviewers assign each item to one of four categories based on the degree of alignment.

- *Challenge.* This criterion is applied to a set of items to determine whether doing well on these items requires students to master challenging subject matter. Reviewers consider two factors in evaluating sets of test items against the challenge criterion: *source* of challenge and *level* of challenge.

    Source of challenge attempts to uncover whether the individual test items in a set are difficult because of the knowledge and skills they target, or for other reasons not related to the subject matter, such as relying unfairly on students' background knowledge. Reviewers rate each item as having an appropriate or inappropriate source of challenge.

    Level of challenge compares the emphasis of performance required by a set of items to the emphasis of performance described by the related standard. In addition to evaluating alignment, reviewers also judge whether the set of test items has a span of difficulty appropriate for students at a given grade level based on the standards, the assessment, and supporting materials.

- *Balance and range.* No one assessment can measure the full range of knowledge and skills required by the state standards. Evaluating balance and range provides both qualitative and quantitative descriptive information about the choices states or test developers have made.

    Balance compares the emphasis of content and performance supplied by an item set to the emphasis of content described by the standards. In addition to evaluating alignment, reviewers also judge whether the set of items emphasizes the more important content at the grade level. Reviewers write a succinct summary of the balance of each item set.

    Range is a measure of coverage or breadth (the numerical proportion of all content addressed).

FINDINGS

THE QUALITY OF STANDARDS

The two studies, the Schmidt study using the TIMSS framework and the Achieve in-depth analyses, found a number of important strengths that suggest that state standards have improved since the early days of the standards movement. In 1996, when only 15 states had standards in core subjects, reviews found that most standards lacked clarity and were not grounded in content (American Federation of Teachers, 1996). Many included expectations that were not measurable, such as goals for students' enjoyment of reading.

These studies suggest that in 2000, when 49 states had standards, the picture was far different (American Federation of Teachers, 2000). Some of the standards that stood out as best in 1996 were at about the average level in 2000. One noticeable improvement is in the language of the standards. The Achieve studies show that the overwhelming majority of the standards are clear and jargon-free, rather than written in such a way that few people other than professional educators could make any sense of them. In addition, the standards for the most part are written in measurable terms.

Despite these positive signs, standards still have room for improvement. The writing of the standards, while better than before, could become more clear. Although the standards are understandable on their face, they are often too vague and all-encompassing to provide sufficient guidance to teachers or test developers. One state, for example, expects all students to "read literally, inferentially, and critically." While this sentiment is laudable, it says nothing about how to craft lessons or exercises to determine whether students can accomplish the goals, or how to determine whether, in fact, a student has achieved the desired result. Almost anything can be caught under that wide net.

In part, this vagueness may reflect states' efforts to set general guidelines at the state level without dictating to local districts or schools how to teach. While this approach represents a laudable effort to respect local control and teacher creativity, it can result in general expectations that can be interpreted in different ways by different teachers. Such varying interpretations run counter to the intention of the standards effort to provide common expectations for all students (American Federation of Teachers, 2000).

Some newer standards, such as Massachusetts's in English/language arts and Arizona's in mathematics, have done a better job of walking the line between state guidance and local control. These standards show that it is possible to provide clear and specific expectations at the state level that provide appropriate guidance and still accommodate multiple programs of study at the local level.

Consider the following contrast between Illinois's standard for measurement in grade 3 with a comparable standard in Arizona:

Illinois:
    "Sort, classify, and compare familiar shapes."

Arizona:

5M-F1: Demonstrate that a single object has different attributes that can be measured in different ways (e.g., length, mass/weight, time, temperature, area, and volume).

5M-F1 PO 1: Determine the characteristics (attributes) that are measurable (e.g., length and weight are measurable; color and texture are not measurable).

5M-F1 PO 2: Identify the type of measure (e.g., weight, height, volume) for each attribute.

As this example makes clear, the Arizona standards provide much clearer guidance to teachers and test developers than the Illinois example, yet do not dictate pedagogy.

Standards are continuing to evolve and a newer generation of standards may represent a substantial improvement. Both Indiana and Oregon, for example, revised their standards following an Achieve review, and reviewers concluded that the newer standards represent a substantial improvement over the previous versions. Consider the following pair of standards for writing applications for grade 4, both from Indiana. The first is from an earlier set of standards, adopted in 1999, which Achieve reviewers found unclear and excessively vague. The second is from a revised set of standards, adopted in 2000 following the Achieve review.

Standard 6: Writing: Application

Write using a variety of forms. Use reference sources to locate information. Use varied word choices. Write for different purposes and audiences.

Students in grade 4 who meet the standard will be able to do the following:

- Write using a variety of forms including responses to literature, informational articles, and reports.
- Use references and resources to find information for a report or description. Include details to support the main ideas.
- Use varied word choices to make writing interesting.
- Write for different purposes.
- Write to a specific audience or person.

Standard 5: Writing: Writing Applications

(Different Types of Writing and their Characteristics)

At grade 4, students are introduced to writing informational reports and written responses to literature. Students continue to write compositions that describe and explain familiar objects, events, and experiences. Student writing demonstrates a command of Standard English and the drafting, research, and organizational strategies outlined in Standard 4—Writing Process. Writing demonstrates an awareness of the audience (intended reader) and purpose for writing.

In addition to producing the different writing forms introduced in earlier grades, such as letters, grade 4 students use the writing strategies outline in Standard 4—Writing Process to:

- Write narratives (stories) that:
    Include ideas, observations, or memories of an event or experience.
    Provide a context to allow the reader to imagine the world of the event or experience.
    Use concrete sensory details.
- Write responses to literature that:
    Demonstrate an understanding of a literary work.
    Support judgments through references to both the text and prior knowledge.
- Write informational reports that:
    Ask a central question about an issue or situation.
    Include facts and details for focus.
    Use more than one source of information, including speakers, books, newspapers, media sources, and online information.
- Write summaries that contain the main ideas of the reading selection and the most significant details.
- Use varied word choices to make writing interesting.
- Write for different purposes (information, persuasion) and to a specific audience or person.

The Achieve studies also suggest that states face challenges in improving the rigor of their standards. When held up to those of high-performing nations, many state standards are not as challenging as the expectations other countries have for their students. In some states, the expectations for eighth graders are equivalent to what other nations expect elementary students to master. For example, Oregon, in its original standards, expected eighth graders to apply measurement formulas that Japan asks students to apply in grades 4 and 5. The state also asked students to add and subtract fractions with like denominators at grade 5; Japan expects students to add and subtract decimals and fractions with *unlike* denominators at grade 3.

These lower expectations reflect, in part, the fact that many states fail to expect students to develop a more sophisticated understanding of content and more complex reasoning skills over time. They simply include the same topics year after year and apparently do not expect students to master the content at all. The resulting standards in later years are crammed with so many expectations that teachers cannot teach any of them in depth—the curriculum thus becomes a mile wide and an inch deep. For example, Schmidt's study showed that states include in their standards as many as 40 mathematics topics in eighth grade; by contrast, high-performing nations like Japan include fewer than 20.

These nations, moreover, expect students to master topics and move on to new topics, while U.S. states tend to hit a plateau. For example, Oregon students in grades 3, 5, 8, and 10 are asked to round numbers (starting with one-, two- and three-digit whole numbers to the nearest 10, 100, and 1,000 in grade 3; moving to rounding with ranges from the nearest hundredth to the nearest ten-thousandth in grade 5, and the nearest thousandth to the nearest millionth in grade 8). Japan introduces the concept of place value in grade 3, when students are expected to understand the place value of 10,000, and completes the concept in grade 4, when students are exposed to "units such as hundred million, trillion, billion, etc." (Achieve 2000c, p. 19).

The Achieve studies also found that, when compared with those of high-performing nations, state standards omit important content. One common omission is clear expectations for early literacy. This omission reflects the fact that many states begin their standards at grade 4, in part to respect local control over the curriculum. By starting in grade 4, these standards assume that students have mastered early literacy essentials such as concepts about print, phonemic awareness, decoding, and word recognition. As a result, they provide little guidance about the early stages of literacy development, particularly systematic phonics. Yet as a growing consensus in the field makes clear, systematic phonics is an essential element of beginning reading instruction (Snow, Burns, & Griffin, 1998). Without guidance for the pre-K–3 curriculum, teachers will have few clues about whether students are prepared to meet the demanding standards for comprehension and fluency outlined in the grade 4 standards. And without that foundation, children will be ill-prepared for higher expectations in the later grades.

A number of states also leave out important content in mathematics. They do not explicitly state that students should learn the fundamental concepts and properties of algebra and geometry. For example, the grade 8 expectations for geometry in the early version of Indiana standards dictate that students will:

Describe and compare two- and three-dimensional shapes. Solve problems using similarity. Apply the Pythagorean theorem. Relate geometric transformations to the real world.

By contrast, comparable expectations in Japan emphasize additional content that the Indiana standards omit:

1. Find the properties of a figure in a plane and confirm them by using the properties of parallel lines and the conditions for congruence of triangles.
   a. The properties of parallel lines.
   b. The conditions for congruence of triangles.
   c. The properties of triangles and parallelograms.
2. Clarify the concepts of similarity of figures and develop the ability to find the properties of figures by using the conditions for congruence or similarity of triangles, and confirm them.
   a. The meaning of similarity and the conditions for similarity of triangles.
   b. The properties of the ratio of segments of parallel lines.
   c. The applications of similarity.
   Terms/Symbols: opposite angle, interior angle, exterior angle, definition, proof, center of gravity.

Many state standards also tend to neglect such topics as congruence, quadratics, slope, and trigonometry, which high-achieving countries emphasize at grade 8.

THE QUALITY OF TESTS

As with the standards, the Achieve studies also suggest that tests have improved substantially in recent years. They demonstrate that the efforts that began in the 1980s to reform testing have taken hold in the states, and that tests in use represent a far cry from the minimum-competency tests of a previous generation.

In two of the states Achieve has examined, Michigan and New Jersey, the tests are particularly strong—in fact, stronger than their standards. In these states, the tests are challenging and measure important knowledge and skills. In English/language arts, the tests ask students to show their comprehension of reading passages and use their understanding to make inferences based on what they have read. In mathematics, the tests pose challenging problems that enable students to demonstrate their understanding of important concepts.

While the other state tests are not as strong as those two, all of them demonstrate significant strengths. Notably, all of the state tests include at least some open-ended items, although states continue to rely largely on multiple-choice questions. In many cases, although not all, the tests use these formats wisely, employing multiple-choice questions for efficiency and open-ended items to tap skills not easily measured by other formats.

Writing assessments are particularly strong. These not only provide a good gauge of students' ability to produce prose, but also send an important signal to teachers that writing ability is expected.

The better writing assessments Achieve reviewed truly tapped the qualities of effective writing. For example, Achieve reviewers found that New Jersey's six-point scoring scale measured the characteristics of writing appropriately and allowed distinctions among gradations of effective writing. Moreover, the sample papers that earned the highest scores were indeed exemplary.

The Achieve alignment studies also found that state tests do, in fact, measure much of the knowledge and skills the standards expect. The first step in the Achieve alignment process is to map the test items to the standards. This step is intended as preparation for the more detailed alignment analysis; however, it also provides information on the extent to which the content on the tests matches the content in the standards. These matches found that, in many cases, state tests and standards show a high degree of agreement. In a number of instances, the match was as high as 95%; that is, nearly all the test items measured content included in the standards.

This degree of matching—which is where many other alignment studies stop—is a positive sign. It suggests that the tests, in fact, measure content and skills the state considers important for all students to learn, and that students and teachers who pay attention to the standards should not be surprised by the material on the tests. However, this finding does not suggest that alignment is exemplary, or that the tests measure the standards well. Moreover, the finding of a high degree of match between standards and tests is not uniform. In one state, for example, 95% of the items on the English tests matched content and skills in the standards, but only 65% of the mathematics items did so.

In addition, in the one instance in which Achieve reviewed a commercially available test, the analysis found a considerable mismatch between the tests and the standards. At grade 10, 25% of the test questions did not match the state standards at all. The match was closer in the earlier grades.

The use of the Achieve protocol to analyze the alignment between the tests and the standards suggests that the match between test items and standards masks some substantial misalignment. Although tests may be "aligned" with standards in a superficial way, they do not always measure all of what the standards expect students to know and be able to do.

In a number of cases, for example, tests measure only the least complex of the skills called for in the standards. In part, this problem reflects the all-encompassing nature of the standards. Some standards ask students to demonstrate a number of skills, such as to identify geometric properties and use them to solve problems. However, the tests may ask students only to identify the properties. The one-to-one match may suggest that such test items are aligned with the standards, but clearly the test does not measure what the standards expect students to demonstrate.

When a state standard includes a number of objectives, it is likely that a test item will measure only one. If the test as a whole included items that measured the full range of objectives, then the test could represent a fair measure of the standard. But this is seldom the case. Often the test includes at best only a few items measuring the standard, and those that do, tend to measure the relatively low-level objectives.

For example, Minnesota's grade 5 standard in English/language arts for literal comprehension includes the following objective:

A student shall demonstrate comprehension of literal meaning by reading, listening, and viewing of nonfiction and fiction selections to identify main ideas and supporting details, retell main events or ideas in sequence, pronounce new words using phonics, demonstrate techniques of improving and expanding vocabulary, and demonstrate an age-appropriate reading rate.

While all of these multiple, distinct concepts are important (although some may be difficult to assess in an on-demand setting), the grade 5 test emphasizes only the first of these—identifying main ideas and supporting details. This is the least complex of the objectives.

The Achieve studies also found that the tests tend to be "unbalanced"; that is, they measure some standards but not others. This is understandable; a test is unlikely to measure all of a state's standards. While in some cases, the topics the states chose to emphasize were the most important ones, in other cases, it was not always clear that standards were deliberately emphasized or de-emphasized. Rather, the choices were sometimes haphazard. In one state, for example, almost half of an eighth-grade reading test assessed a single standard: "make inferences and draw conclusions." While this objective is worthwhile, it leaves little room for other standards that are also important and that could be assessed but are not on the test, such as word recognition, vocabulary, and an understanding of different reading genres.

Similarly, in mathematics, some state tests tend to focus on number and measurement, leaving little room for important standards like algebra and geometry. And what is measured, at the eighth-grade level, is often arithmetic, which high-achieving countries expect students to master in elementary school. In one state in Schmidt's study, for example, nearly half the test items in eighth grade measured whole number operations, and 40% included questions on measurement (some could have tapped both topics). By contrast, only a fourth of the items measured two-dimensional geometry, and a fourth measured functions, relations, and equations—the fundamentals of algebra.

This finding is fairly consistent across the states that Achieve has examined. In another state, for example, the reading comprehension tests do a good job of measuring vocabulary, literal interpretations of reading passages, and inference. However, there are few items that measure literary analysis or that ask students to distinguish among genres, identify or organize main ideas, or compare and contrast. These important concepts are included in the standards, but are not assessed. The state's mathematics tests in grades 5 and 8, meanwhile, overemphasize computation and exclude content that requires higher-order thinking.

The lack of balance in the assessments sometimes is exacerbated by the injudicious use of item formats. Many, although not all, states use multiple-choice and open-ended items inappropriately. Indiana's ISTEP+, for example, commendably includes a substantial number of open-ended items, yet the test assesses writing conventions through the use of multiple-choice items, rather than open-ended items that would enable students to demonstrate their understanding of conventions through their use in writing.

One of the most serious shortcomings of the tests Achieve has analyzed involves the level of challenge they pose for high school students. Simply put, the level of challenge in tests tends to reach a plateau or decline between middle school and high school. While this is not true in every state Achieve has examined, it raises questions about states' expectations for high school students—particularly in states where students will be required to pass a test to graduate.

In New Jersey, for example, where Achieve reviewed a field test of the grade 11 examination, which eventually will be used as a graduation requirement, the level of challenge on the mathematics test was weak. This represented a sharp contrast from the fourth- and eighth-grade tests, which were demanding and asked students to demonstrate knowledge and skills that are important and appropriate for their grade level.

Of the four strands of mathematics assessed on the eleventh-grade test, only number sense came close to the level of challenge the reviewers considered appropriate for eleventh graders. There was a moderate range of difficulty among the items within the set, although there were no items the reviewers characterized as having a high level of challenge. In the other strands, particularly geometry and data analysis, the level of challenge was too low for high school students and did not match the level of rigor denoted by the standards. Overall, the test contained an abundance of low-level demands and in many cases a revisiting of content taught in the middle grades.

In some cases, in fact, items on the test appeared more appropriate for eighth graders than for students about to enter their final year of high school. Items assessing patterns, functions, and algebra emphasized linear relationships, a concept that should have been mastered earlier.

CONCLUSIONS AND IMPLICATIONS

The in-depth analyses of standards and assessments in nine states conducted by Achieve, as well as the 21-state study conducted by Schmidt, came up with similar findings. They found that the standards and tests represent a considerable step forward from the early 1990s, when standards tended to be lists of jargon-filled vague aspirations, and tests for the most part measured minimum competencies only. The newer standards are relatively clear and focus on academic content, and the newer tests at least attempt to measure a broad range of knowledge and abilities, many incorporating constructed-response items to better assess higher-order skills and model effective classroom practice.

However, the reviews show clearly that both standards and tests could use improvement. This is particularly true in the area of alignment. While a relatively superficial analysis would suggest that tests measure the content included in state standards, the deeper analysis probed by the Achieve protocol demonstrates that this degree of alignment is misleading. In nearly every case Achieve has examined, tests do not measure what the standards expect, either in the content and performances expected of students or in the breadth of knowledge and skills outlined in the standards. In addition, the level of rigor in the tests, particularly high school tests, tends to be relatively low.

Moreover, the way the tests are misaligned with the standards tends to follow a regular pattern. More often than not, test items tend to measure the least cognitively complex of the expectations outlined in a standard, and item sets tend to focus on relatively low-level knowledge and skills. And the high school tests tend to measure content that should have been mastered earlier.

To be sure, these patterns have not manifested themselves in every state Achieve or the TIMSS researchers have examined; as noted above, at least two state tests measure challenging expectations. Yet taken together, the findings from the Achieve studies suggest that many state tests do not measure the full range of knowledge and skills states expect all students to master, and what they do measure tends to be the least complex of those expectations.

These findings hold a number of significant implications for policy and practice. First, they call into question the validity of reports on student performance. If a test measures only some of the expectations the standards hold for all students, can a score on the test truly represent a measure of performance against the standards? Has a student who performs well on the test mastered what the state expects all students to know and be able to do? Is a school with a high proportion of students who perform well on the test truly a school that is enabling students to meet challenging standards?

This problem is exacerbated by the way some states report results. Illinois, for example, reports student performance according to clusters of standards, rather than by individual standards or as a whole. But as the Achieve review in Illinois found, this practice masked the imbalance in the test. In many cases, items measured only one or two standards within a cluster. As a result, the reports of student performance may be misleading by suggesting that students have mastered a certain group of standards when in fact they may have mastered only a few of these.

The use of passing scores further complicates the validity of the results. If a test measures only some of the knowledge and skills expected for all students, what does a passing score indicate? Does it mean that students who attain the score have demonstrated proficiency on the test, or on the standards? Although Achieve's protocol has focused on the test instrument, in future work the organization plans to examine the passing standards as well to provide an indication of the alignment of passing scores with expectations for student performance.

In addition to the validity problem, the mismatch between standards and assessments also has implications for the allocation of educational resources. If test results reveal that a school is performing relatively poorly in one area of mathematics, say patterns and functions, how should the school address the problem? Should it try to obtain professional development on the broad range of content and skills included in the standards for that topic, or should it focus on the relatively narrow range included on the test?

Similarly, how should teachers respond to the mismatch between standards and tests? Should they focus on the knowledge and skills the standards expect and hope that by doing so students will perform well on the tests? Undoubtedly many teachers do so. But some will likely focus only on the material on the test, thereby shortchanging their students of higher-level knowledge and skills the state expects all students to master.

WHAT IS A STATE TO DO?

Faced with these challenges, what can a state do? One response is to augment the state test with a set of items that broaden the balance, range, and level of challenge of the test. The Achieve studies did not find that the state tests measure unimportant content or, for the most part, content and skills not included in the standards. What they did find was that the tests placed too much emphasis on certain (low-level) content and skills at the exclusion of higher-level abilities and more challenging standards. By including additional items, states can help ensure that their tests have a broader representation of their standards.

This is the approach California took in 1999 when the state acknowledged that the off-the-shelf test it was using to assess student performance (the Stanford Achievement Test—9th Edition, or SAT-9) was not aligned with the state standards. Making the determination of misalignment on its own—Achieve did not review the California test—the state administered an augmentation, or additional items in English/language arts and mathematics, that measured standards not tapped by the SAT-9. (However, until 2001, only the SAT-9 was considered for accountability purposes.) The state plans to place greater emphasis on the standards-based tests and less emphasis on the SAT-9 in the future.

While an augmentation may help address some of the limitations of the current level of alignment, it has some drawbacks. The biggest is the additional testing burden. States will have to consider whether additional items or tests are worth the benefit of measuring a broader range of the standards, or whether another approach might be more cost-effective.

A second, longer-term approach to improving alignment is to build alignment into tests from the outset. By using the Achieve protocol or one like it, test developers can determine whether their items and sets of items measure what the standards expect. Such an approach yields much better information than a simple checklist that indicates whether a test item measures a standard or not.

Achieve has held workshops in several states to acquaint test developers and curriculum developers with its alignment methodology. The hope is that these and other efforts will enable states to develop assessments that truly measure what all students should know and be able to do.

REFERENCES

Achieve. (1998). *Academic standards and assessment benchmarking evaluation for Michigan*. Washington, DC: Author.

Achieve. (2000a). *Measuring up: A report on education standards and assessments for Indiana*. Washington, DC: Author.

Achieve. (2000b). *Measuring up: A report on education standards and assessments for New Jersey*. Washington, DC: Author.

Achieve. (2000c). *Measuring up: A report on education standards and assessments for Oregon*. Washington, DC: Author.

Achieve. (2000d). *Taking stock: A report to education policymakers in Illinois*. Washington, DC: Author.

Achieve. (2001). *Measuring up: A report on education assessments for Minnesota*. Washington, DC: Author.

American Federation of Teachers. (1996). *Making standards matter*. Washington, DC: Author.

American Federation of Teachers. (2000). *Making standards matter*. Washington, DC: Author.

Elmore, R. F., & Rothman, R. (Eds.). (1999). *Testing, teaching, and learning: A guide for states and school districts*. Washington, DC: National Academy Press.

Finn, C. E., & Petrelli, M. J. (Eds.). (2000). *The state of state standards 2000*. Washington, DC: Thomas B. Fordham Foundation.

Gaining ground. Quality counts 2001: A better balance. (2001, January 11). *Education Week, 20*(17), 33–40.

O'Day, J. A., & Smith, M. S. (1993). Systemic reform and educational opportunity. In S. H. Fuhrman (Ed.), *Designing coherent education policy: Improving the system* (pp. 313–322). San Francisco: Jossey-Bass.

Ravitch, D. (1995). *National standards in American education: A citizen's guide*. Washington, DC: Brookings Institution Press.

Schmidt, W. H., McKnight, C., Houang, R. T., Wang, H., Wiley, D. T., Cogan, L. S., & Wolfe, R. G. (2001). *Why schools matter: A cross-national comparison of curriculum and learning*. San Francisco: Jossey-Bass.

Schmidt, W. H., McKnight, C., & Raizen, S. (1997). *A splintered vision: An investigation of U.S. science and mathematics education*. Boston: Kluwer.

Schmidt, W. H., McKnight, C., Valverde, G. A., Houang, R. T., & Wiley, D. T. (1997). *Many visions, many aims: Vol. I. A cross-national investigation of curricular aims in mathematics*. Boston: Kluwer.

Schwartz, R. B., & Robinson, M. A. (2000). Goals 2000 and the standards movement. In D. Ravitch (Ed.), *Brookings papers on education policy: 2000*. Washington, DC: Brookings Institution.

Snow, C. E., Burns, M. S., & Griffin, P. (1998). *Preventing reading difficulties in young children*. Washington, DC: National Academy Press.

Webb, N. L. (1997). Determining alignment of expectations and assessments in mathematics and science education. *NISE Brief, 1*(2), 1–8. Madison: National Center for Improving Science Education, University of Wisconsin–Madison.

Chapter 6

Biting the Bullet: Including Special-Needs Students in Accountability Systems

Martha L. Thurlow

The U.S. educational system is distinguished by its historic commitment to free, universal public education. It has long struggled to fulfill this mission by improving services offered to students of diverse racial, ethnic, and economic backgrounds. In 1975, the United States explicitly extended this commitment with the enactment of the Education for All Handicapped Children Act (Public Law 94-142), which ensured that children with all types of disabilities could attend school and receive a public education. There is no doubt that today's schools are more diverse than they have ever been (Hodgkinson, 1996; Lollock, 2001). This diversity presents many challenges; among the most difficult are those associated with educating students with disabilities and English language learners (ELLs), referred to in this chapter as special-needs students.

Education of special-needs students takes on added significance in the current context of standards-based accountability systems that aim to improve the education of all students through the systematic reporting, analysis, and use of student assessment data. The National Research Council (NRC) of the National Academy of Sciences (August & Hakuta, 1997; McDonnell, McLaughlin, & Morison, 1997) cited several benefits to including students with disabilities and ELLs in educational assessments and accountability systems, including: (1) a more accurate picture of education; (2) the relevance of reforms, interventions, and other variables that reflect students' opportunity to learn; and (3) the potential for raised expectations for students. These reports reflected increasing concern about the importance of having good outcome data on students with disabilities who received extensive federal and state funds and on ELLs who missed out on content instruction because of the attention given to teaching them English. Good outcome data also were recognized as important in setting high standards, ensuring appropriate opportunities to learn, developing effective interventions, and improving student achievement.

The need to include all students in assessments and accountability also was prompted by documented variability in the characteristics of students excluded from assessment systems—variability that resulted in noncomparable data, inappropriate conclusions, and an avenue for excluding ever-increasing numbers of students. The work of Allington and McGill-Franzen (1992) in New York clearly showed the tendency for educators to find ways to not be held accountable for students expected to perform poorly by systematically excluding them from assessments through grade retention or special education referral. To add to the New York revelations, others found evidence of variability in exclusion rates across districts (Zlatos, 1994) and states (McGrew, Thurlow, Shriner, & Spiegel, 1992). Similar concerns about the participation of ELLs in assessments and accountability systems emerged in the mid-1990s with documentation, for example, of only five states requiring ELLs to take state assessments, and at least 36 states exempting students for up to 3 years (August & Lara, 1996).

The likelihood that overexclusion of both students with disabilities and ELLs would occur in some places but not in others was a turning point in discussions about the need to include all students in assessments and accountability systems. The conclusion that there could be no exclusion loopholes was reached by the special study conducted by the NRC (McDonnell, McLaughlin, & Morison, 1997).

> *If students with disabilities are to gain any benefits from standards-based reform, the education system must be held publicly accountable for every student's performance....*
>
> *The presumption should be that all students will participate in assessments associated with standards-based reform.* Assessments not only serve as the primary basis of accountability, but also they are likely to remain the cornerstone and often the most well-developed component of the standards movement. (p. 192, emphasis in original)

Despite the logic of this conclusion, it has proved to be difficult for administrators and educators to accept.

This chapter addresses the challenge of including students with disabilities and ELLs in school accountability systems—those that determine consequences for educators and their schools—rather than those used to determine consequences for students (grade promotion or graduation). Because the knowledge in the field is greater for students with disabilities, I focus primarily on these students, bringing in information on ELLs along the way.

A simple way to approach the topic of including special-needs students in assessments and accountability is to recognize that students with disabilities (and ELLs) can participate in assessment systems in a variety of ways—in the same way as other students (standard assessment), with accommodations, or in an alternate assessment. This chapter focuses primarily on accommodated and alternate assessment students because they represent the two largest groups of students who have been added to educational assessment systems, and therefore must be added to accountability systems.

In this chapter, I first identify the laws that support the development of accountability systems that are inclusive of *all* students. After addressing the unique challenges of including accommodated and alternate assessment students, I explore current approaches to their inclusion in school accountability systems and the intended and potential unintended effects of this inclusion.[1]

FEDERAL LAWS SUPPORTING INCLUSIVE ACCOUNTABILITY SYSTEMS

Two federal laws provide the primary impetus for the inclusion of all students in accountability systems—the 1994 reauthorization of the Elementary and Secondary Education Act (ESEA), and the 1997 reauthorization of the Individuals with Disabilities Education Act (IDEA), formerly the Education of All Handicapped Children Act. While IDEA focuses just on students with disabilities who have Individualized Education Programs (IEPs), ESEA focuses on all children—particularly in its Title I funding provisions.

IDEA. Special education funding is provided through Part B of IDEA. Historically, this law provided children with disabilities the right to a free and appropriate public education, with provisions for receiving services in the least restrictive environment that are driven by IEPs and plans for transition from school to postsecondary education and work. These provisions are supported by a range of other requirements related to discipline, mediation, and more.

When IDEA was reauthorized in 1997, new requirements addressed the need for accountability for the results of education for students with disabilities. Four aspects of IDEA are relevant to accountability systems, some more directly than others. First, IDEA requires consideration of student access to the general curriculum. Second, IDEA requires the participation of all students with disabilities in state and district assessments, with accommodations if needed, or through the development and implementation of an alternate assessment. Third, IDEA requires that the IEP specifically address access to the general curriculum and how the student will participate in assessments and what accommodations the student needs in instruction and assessments. Fourth, IDEA requires the public reporting of performance results of students with disabilities whenever the performance of other students is reported, both included in the aggregate performance, and disaggregated for students with disabilities.

While there is no language in IDEA that specifically requires inclusion of students with disabilities in formal accountability systems, there is language that confirms this intent in the regulations that accompany IDEA (Federal Register, 64 (48), Friday, March 12, 1999, pp. 12564, 12565). Furthermore, both the requirement for public reporting and the requirement that states prepare biennial reports that include data on assessment performance reflect a commitment to inclusion of students with disabilities in accountability systems.

ESEA. Title I of the Elementary and Secondary Education Act provides funding to states to support programs for disadvantaged students. When reauthorized in 1994, it included important changes relevant to the inclusion of all students in accountability systems. ESEA used the phrase "all students" to specifically include students with disabilities and students with limited English proficiency (the federal term that corresponds to ELLs) when it clarified the new way in which Title I programs were to be evaluated. Instead of allowing the former approach of using locally determined tests to collect pre- and posttest data, with no central accountability for results, ESEA required that states base their evaluation process on the performance of all students on state assessments aligned with state standards. States were required to meet the 1994 Title I provisions by summer 2001.

The Department of Education's review of states' Title I materials indicate that 36 of the 41 states initially not approved were cited for problems with including students with disabilities, and 33 were cited for problems with including students with limited English proficiency (the Department of Education's decision letters can be viewed at www.ed.gov/offices/OESA/saa). While some of these problems have since been resolved, only 19 states had received full Title I approval by the end of August 2002.

The Title I findings, coupled with the increased emphasis on assessment and accountability for all students in the 2001 reauthorization, suggest that states are going to have to "bite the bullet" and include students with disabilities and limited English proficient (LEP) students in their assessments and accountability systems. They are going to have to include students who so far have been excluded.

WHICH SPECIAL-NEEDS STUDENTS HAVE BEEN EXCLUDED?

Students who were excluded in the past included primarily: (1) students now in alternate assessments who previously had no large-scale assessment system in which to participate, and (2) students who require the use of accommodations during assessments. There are other students who have not been fit into the accountability system (e.g., highly mobile students, students who take out-of-level tests); these students are addressed in the section on intended and unintended consequences.

The number of students excluded from traditional state and district assessments has changed dramatically in the past 5 to 10 years. While IDEA requires that an alternate assessment be developed for students with disabilities who are unable to participate in state or district assessments, there is no corresponding requirement for ELLs. In fact, by 2001 only two states (Arkansas and Delaware) had developed standards-based alternate assessments (not language proficiency measures) for ELLs not included in general state assessments. These states have opted to use a portfolio or body of evidence approach to measure the progress of ELLs on content standards at the same time that the students are gaining English language proficiency.

Changes in participation in general state assessments are evident for students with disabilities. In the early 1990s, researchers and policy makers first uncovered the extent to which exclusion existed. Revelations of large numbers of excluded students emerged from both national data collection programs, such as the National Assessment of Educational Progress (NAEP), and state data collection programs (McGrew, Thurlow, & Spiegel, 1993). Significant attention was given to the issue of exclusion from NAEP of students with disabilities (Ysseldyke, Thurlow, McGrew, & Vanderwood, 1994) and students with limited English proficiency (August & McArthur, 1996).

Analyses of state policies on participation in assessments confirmed that in many states, the participation of students with disabilities was discouraged at a policy level (Thurlow, Ysseldyke, & Silverstein, 1995). Further, early surveys found most states estimating participation rates from 0–10% of students with disabilities (Shriner & Thurlow, 1994). These estimates often were just guesses; many states revealed that they did not have the data management systems in place to know whether students who took tests had disabilities, or, on the other hand, whether students with disabilities took the state tests (Almond, Tindal, & Stieber, 1997).

Data available from states changed dramatically as awareness of the problem of exclusion grew, to the point that just after the enactment of the reauthorized IDEA in 1997, 23 states indicated that they knew the participation rates of students with disabilities. For many of these states, the participation rates had changed considerably from 1992 to 1999 (see Table 6.1), and in several states they approached 90–100% of students with disabilities. Since the students included in state assessments in the early 1990s tended to be those perceived to be the highest-performing students, the increasing percentages meant that more low-performing students and students who needed accommodations were being included in assessments. Trying to include these students in accountability systems creates several challenges.

Table 6.1. Estimates of Participation Rates of Students with Disabilities in Statewide Assessments

Participation Rates	1992 [1]	1999 [2]
< 10%	Florida, Georgia, Minnesota, Missouri, Washington, Wisconsin	
10–24%	Kansas, New York	Wisconsin
25–49%	Connecticut, Tennessee, Texas	Connecticut, Pennsylvania, Texas
50–74%	Rhode Island, South Dakota	Florida, Georgia, Kansas, Ohio*, South Dakota
75–90%	Indiana, Maryland	Indiana, Minnesota, Missouri, Nevada*, New York, Oklahoma*, Tennessee, Vermont*, West Virginia*
> 90%	Kentucky	Kentucky, Maryland, Rhode Island, Washington

Notes: States with an asterisk (*) did not know the participation rate for students with disabilities in 1992.

[1] From Shriner & Thurlow, 1994.

[2] From Thompson & Thurlow, 1999.

THE CHALLENGE OF INCLUDING ALTERNATE ASSESSMENT STUDENTS

Students for whom states and districts are developing alternate assessments generally are students with significant cognitive disabilities, such as severe mental retardation, and students with multiple disabilities, including mental retardation, autism, or deaf-blindness. Such students constitute about 0.5–2% of all students (which translates to about 5–20% of students with disabilities).

An issue that quickly emerged with the IDEA 97 requirement for the development of alternate assessments was whether too many students would be included in the alternate assessments, perhaps even removing students from the regular assessment so that they could be in an alternate assessment. In many states, moving students into the alternate assessment removed them from the accountability system. IDEA 97 and its regulations do not provide much guidance; they simply refer to the alternate assessment as being for those students unable to participate in general state and district assessments. While percentages of .5–2% of all students frequently are mentioned in the literature (Thurlow, Elliott, & Ysseldyke, 1999), many educators believe that this represents too few students, and that many more students really are unable to *meaningfully* participate in traditional assessments (Quenemoen, Massanari, Thompson, & Thurlow, 2000). States' estimates of the percentage of the total school population expected to participate in alternate assessments (Thompson & Thurlow, 1999) ranged from 0.5% to 4% of all students, further indicating that alternate assessments have been developed for a range of students, not just those with significant cognitive disabilities, and will include many more students with disabilities than originally intended.

When the types of students included in an alternate assessment vary, so do the assessments developed. For example, most states have chosen to use some type of portfolio or body of evidence for their alternate assessments, but others have selected checklists or rating scales, and still others are relying on an analysis of IEP goals (Thompson & Thurlow, 2001). A few states are allowing IEP teams to determine how they will collect data for individual students, which may or may not then be scored and aggregated. Of course, when there are no scores, it is unlikely that student performance will be represented in the accountability system.

The extent to which alternate assessments are aligned with state standards varies (Thompson & Thurlow, 2001). Most states have attempted to align their alternate assessments with the broad domains of their standards by "extending" or "expanding" the essence of those standards to apply to students with significant cognitive disabilities (20 states), by linking skills to standards (14 states), or by adding them to standards (9 states). Yet, other states focus on non-standards-based functional or other skills (7 states). Studies of the reliability and validity of the various approaches taken by states are just beginning to occur (see Kleinert & Kearns, 2001).

Supposedly, the requirement that an alternate assessment be developed will block the final avenue for exclusion of students with disabilities from assessments. In reality, however, the existence of alternate assessments does not yet mean that all students' scores are reported or included in accountability mechanisms.

The Title I requirement that alternate assessments be in the accountability system may change this, but how this inclusion will occur is not yet clear (Rigney et al., 2001). The development of alternate assessments also has revealed in some states a group of students for whom neither the regular assessment, even with accommodations, nor the alternate assessment seems appropriate (Almond, Quenemoen, Olsen, & Thurlow, 2000). Although the number and characteristics of these students vary somewhat from one location to the next, explanations of the problem often refer to students who have mild mental retardation or students with significant learning disabilities. In some states these "gap" students have been addressed by developing a second alternate assessment; in other states they have been addressed by moving to out-of-level testing or, more recently, to juried assessments (Elliott & Schrag, 2001) that involve a panel of educators who judge a portfolio of evidence or a student demonstration of performance to determine whether a student has met defined proficiency standards. Whether or how the "gap assessments" will be included in accountability systems is unclear.

THE CHALLENGE OF INCLUDING STUDENTS WHO NEED ASSESSMENT ACCOMMODATIONS

Assessment accommodations are changes in assessment materials or procedures that enable the student's knowledge and skills to be assessed rather than the student's disabilities or limited English proficiency. Common types of accommodations include extended time, repeating directions, individualized setting, reading the test to the student, and Braille or translated editions of the test. But there are hundreds more accommodations that students may use as they participate in assessments. It is usually assumed that there should be a connection between the accommodations that a student uses during instruction and those used during assessments. While the right to accommodations emerged long ago for students with disabilities, they now are recognized also as a way to provide ELLs access to assessments.

In the early 1990s, when the National Center on Educational Outcomes began looking at state accommodation policies, less than half of the states had written policies or guidelines (Thurlow, Ysseldyke, & Silverstein, 1993). Today, all states (even those without state-level assessments) have written policies on assessment accommodations for students with disabilities (Thurlow, House, Scott, & Ysseldyke, 2000). Current policies look quite accommodating—many accommodations are listed by states. Other aspects of the policies have changed as well. For example, in the early 1990s, most of the guidelines limited the use of accommodations, whereas current guidelines reflect the view that students with disabilities need certain accommodations to demonstrate their knowledge and skills rather than their disabilities (Thurlow, 1999). Many states are now collecting data on the specific accommodations or types of accommodations that students are using (Thurlow, 2001).

Students with testing accommodations increasingly are being included in public reporting of assessment data. In the early 1990s, it was not uncommon for states to exclude all students with testing accommodations. By the year 2000, in most states, only students with certain accommodations were excluded—those with accommodations deemed to change the validity of the assessment or the comparability of scores (see also Krentz, Thurlow, & Callender, 2000). States were still inconsistent, however, in their identification of which specific accommodations affected score comparability or test validity—even when the very same test was being used. For example, Braille is a commonly allowed accommodation, but is considered to produce invalid scores in 14 of the 49 states that allow its use (Thurlow, Lazarus, Thompson, & Robey, 2002).

Changes in NAEP also demonstrate some evolution in testing and reporting results for students using accommodations. Following strong recommendations that students using testing accommodations be included (Ysseldyke et al., 1994), NAEP first introduced accommodations in its 1995 mathematics field test. Studies of this test as well as the 1996 assessments of math and science indicated that these accommodations increased the participation of students with disabilities in NAEP. Scores of accommodated students initially were not reported, however, ostensibly because of their uncertain effect on item characteristic curves and the need to maintain trend lines (Anderson, Jenkins, & Miller, 1996; Mazzeo, Carlson, Voekl, & Lutkus, 2000). The 2000 NAEP reading assessment reported scores of accommodated students; these scores were reported separately, rather than merged with all test scores as they will be in the future.

Federal IDEA guidance also brought forth new approaches to accommodations. In a Q&A released in August 2000, the Office of Special Education Programs (Heumann & Warlick, 2000) made it clear that state policies could not prevent IEP teams from determining that a student might need a certain "nonapproved" accommodation to participate in an assessment. Accommodations that were identified as nonapproved by states were the ones that they had decided resulted in noncomparable scores—the specific accommodations varied from state to state, but across states the most frequently nonapproved accommodations were having the test read to the student, allowing student use of a calculator, having the test recorded for the student, and providing extended time for a timed test (Thurlow et al., 2002). This created yet another challenge for states as they struggled with how to include *all* scores in accountability formulas: how to include scores of students tested with nonapproved accommodations when those scores might not really reflect progress on the standards-based learning constructs.

Other dramatic changes were occurring in states as well. Increasingly, legal battles were viewed as the pathway to solving disagreements about whether accommodations were appropriate for use during assessments. Most of the legal battles focused on high-stakes testing for students, in which a high school diploma was the focus of the suit. Still, the legal resolutions in this arena have implications for assessments used for school accountability.

Recent lawsuits aimed at state tests have been brought in California, Indiana, and Oregon. The Indiana lawsuit was on behalf of students who were viewed as needing accommodations that the state did not allow and not having enough time to prepare for the exams (Olson, 2000). This suit was decided in the state's favor, with the rationale for the decision being that states should determine accommodation policies and that 4 years is enough time for any student to prepare for a high school exam; the decision is under appeal (Keynes, 2001). Another suit brought by an advocacy organization (Disability Rights Advocates) on behalf of five Oregon students with learning disabilities was settled after a Blue Ribbon Panel produced a set of recommendations (Disability Rights Advocates, 2001; Fine, 2001).

In relation to accommodations, the Oregon settlement seemed to turn the validity argument on its heels. The *Standards for Educational and Psychological Testing* suggest that states assume the responsibility of establishing the validity of assessment accommodations (American Educational Research Association, American Psychological Association, & National Council on Measurement in Education, 1999). The Oregon decision took the burden of proof off the state in establishing the validity of the accommodation and agreed to assume that all accommodations were valid until proven otherwise.

These are just a few examples of the swirl of activities and dramatic changes that have occurred around the policy and practice of accommodations for students with disabilities. The notion that LEP students need accommodations in order to participate in assessments has emerged at a much slower pace than for students with disabilities. This is due, in part, to the lack of a broader legal basis for access to accommodations for individuals who speak other languages. Still, the conversations about participation in large-scale assessments like NAEP have reached the same conclusion—that accommodations are one avenue to increased participation of LEP students. NAEP undertook a parallel line of investigation on accommodations for LEP students. Stancavage, Allen, and Godlewski (1996) concluded that "NAEP should continue efforts to identify appropriate adaptations or accommodations that would permit the inclusion of even larger proportions of LEP students in the assessments" (p. 178).

Researchers also have studied state policies on accommodations for ELLs that are allowed during statewide assessments (Rivera, Stansfield, Scialdone, & Sharkey, 2000). In doing so they found that while 48 states had participation policies, just 40 had accommodations policies and, of these, only 37 actually allowed accommodations to be used by LEP students. These numbers are up considerably from the past, however (e.g., Thurlow, Liu, Erickson, Spicuzza, & El Sawaf, 1996), and probably will continue to change. There is considerable evidence that most states now recognize that accommodations for LEP students should not be exactly the same as accommodations for students with disabilities; LEP students may not need all of the accommodations that are available to students with disabilities but may need others (e.g., translations, glossaries, familiar examiner).

Despite the dramatic shifts in accommodation policies for both students with disabilities and ELLs, there are a number of implementation issues that generate continued concerns about accommodated testing. Three primary concerns are: (1) the tendency to "overaccommodate," (2) poor criteria or decision-making skills for determining needed accommodations, and (3) inappropriate use of accommodations as a means for excluding student scores from reporting or accountability systems.

Accommodations are intended to provide students access to assessments, so that tests measure the constructs intended rather than the student's disabilities or limited English proficiency. This simple-sounding intent is difficult to translate into practice. As a result, educators tend to select all possible accommodations for individual students, with the apparent hope that they will result in improved performance (Fuchs et al., 2000).

Typically, accommodations criteria indicate that assessment accommodations should be related to accommodations used in instruction. Yet, there is evidence of a significant disconnect between the two (Shriner & DeStefano, 2001). Students often do not receive the same accommodations in the classroom that the IEP team determined were needed for assessments. Few states have developed criteria for determining which accommodations are appropriate for which student. The confusion about accommodations in the classroom translates to confusion during assessments and, indeed, to considerable controversy about what should be done with scores from accommodated assessments.

As the consequences imposed on educators resulting from students' performance on state and district assessments increase, so do concerns about including low-performing students in assessments. The fact that some accommodations must be provided to students even though they are not approved (and, then, usually not counted in accountability) opens up a way to remove students from the accountability system. A significant potential unintended consequence of liberal accommodation policies coupled with conservative accountability policies is that large numbers of students will be able to participate in assessments, but their scores will not factor into accountability measures.

As is obvious from this discussion, there often is not a direct relationship between testing policies and accountability policies for special-needs students. States were informed through a memorandum from the U.S. Department of Education (Cohen & Heumann, 2001) that they had to allow students to use accommodations in assessments that were listed on the students' IEPs, regardless of whether the state education agency considered the scores from them to be valid. On the other hand, the memorandum also acknowledged that states could determine which of the "nonapproved" accommodations that students might use would be included in accountability indices; they also could develop other ways to include these students in accountability indices. The potential outcome is that more students will be excluded from accountability systems than were ever excluded from assessments—that is, unless all students are included in accountability systems regardless of how they participate in assessment systems.

CURRENT APPROACHES TO INCLUDING STUDENTS IN STATE ACCOUNTABILITY SYSTEMS

Are the concerns about exclusion from accountability systems realized in actual practice? Are states already including special-needs students in their accountability systems? Both IDEA and ESEA require that the scores of students with disabilities be reported so that educators and others know whether programs are meeting those students' needs, and ESEA requires the same for LEP students. This public reporting is beginning to occur (Bielinski, Thurlow, & Callender, 2001; Thurlow, Albus, & Liu, in press); more and more states each year are disaggregating and reporting the performance of these subgroups. But are these special-needs students being included in accountability systems in the same way as other students?

Krentz, Thurlow, and Callender (2000) examined information available on state websites about inclusion of students with disabilities in accountability systems and found that it is not always clear who is included and who is excluded. Their analysis indicated that of the 38 states whose accountability systems have significant consequences for schools, only seven clearly included all students with disabilities in their accountability systems. Seventeen states indicated that a subset of students with disabilities was excluded from their accountability systems. Nine states were not clear about which students were excluded. Seven states indicated that students who used nonstandard accommodations were excluded. Other exclusions were extremely diverse in focus (e.g., extended absence, parent request, not expected to meet curriculum objectives).

Only for a few states did Krentz, Thurlow, and Callender (2000) find specifically how various accountability indicators were put together to determine consequences for schools. The devil may be in the details—as suggested by the details in those states that were most specific about how consequences were assigned to specific schools. For example, among the details was the revelation that often a subset of students with disabilities is excluded. Thus, students with one category of disability (e.g., those with speech impairments) might be included, while those labeled with other categories (e.g., learning disabilities) were excluded. Or, schools might be given longer to be accountable for students with disabilities than for other students, essentially cutting the impact of these students. Further, students who take tests for a grade below the grade in which they are enrolled (out-of-level testing) often are excluded from accountability indices (Thurlow & Minnema, 2001).

Thompson and Thurlow (2001) surveyed state directors of special education about various aspects of the participation of students with disabilities in state assessments. In an attempt to clarify the extent to which state assessment components included in accountability systems actually included students with disabilities, they found a total of 24 states indicating that all of their assessment components included students with disabilities. Most of the remaining states indicated that they were uncertain about how students with disabilities in general, but more often students with disabilities who were alternate assessment participants, were going to be included. Only nine states (Alaska, Florida, Idaho, Louisiana, Maryland, North Carolina, South Carolina, West Virginia, and Wisconsin) had specifically decided that students with disabilities would be included in fewer components than other students; one state (Iowa) indicated that students with disabilities would be included in *more* components than the required number of components. Most of the states including students with disabilities in fewer components were specifically limiting the number of components only for those students in the alternate assessment.

INTENDED AND POTENTIAL UNINTENDED EFFECTS
OF INCLUSION IN ACCOUNTABILITY

The inclusion of students with disabilities and ELLs in accountability systems is still a work in progress. There has been considerable discussion, nonetheless, about the potential negative effects of this inclusion, ranging from higher rates of dropping out, retention, and absenteeism, and lower rates of graduation among these populations, to cheating on tests and teacher burnout (Quenemoen, Lehr, Thurlow, & Massanari, 2001). On the other hand, some have suggested that the positive consequences are beginning to outweigh the negative consequences, at least for students with disabilities (Thompson & Thurlow, 2001), with two-thirds of the state directors of special education reporting stable or increased performance levels of students with disabilities on state tests.

Actual data on either the intended or potential unintended consequences of inclusion of special-needs students in accountability are few and far between. Still, recently New York has reported that more students with disabilities are now passing the Regents examinations than have taken them in past years (New York State Education Department, 2001). Moreover, analyses of trends over time reveal that when the same students with disabilities are followed over several years, they show a slight narrowing of the gap relative to their peers without disabilities (Bielinski & Ysseldyke, 2001).

At the same time that we are awaiting data on the effects of including special-needs students in accountability systems, it is important to remember that it is a work in progress and that accountability systems are varied and complex (Education Commission of the States, 1999; Goertz & Duffy, 2001; Krentz, Thurlow, & Callender, 2000). States are still struggling a great deal with the notion that all students can be included in their reporting and accountability systems. States are currently more willing to include students in assessment systems than in accountability systems. It is particularly difficult for states to consider how to report and count students who participate in assessments that are different in some way from the standard assessment. States also have bought into a number of "nonstandard" ways of including students with special needs, most notably the use of out-of-level testing with tests for which there do not exist equated levels (Thurlow & Minnema, 2001).

Five of the challenging situations that states face as they try to include all students in their accountability systems are what they will do with students who: (1) do not take the test, (2) take the test using approved assessment accommodations, (3) take the test using nonapproved assessment accommodations, (4) participate in an alternate assessment, and (5) take out-of-level or hybrid tests. Each of these is discussed in brief here. The fact that most of the examples are of students with disabilities does not indicate that the issues are any less important for LEP students. Rather, it indicates that the issues have not yet been subjected to as much investigation as they have for students with disabilities. The issues clearly apply to both groups, and to those students who have both limited English proficiency and disabilities (see Thurlow & Liu, 2000).

INCLUDING STUDENTS WHO DO NOT TAKE THE TEST

Until nonparticipating students are factored into accountability systems, schools have very little incentive to increase the percentage of students taking tests. This may result in unintended consequences such as excessive absenteeism, particularly among certain groups of students, most often those who are lower performing. Nearly half the states (21) currently have no way of accounting for nonparticipating students in their accountability systems (Thompson & Thurlow, 2001). In contrast, six states (Delaware, New Hampshire, New York, South Carolina, Vermont, and Wyoming) score nonparticipating students as a zero score, and two states (Kentucky and Massachusetts) score nonparticipating students as the lowest score possible. These states provide an incentive for including more students in assessments—under the assumption that a student will be able to obtain a score, albeit perhaps low, that is better than a zero or lowest score possible.

INCLUDING STUDENTS WHO TAKE THE TEST USING APPROVED ASSESSMENT ACCOMMODATIONS

In all but one state (and that state had not yet decided), scores from tests taken with approved accommodations are considered to be the same as scores from standard test administrations (Thompson & Thurlow, 2001). Given this, the finding that there is variability in which accommodations are considered to be "approved" (Thurlow et al., 2000) is somewhat disconcerting.

INCLUDING STUDENTS WHO TAKE THE TEST USING NONAPPROVED ASSESSMENT ACCOMMODATIONS

Including students who take assessments with nonapproved accommodations is another matter altogether. As indicated by Krentz, Thurlow, and Callender (2000), at least seven websites publicly indicated that students who use "nonstandard" accommodations are excluded from accountability systems. When asked about their inclusion in reporting (Thompson & Thurlow, 2001), 12 states (Georgia, Hawaii, Idaho, Illinois, Louisiana, Massachusetts, Missouri, Nebraska, New York, North Dakota, Rhode Island, and Virginia) indicated that these scores were aggregated; in some cases, these states also separated these scores and reported them separately. Other states either did not count them, gave them the lowest score possible, reported them separately, or were still making a decision about what to do.

Unless states figure out a way to include students with nonapproved accommodations in accountability systems, they may create incentives to designate students as needing nonapproved accommodations solely as a way of excluding them. Thurlow and Wiener (2000) suggested that one way to include nonapproved accommodations was to use the score from a test taken with nonapproved accommodations as one piece of evidence and to rely on a variety of other performance measures to assign a proficiency-level score that then could be included in the accountability system. It will be important for states that are simply aggregating and counting these scores to keep track of how many such scores are appearing. Further, it seems critical that special studies be conducted on the impact of this approach on the students who earn the scores (have they really met standards when their scores indicate that they have?) and on the educational system (do these students continue to receive needed instructional interventions or eventually stop needing nonapproved accommodations?). A host of critical research and policy issues hinge on the decision to count scores from assessments taken with nonapproved accommodations as equal to other scores.

INCLUDING STUDENTS WHO PARTICIPATE IN AN ALTERNATE ASSESSMENT

Alternate assessments constitute the newest component of states' assessment systems. To the extent that these assessments are used with a tightly defined set of students (e.g., students with significant cognitive disabilities), the inclusion of these scores becomes a policy issue rather than a technical one (Hill, 2001). In fact, Hill demonstrated that as long as the percentage of students in the alternate assessment remains the same from one year to the next, the effect of simply scoring the alternate assessment on the entire range of proficiency levels available to students in the regular assessment is negligible.

Given that alternate assessments are just now being implemented to the point where some states have scores that could be included in an accountability system, states seem to be far down the pathway to accountability—in their plans at least. When Thompson and Thurlow (2001) asked about the inclusion of alternate assessment scores in the accountability system, 28 states indicated that they did include them currently, or that they planned to include them. States have identified a variety of ways to assign proficiency levels to alternate assessments (Bechard, 2001), which in turn affects the extent to which they count in accountability systems.

When the scores of alternate assessment students are included in accountability systems, several positive consequences are possible. The most obvious, perhaps, is that these students become part of the educational system. Anecdotal evidence of the impact of including alternate assessment students in accountability systems is trickling in, generally focused on both the increased sense of professionalism experienced by the teachers and aides working with these students, and the improved skills of students participating in the alternate assessment (Kleinert & Kearns, 2001; Thompson, Quenemoen, Thurlow, & Ysseldyke, 2001).

Many problems may arise, however, if the population of students in the alternate assessment is not well defined and consistent. Among them is the possibility that more and more students will be relegated to the alternate assessment so that they can earn higher proficiency levels than they could if they were in the appropriate assessment. This can have significant implications for what happens instructionally for these students. States are going to have to keep good data on the numbers and characteristics of students who are in their alternate assessments to ensure that these students are not inappropriately identified and assessed.

INCLUDING STUDENTS WHO TAKE OUT-OF-LEVEL OR HYBRID TESTS

There are a few approaches to state testing that have been added to the mix of state assessment systems. Out-of-level testing is an approach that has increased dramatically in states—from just one state allowing out-of-level testing in 1993 and five states in 1995 (Thurlow, Elliott, & Ysseldyke, 1999) to 17 states in 2001 (Thompson & Thurlow, 2001). In nearly all of the states, out-of-level testing is designated for students with disabilities only, and is always defined as testing students at a level below a student's assigned grade level (Thurlow & Minnema, 2001). Nearly all the states that have implemented out-of-level testing indicate that they are able to report the scores in some way (Thompson & Thurlow, 2001; Thurlow & Minnema, 2001), but it is unclear whether they include them in the accountability system.

Another relatively recent phenomenon in state assessment systems is the hybrid test. This approach involves identifying other assessments that are related in some way to the content areas being tested—usually these are off-the-shelf, individualized diagnostic assessments (such as an achievement battery or a test designed to diagnose reading or math problems)—and then using them in place of the standards-based state assessment. Only a few states have made the move to these assessments, and those that have, are unclear about whether they would report those scores aggregated for groups of students and whether they would factor the scores into an accountability system.

BITING THE BULLET

Significant changes are occurring in the inclusion of special-needs students in assessment and accountability systems. States and districts are beginning to "bite the bullet," despite the pain that they think it will create. Because of the flurry of change, it is difficult to describe exactly where states and districts are in the process of including students with disabilities and ELLs in their accountability systems. Some states have moved far along in the process, as indicated by the large number of students with disabilities participating in their assessments and included in their accountability formulas; these states are also more likely to have received Title I approval. Other states are just beginning to move in that direction.

We still do not have clear answers, however, even to simple questions like: Are many students still excluded from assessments and accountability systems? Are accommodations a good thing, or are they being used inappropriately to give some students an advantage in testing? Knowledge gaps remain, particularly in the areas of decision making (e.g.,What criteria are needed to support good decisions about which students should take a general assessment and which should take an alternate assessment? What criteria can guide good decisions about what accommodations a student needs for instruction and for assessments?).

The saying "all means all" creates numerous difficulties when it comes to accountability systems because not "all" students can take the same assessment in the standard way. As we move away from standard assessments, inclusion in accountability systems becomes more complex. Students who have been excluded or are still being excluded, and students who use certain accommodations during the assessment process, create significant challenges for accountability systems. These students tend to be those with disabilities, particularly those on IEPs, those who are ELLs, and those who are both ELLs and students with disabilities. Many schools continue to educate these students without a strong sense of accountability for their learning. As we have seen, this separation can lead to many unintended consequences that have an impact not just on students with disabilities and ELLs, but on other students as well. Once the floodgate of exclusion from accountability is opened, the leak continues to encompass more and more students with whom the educational system has not been successful.

Solutions to taking responsibility for all are emerging, but they do not satisfy everyone. The challenge is to design systems with higher expectations and fair assessments for all students, while avoiding including students with special needs in a way that actually lowers the standards that are held for them (Freedman, 2001). There are several steps that can be taken toward a truly inclusive accountability system (Thurlow, Quenemoen, & Minnema, 2001). Requiring that test contractors design assessments that are inclusive of all students and that move toward universal designs is one part of the solution, as is ensuring that multiple measures of students become a reality, not an ideal. Reaching consensus among assessment personnel about a set of methods for aggregating diverse types of scores is another. Even with these steps, however, accepting accountability for all (including special-needs students) in a fair and equitable way is likely to continue to be a challenge and balancing game for some time to come.

ACKNOWLEDGMENTS

The preparation of this chapter was supported, in part, by cooperative agreements (H159C50004 and H326G000001) between the University of Minnesota, National Center on Educational Outcomes, and U.S. Department of Education, Office of Special Education Programs, Division of Research to Practice. Opinions expressed in this chapter are those of the author and do not necessarily reflect those of the U.S. Department of Education or offices within it.

NOTE

1. The reader should note that this chapter was written in 2001. Therefore, much of the content presented here may be dated as the topic is continually changing.

REFERENCES

Allington, R., & McGill-Franzen, A. (1992). Unintended effects of reform in New York. *Educational Policy*, 6(4), 397–414.

Almond, P., Quenemoen, R., Olsen, K., & Thurlow, M. (2000). *Gray areas of assessment systems* (Synthesis Report 32). Minneapolis: National Center on Educational Outcomes, University of Minnesota.

Almond, P., Tindal, G., & Stieber, S. (1997). *Linking inclusion to conclusions: An empirical study of participation of students with disabilities in statewide testing programs* (Oregon Report 1). Minneapolis: National Center on Educational Outcomes, University of Minnesota.

American Educational Research Association, American Psychological Association, & National Council on Measurement in Education. (1999). *Standards for educational and psychological testing*. Washington, DC: Authors.

Anderson, N. E., Jenkins, F. F., & Miller, K. E. (1996). *NAEP inclusion criteria and testing accommodations: Findings from the NAEP 1995 field test in mathematics*. Princeton, NJ: Educational Testing Service.

August, D., & Hakuta, K. (1997). *Improving schooling for language minority children: A research agenda*. Washington, DC: National Academy Press.

August, D., & Lara, J. (1996). *Systemic reform and limited English proficient students*. Washington, DC: Council of Chief State School Officers.

August, D., & McArthur, E. (1996). *Proceedings of the conference on inclusion guidelines and accommodations for limited English proficient students in the National Assessment of Educational Progress, December 5–6, 1994* (NCES 96-861). Washington, DC: U.S. Department of Education, Office of Educational Research and Improvement and National Center for Education Statistics.

Bechard, S. (2001). *Models for reporting the results of alternate assessments within state accountability systems* (Synthesis Report 39). Minneapolis: National Center on Educational Outcomes, University of Minnesota.

Bielinski, J., Thurlow, M., & Callender, S. (2001). *On the road to accountability: Reporting outcomes for students with disabilities* (Technical Report 32). Minneapolis: National Center on Educational Outcomes, University of Minnesota.

Bielinski, J., & Ysseldyke, J. E. (2001). *Interpreting trends in the performance of special education students* (Technical Report 27). Minneapolis: National Center on Educational Outcomes, University of Minnesota.

Cohen, M., & Heumann, J. E. (2001). *Clarification of the role of the IEP team in selecting individual accommodations, modifications in administration, and alternate assessments for state and district-wide assessments of students with disabilities*. Washington, DC: U.S. Department of Education, Office of Elementary and Secondary Education and Office of Special Education Programs.

Disability Rights Advocates. (2001). *Do no harm: High-stakes testing and students with learning disabilities*. Oakland, CA: Author.

Education Commission of the States. (1999). *Education accountability systems in 50 states*. Denver: Author.

Elliott, J. L., & Schrag, J. (2001). Accommodations: The good, the bad, and the ugly. *Perspectives, 27*(4), 12–14.

Fine, L. (2001, February 14). Oregon special-needs students to get testing assistance. *Education Week, 20*(22), 5.

Freedman, M. (2001, March 23). Recommended accommodations for assessment may erode standards. *The Special Educator, 16*(16), 1–3.

Fuchs, L. S., Fuchs, D., Eaton, S. B., Hamlett, C., Binkley, E., & Crouch, R. (2000). Using objective data sources to enhance teacher judgments about test accommodations. *Exceptional Children, 67*(1), 67–81.

Goertz, M. E., & Duffy, M. C., with Le Floch, K. C. (2001). *Assessment and accountability systems in the 50 states: 1999–2000* (Research Report No. RR-046). Philadelphia: Consortium for Policy Research in Education, University of Pennsylvania.

Heumann, J. E., & Warlick, K. R. (2000). *Questions and answers about provisions in the Individuals with Disabilities Education Act Amendments of 1997 related to students with disabilities and state and district-wide assessments* (Memorandum OSEP 00-24). Washington, DC: U.S. Department of Education, Office of Special Education Programs.

Hill, R. (2001, June). *Impact of including special education students.* Paper presented at the annual Council of Chief State School Officers' Large-Scale Assessment Conference, Houston.

Hodgkinson, H. L. (1996). *Bringing tomorrow into focus: Demographic insights into the future.* Washington, DC: Center for Demographic Policy, Institute for Educational Leadership.

Keynes, A. (2001, June 25). Court: Disabled must take Ind. exit exam. *Education Week, 34*(121), 1, 4.

Kleinert, H. L., & Kearns, J. F. (2001). *Alternate assessment: Measuring outcomes and supports for students with disabilities.* Baltimore: Brookes.

Krentz, J., Thurlow, M. L., & Callender, S. (2000). *Accountability systems and counting students with disabilities* (Technical Report 29). Minneapolis: National Center on Educational Outcomes, University of Minnesota.

Lollock, L. (2001). *The foreign-born population in the United States: Population characteristics, March 2000* (Current Population Reports, P20-534). Washington, DC: U.S. Census Bureau.

Mazzeo, J., Carlson, J. E., Voekl, K. E., & Lutkus, A. D. (2000). *Increasing the participation of special-needs students in NAEP* (NCES 2000-473). Washington, DC: U.S. Department of Education, Office of Educational Research and Improvement.

McDonnell, L., McLaughlin, M., & Morison, P. (1997). *Educating one and all: Students with disabilities and standards-based reform.* Washington, DC: National Academy Press.

McGrew, K. S., Thurlow, M. L., Shriner, J. G., & Spiegel, A. N. (1992). *Inclusion of students with disabilities in national and state data collection programs* (Technical Report 2). Minneapolis: National Center on Educational Outcomes, University of Minnesota.

McGrew, K. S., Thurlow, M. L., & Spiegel, A. N. (1993). An investigation of the exclusion of students with disabilities in national data collection programs. *Educational Evaluation and Policy Analysis, 15*(3), 339-352.

New York State Education Department. (2001). *Report to the Board of Regents on special education data.* Albany: Office of Vocational and Educational Services for Individuals with Disabilities.

Olson, L. (2000, May 31). Indiana case focuses on special ed. *Education Week, 19*(38), 1, 14-15.

Quenemoen, R. F., Lehr, C. A., Thurlow, M. L., & Massanari, C. B. (2001). *Students with disabilities in standards-based assessment and accountability systems: Emerging issues, strategies, and recommendations* (Synthesis Report 37). Minneapolis: National Center on Educational Outcomes, University of Minnesota.

Quenemoen, R., Massanari, C., Thompson, S., & Thurlow, M. (2000). *Alternate as-*

sessment forum: Connecting into a whole. Minneapolis: National Center on Educational Outcomes, University of Minnesota.

Rigney, S., Thurlow, M., Trimble, S., Marion, S., Fabrizio, L., Hill, R., et al. (2001, June). *How do you count alternate assessment results in accountability?* Symposium presented at the annual Council of Chief State School Officers' Large-Scale Assessment Conference, Houston.

Rivera, C., Stansfield, C. W., Scialdone, L., & Sharkey, M. (2000). *An analysis of state policies for the inclusion and accommodation of English language learners in state assessment programs during 1998–1999.* Arlington, VA: Center for Equity and Excellence in Education, George Washington University.

Shriner, J. G., & DeStefano, L. (2001, April). *Curriculum access and state assessment for students with disabilities: A research update.* Paper presented at the annual conference of the Council for Exceptional Children, Kansas City, MO.

Shriner, J. G., & Thurlow, M. L. (1994). *1993 state special education outcomes.* Minneapolis: National Center on Educational Outcomes, University of Minnesota.

Stancavage, F., Allen, J., & Godlewski, C. (1996). Study of exclusion and accessibility of limited English proficient students in the 1994 Trial State Assessment of the National Assessment of Educational Progress. In National Academy of Education Panel on the Evaluation of the NAEP Trial State Assessment, *Quality and utility: The 1994 Trial State Assessment in reading* (pp. 176–178). Stanford: National Academy of Education, Stanford University.

Thompson, S. J., Quenemoen, R. F., Thurlow, M. L., & Ysseldyke, J. E. (2001). *Alternate assessments for students with disabilities.* Thousand Oaks, CA: Corwin Press.

Thompson, S. J., & Thurlow, M. L. (1999). *1999 state special education outcomes: A report on state activities at the end of the century.* Minneapolis: National Center on Educational Outcomes, University of Minnesota.

Thompson, S. J., & Thurlow, M. L. (2001). *2001 state special education outcomes: A report on activities at the beginning of a new decade.* Minneapolis: National Center on Educational Outcomes, University of Minnesota.

Thurlow, M. L. (1999, April). *Inclusion of students with disabilities in state assessments.* Paper presented at the annual meeting of the American Educational Research Association, Montreal.

Thurlow, M. L. (2001, April). *Use of accommodations in state assessments: What data bases tell us about differential levels of use and how to document the use of accommodations.* Paper presented at the annual meeting of the National Council on Measurement in Education, Seattle.

Thurlow, M. L., Albus, D., & Liu, K. K. (in press). *State assessment participation and performance of English language learners.* Arlington, VA: Center for Equity and Excellence in Education, George Washington University.

Thurlow, M. L., Elliott, J. L., & Ysseldyke, J. E. (1999). *Out-of-level testing: Pros and cons* (NCEO Policy Directions 9). Minneapolis: National Center on Educational Outcomes, University of Minnesota.

Thurlow, M. L., House, A. L., Scott, D. L., & Ysseldyke, J. E. (2000). Students with disabilities in large-scale assessment: State participation and accommodation policies. *Journal of Special Education, 34*(2), 154–163.

Thurlow, M. L., Lazarus, S., Thompson, S., & Robey, J. (2002). *2001 state policies on assessment participation and accommodations* (Synthesis Report 46). Minneapolis: University of Minnesota, National Center on Educational Outcomes.

Thurlow, M. L., & Liu, K. K. (2000, November). *State and district assessments as an avenue to equity and excellence in education for English language learners with disabilities.* Paper presented at Harvard Civil Rights Conference, Boston.

Thurlow, M. L., Liu, K. K., Erickson, R. N., Spicuzza, R., & El Sawaf, H. (1996). *Accommodations for students with limited English proficiency: Analysis of guidelines from states with graduation exams* (Minnesota Report 6). Minneapolis: National Center on Educational Outcomes, University of Minnesota.

Thurlow, M. L., & Minnema, J. (2001). *State out-of-level testing policies* (Out-of-Level Testing Report 4). Minneapolis: National Center on Educational Outcomes, University of Minnesota.

Thurlow, M. L., Quenemoen, R., & Minnema, J. (2001). *Meeting the challenge of the Title I requirement for inclusion of students with disabilities in state assessments.* Paper prepared for the National Research Council.

Thurlow, M. L., & Wiener, D. J. (2000). *Non-approved accommodations: Recommendations for use and reporting* (NCEO Policy Directions 11). Minneapolis: National Center on Educational Outcomes, University of Minnesota.

Thurlow, M. L., Ysseldyke, J. E., & Silverstein, B. (1993). *Testing accommodations for students with disabilities: A review of the literature* (Synthesis Report 4). Minneapolis: National Center on Educational Outcomes, University of Minnesota.

Thurlow, M. L., Ysseldyke, J. E., & Silverstein, B. (1995). Testing accommodations for students with disabilities. *Remedial and Special Education, 16*(5), 260–270.

Ysseldyke, J., Thurlow, M., McGrew, K., & Vanderwood, M. (1994). *Making decisions about the inclusion of students with disabilities in large-scale assessments: A report on a working conference to develop guidelines on inclusion and accommodations* (Synthesis Report 13). Minneapolis: National Center on Educational Outcomes, University of Minnesota.

Zlatos, B. (1994). Don't test, don't tell: Is "academic red-shirting" skewing the way we rank our schools? *American School Board Journal, 181*(11), 24–28.

PART III

Effects of Accountability Systems

Chapter 7

The Effects of Testing on Instruction

Joan L. Herman

Standards-based reform represents not only high expectations for student performance, but equally high expectations for how assessment-based accountability policies can influence teaching and learning in schools. Much is expected of standards-based assessment at the policy level. As is noted in many chapters in this volume, such assessments are expected to serve as both a lever for improvement and a measure of such improvement. Based on available research, this chapter explores how well assessments serve these functions from the perspective of elementary schools. The chapter begins with the basic vision of what standards-based assessment is expected to accomplish and then reviews major themes emerging from the literature that show the extent to which this vision is being realized. The chapter concludes with recommendations for improving policy and practice.

A VISION OF STANDARDS-BASED ASSESSMENT REFORM

In brief, the basic vision of standards-based assessment starts with consensus on what is important for *all* students to know and be able to do if they are to be successful in the twenty-first century. The idea is that if society and its stakeholders are clear on what is expected, it is possible to hold everyone in the system—from policy makers to educators and students—accountable for meeting those expectations. What is particularly new in standards-based assessment reform is being clear not only on the "what" of what is expected (the content standards), but also on "how well" it should be accomplished (the performance standards) (Linn & Herman, 1997).

THE MULTIPLE FUNCTIONS OF ASSESSMENT

The performance standards really come to life as large-scale assessments are developed and put into place. Emanating from the state and/or local level, the assessments make explicit what kinds of learning are expected and, as performance levels and minimum passing scores are established, make clear how well students have to do to meet the standards. The assessments thus become a primary vehicle for communicating what the standards really mean, and provide a strong signal to teachers and schools about what they should be teaching and what students should be learning. Unique to standards-based assessment as well is the intention not only to signal to teachers what to teach but, with the use of multiple types and forms of assessment, to provide clues of how to teach as well. That is, with the incorporation of more performance-based and open-ended items, assessments also are expected to communicate models of good teaching and learning practice.

The results also are supposed to provide information value to schools and policy makers by measuring the status and progress of student learning. Results from the assessment are intended to support important insights on the nature, strengths, and weaknesses of student progress relative to the standards, and educators are expected to use this feedback to understand and to direct their efforts toward improving relevant aspects of student learning.

Policy makers try to strengthen the accountability aspects of the system by establishing specific goals for school performance and attaching incentives and sanctions to achieving or surpassing these results. Across the country and spurred at least in part by federal policy, states have created sizeable incentives for performance; there are substantial cash awards for schools and teachers that meet or exceed their goals, and, at the other extreme, takeovers of schools that don't make the grade. Dramatic incentives for students also have been added to the mix, as a growing number of states adopt policies that require students to meet a performance standard to be promoted to the next grade or to be granted a high school diploma. Through such rewards and sanctions, policy makers seek to motivate teachers, students, and the community to pay attention—to the standards, to the assessment results, and to the analysis of results to improve subsequent performance. The system thus promotes a continuous improvement model aimed at enabling all children to reach the standards: establish and monitor goals and benchmarks, assess progress, and use results on goal attainment to improve.

ESSENTIAL ALIGNMENT WITH STANDARDS

The idea is not really to teach to the test, but to motivate everyone in the system to focus on the standards and enable children to reach them (see Figure 7.1). Reaching the goal requires the broad alignment of system components and the specific alignment of the assessment with the standards (see Chapter 5 for a detailed discussion of this issue), but more important, and of special significance to the content of this chapter, reaching the goal

Figure 7.1. A Model of Standards-Based Assessment Reform

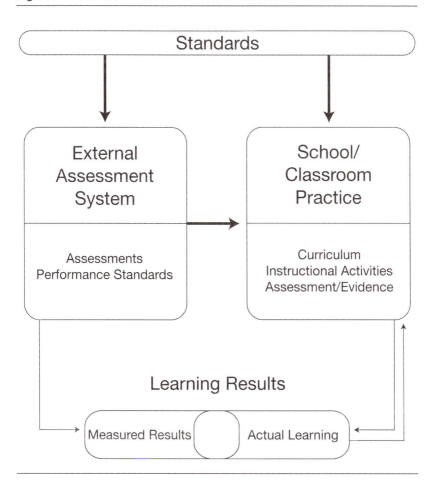

requires the alignment of classroom instruction with the standards and their assessments. It is only when the content and process of teaching and learning correspond to the standards that students indeed have the opportunity to learn what they need in order to be successful. Under these conditions, too, an assessment provides information on how well students are doing relative to the standards and on the extent to which classroom teaching and learning are helping students to attain the standards. All parts of the system are focusing on the same or a similar conception of standards and are in sync with a continuous improvement model.

Without such a correspondence, the logic of the standards-based system falls apart. The inferences that can be drawn from assessment results about how well schools are doing and what progress is being made also become tenuous. For example, if there is little alignment between what is being taught and what is being tested, the value of using results to determine the strengths and weaknesses or overall effectiveness of instruction is significantly undermined. That is, if what is tested is not taught, the information can tell us little if anything about what students learned in school because what they might have learned was not assessed.

Similarly, if the assessment and the standards are not aligned, the results can provide little information about whether students are attaining specified standards or whether instruction is helping them to make the grade. Worse yet, rather than being mutually reinforcing, the standards and the assessment may push teachers and schools in different directions. With incentives or sanctions attached to performance results, there is little doubt about which direction teachers and schools are most likely to heed.

Of course, even in the best of circumstances, a test measures only a part of what students are learning—what can be measured in a finite and limited period of time and by the types of formats that are included in the test. All measures also are fallible and include error; they thus provide only an imperfect measure of student performance. Recognizing the limits of the information that can be derived from any single measure, measurement experts advise that good assessment systems really need to include multiple measures to assess the range of knowledge and skills we really want children to achieve.

THE RESEARCH BASE

Interestingly, the current vision of standards-based assessment reform and the high hopes it holds for large-scale, standards-based assessment have their roots in research conducted during the late 1970s and 1980s showing the unfortunate effects of traditional, standardized tests. The research showed the power of these tests, built to assess general achievement and based solely on multiple-choice items, to influence teachers and schools.

PRE-REFORM LITERATURE

A number of researchers, using surveys of teachers, interview studies, and extended case studies, provided evidence that traditional standardized tests were having adverse effects on the quality of curriculum and classroom learning. Under pressure to help students do well on such tests, teachers and administrators tended to focus their efforts on test content, to mimic the tests' multiple-choice formats in classroom curriculum, and to devote more and more time to preparing students to do well on the tests (Corbett & Wilson, 1991; Dorr-Bremme & Herman, 1986; Kellaghan & Madaus, 1991). The net effect was a narrowing of the curriculum to the basic skills assessed and a neglect of complex thinking skills and other subject areas that were not assessed.

Furthermore, the research suggested that schools and teachers used the test format as a model for curriculum and instruction. Preparing students for the test meant lots of practice with test-like, multiple-choice items, with more and more of the curriculum given over to test preparation as the pressure to do well increased. To many, testing was encouraging "drill and kill" worksheets and outmoded, behaviorist pedagogy. Such pedagogy viewed students as black boxes to be filled with discrete bits of knowledge, learning as a linear progression of discrete skills from rote to complex, and connections to students' existing knowledge and experience as unimportant (Resnick & Resnick, 1992; Shepard, 1991). There also was concern that over-reliance on testing gave short shrift to content areas such as science, social studies, and the arts, which often were not the subject of testing (Darling-Hammond & Wise, 1988; Shepard, 1991). Herman and Golan (1993), among others, noted that such narrowing was likely to be greatest in schools serving at-risk and disadvantaged students because test scores in these schools were typically very low, and educators in these schools were likely to be under great pressure to improve their scores.

Effects on instruction, however, appeared very different when tests or other assessments used more performance-oriented items, rather than multiple-choice formats. Direct writing assessment—asking students to actually compose an essay rather than to answer multiple-choice questions about the quality or grammar of a given piece—was the first example. Large-scale writing assessment had begun to gain popularity in the late 1970s with its inclusion in the National Assessment of Educational Progress (NAEP); then, throughout the 1980s, more and more states and locales gradually moved to include this type of assessment in their programs. At the time, arguments for this mode of testing were based primarily on evidence of validity—evidence suggesting that multiple-choice tests did not provide accurate measures of students' ability to write (Quellmalz & Burry, 1983). However, as experience with these direct measures grew, their potential for influencing teaching and learning became more apparent. Studies of the effects of California's eighth-grade writing assessment program, for example, indicated that the program encouraged teachers both to require more writing assignments of students and to give students experience in producing a wider variety of genres. Beyond impact on instruction, studies showed that student performance in some states and districts improved over time with the institution of the new assessment programs (Chapman, 1991; Quellmalz & Burry, 1983).

POST-REFORM STUDIES

Armed with the research, educational reformers aimed to use the power of assessment intentionally to achieve their goals, first in promoting the use of performance assessment in large-scale assessment during the 1990s and more recently in adopting standards-based assessment systems. Coincident with these reforms have been a number of studies of their implementation and impact. These studies cross states and locales and represent significant variation in terms of the nature of tests used, the strength of incentives and sanctions, and research methodology. For example, at the state level, there have been studies of the effects of systems in Arizona (Smith & Rottenberg, 1991), California (Herman & Klein, 1996; McDonnell & Choisser, 1997), Kentucky (Borko & Elliott, 1998; Koretz, Barron, Mitchell, & Stecher, 1996; Stecher, Barron, Kaganoff, & Goodwin, 1998; Wolf & McIver, 1999), Maine (Firestone, Mayrowetz, & Fairman, 1998), Maryland (Firestone et al., 1998; Goldberg & Rosewell, 2000; Lane, Stone, Parke, Hansen, & Cerrillo, 2000), New Jersey (Firestone, Camilli, Yurecko, Monfils, & Mayrowetz, 2000), North Carolina (McDonnell & Choisser, 1997), Vermont (Koretz, McCaffrey, Klein, Bell, & Stecher, 1993), and Washington (Borko & Stecher, 2001; Stecher, Barron, Chun, & Ross, 2000).

MAJOR THEMES IN RECENT RESEARCH

Echoing themes from earlier studies, findings from these post-reform studies provide a surprisingly consistent picture of how these new assessment systems are working and the extent to which they are working as intended, in the sense of encouraging good teaching and learning and helping students achieve the standards.

TEACHERS LISTEN TO THE SIGNAL

Results from nearly every study indicate, indeed, that teachers pay attention to what is tested and adapt their curriculum and teaching accordingly. For example, Lane and colleagues (2000), in a survey of Maryland elementary and middle schools, found teachers and principals reporting that the Maryland State Performance Assessment Program (MSPAP) was having substantial impact on classroom activities (including incorporation of MSPAP-type problems), subject-area instruction, and assessment. A recent statewide study of the Washington State reform shows similar responses to testing. Principals reported developing schoolwide plans and implemented test-preparation activities and policies based on Washington Assessment of Student Learning (WASL) results. Teachers reported significant impact of the WASL on their teaching of writing and mathematics (Stecher et al., 2000). These findings mirror earlier studies in Kentucky that found principals strongly encouraging teachers to focus their instruction on the content and skills likely to be on the Kentucky Instructional Results Information System (KIRIS), and teachers reporting an increase in the match between the content of their instruction and that of the assessment (Koretz, Barron, et al., 1996).

TEACHERS MODEL TEST CONTENT AND PEDAGOGY

Research, furthermore, shows that, in addition to modifying their classroom curriculum and instruction to include the content of what is tested, teachers tend to model the pedagogical approach represented by the test. Thus, when a large-scale assessment is composed of multiple-choice tests, teachers tend to use multiple-choice worksheets in their practice, but when the assessments use open-ended items and/or extended writing and rubrics to judge the quality of student work, teachers incorporate these same types of activities into their classroom work. For example, teachers responded to implementation of Vermont's statewide portfolio assessment by increasing the amount of class time they devoted to teaching problem solving and increasing the focus on written communication and applications in mathematics (Koretz, Stecher, & Deibert, 1992). Subsequent studies in Kentucky similarly found that its innovative assessment system stimulated teachers to focus more on tested subjects and to increase their use of instructional practices intended by the test reformers (Stecher et al., 1998).

Findings from Maine and Maryland echo these trends. Firestone and colleagues (1998) found teachers *adding to* their curriculum the types of problem-solving tasks the teachers expected to be on the statewide assessment. In the case of Maryland, these were extended projects that asked students to apply mathematics concepts, reason mathematically, and use multiple forms of representation.

TEST PREPARATION MERGES INTO INSTRUCTION

The match between test format and instructional format is most apparent in direct test-preparation activities. Here the intent is to engage students in practice activities explicitly designed to mirror the given assessments as closely as possible, with the explicit purpose of getting students familiar with the test format and enabling them to do better on the test. Such practice activities typically are derived from sample items and practice materials provided by the state or district and from commercially available materials developed by test publishers.

The extent and nature of such test preparation vary considerably from study to study. Smith, Edelsky, Draper, Rottenberg, and Cherland's (1990) case study of Arizona elementary schools found regular curriculum virtually shutting down in some schools for several weeks prior to the mandated, standardized test period, as teachers directly prepared their students for the coming test. Smith and colleagues viewed this as an obvious interruption and detraction from regular instruction.

Similar at the extreme, but different in process, Herman, Klein, Heath, and Wakai's (1995) study of California's then-eighth-grade mathematics assessment found that virtually all surveyed teachers reported using sample items with their students. The assessment emphasized complex thinking and problem solving, and the sample items were open-ended, requiring extended time. On average, teachers spent three to five class periods on these practice items, but notably, about a third of respondents reported spending nine or more class periods, the equivalent of nearly 2 weeks, in such practice. Anecdotal evidence suggested that in some classrooms these practice items were amassed near testing time, but in other cases they were distributed throughout the school year.

More recently, Stecher and colleagues' (2000) study of Washington explicitly documents how time spent in test preparation may vary with the time of the year, with teachers increasing the amount of time they spent in direct preparation for the WASL as the test approached in the spring. Firestone and colleagues (2000) also found a similar pattern of increased attention to test preparation just prior to testing in New Jersey, and noted sizeable socioeconomic differences in such practices as well. Teachers from schools in high-poverty districts reported substantially more time devoted explicitly to test-preparation activities than did teachers in wealthy districts.

Of course, it can be difficult to differentiate between special test-preparation efforts and "regular" curriculum and instruction activity that has been influenced by the standards and assessments mandated by external authorities. Part of the issue is one of intent: The former is enacted especially to increase test performance; its value in real learning is not a primary issue. The latter is ongoing curriculum activity that is influenced in content and format by important assessments but is intended to promote student learning. Sometimes an activity may start as one and merge into the other. For example, Herman and colleagues' (1995) study of eighth-grade mathematics found a number of teachers instituting "[state assessment] problem of the week," which initially was intended to prepare students for the test. However, some teachers reported anecdotally that, over time, the attention to problem solving became more integrated with regular instruction and became part of teachers' routine repertoire.

Many states' and locales' experiences incorporating state assessment rubrics into their instruction tell a similar story. For example, Borko and Stecher's (2001) study of exemplary sites in Washington reveals teachers consciously using WASL rubrics for writing and mathematics to prepare their students for the test. Borko describes the example of Ms. Alexander, who asked her students repeatedly over the course of the year to write to the sample prompts provided by the state, scored their pieces using the state rubrics, and engaged students in discussion about what skills they used, where they might have gotten stuck, and what strategies might help them to do better (Stecher & Borko, 2001, pp. 25–26).

TEST DRAWS MORE ATTENTION THAN STANDARDS

The time many teachers acknowledge spending in test preparation makes obvious that the test, rather than the standards, may become the primary target in teachers' curricular plans, at least at some times during the year. That the test rather than the standards may get primary attention *throughout* the year is a point Stecher and colleagues (2000) make forcefully using data from their Washington State study. For example, principals reported greater alignment of their schools' curricula with state standards in tested subjects, indicating that tests rather than the standards themselves commanded attention. Similarly, in the Washington State study more teachers reported strong understanding of the state assessment than reported confidence in the alignment of their curriculum and instruction with the state standards, while two-thirds of teachers identified their teaching as more like "teach(ing) to the WASL," than "teach(ing) to the EALRs [Essential Academic Learning Requirements]" (Stecher & Borko, 2001, p. 22).

Stecher and Barron (1999) examined how teachers allocate classroom time as a function of what was tested on the now-defunct KIRIS at their grade level. Their results show that the amount of time teachers engaged their students in various subjects each week seemed to be highly related to whether the subject was tested at their grade level. In open-ended response questions, teachers cited KIRIS as the primary influence on their reallocation of time. Stecher and colleagues (2000) reported similar results in Washington. Although standards are supposed to be continuous across grade levels, teachers tended to involve their students in more extended writing and to address a greater number of writing objectives in tested grades than in the grades that were not part of the writing portfolio assessment. There were similar findings in mathematics, where teachers tended regularly to teach a greater number of mathematics topics when their grade was assessed in mathematics.

However, Borko's case studies of *exemplary* sites in the same state suggests that the picture of test-focused curriculum may not be as stark as Stecher and colleagues' findings suggest. Here, principals and teachers certainly paid close attention to test results, analyzed them class by class, and used them to help identify curriculum strengths and weaknesses, but the analysis was a point of departure for reflecting on practices and identifying concrete ways to improve instruction. As the principal commented, WASL scores "raised our awareness level in terms of where we need to put our energies," but did not dictate the what and how of instruction (Stecher & Borko, 2001, p. 24).

Nontested Content Gets Short Shrift

A focus on the test rather than the standards also means that what gets tested gets taught, and what does not get tested may get less attention or may not get taught at all. WYTIWYG—what you test is what you get—is a continuing truism in the world of standards-based assessment. Again, Stecher and colleagues' (2000) survey data from their Washington study provide a strong case demonstrating how teachers increased the time they spent on tested subjects at the expense of nontested subjects. Moreover, teachers attributed the cause of these changes to WASL. Again, this mirrors earlier findings from Kentucky, where the great majority of teachers agreed that, because of KIRIS, they were de-emphasizing or neglecting content that was not on the test (Koretz, Mitchell, Barron, & Keith, 1996).

The findings thus suggest that teachers and schools may focus excessively on what is tested to the neglect of both the broader domain of the tested discipline and important subjects that are not tested. To the extent that a state or district test is truly representative of its standards, this focus on the test may not be a problem. However, the reality is that there are limits to how much time can be spent testing and limits to the kinds of academic and intellectual capacities that can be well, efficiently, and accurately assessed with the most commonly used test formats. Recent reports about the nature of current state assessment programs, for example, show a trend toward more traditional types of tests. The rich performance assessment experiments of the 1990s seem to have devolved, at most, into some attention on state assessments to limited open-ended, short-answer items. Multiple-choice items continue to predominate. *Quality Counts 2001*, for example, shows only eight states including extended-response items outside of English/writing (see the chart, "Measurement of Student Performance," Orlofsky & Olson, 2001).

Furthermore, the alignment between states' standards and what actually is tested continues to be problematic. Despite test developers' assurances that their tests match specified standards, relatively few states have undergone serious alignment review. The Achieve studies of nine states' systems represent an exception, but these show uneven results (Rothman, Slattery, Vranek, & Resnick, 2000). Even at the simplest level of alignment, where results tend to be the strongest, there was variable alignment between assessments and state standards. For example, while 95% of the items on the English tests in one state matched content and skills found in its standards, only 65% of the mathematics items were so aligned. Furthermore, the tests tended mostly to measure the lowest-level objectives and not the depth of complexity the standards articulated. Nor did the Achieve studies tend to find that the tests were balanced in their representation of each state standard. So teaching to the test does not necessarily mean teaching to the standards, and with increasingly great incentives and punishments attached to test performance, there is little doubt about whether the standards or the tests are the greater focal point.

ARE THE LEARNING GAINS REAL?

The potential narrowing of the curriculum to focus only on what is tested also has implications for the validity of the assessment results and the credibility of gains that almost always appear in the first several years of a new state assessment program. We care about students' performance on a test, after all, because we believe that it represents something larger than the specific items and content covered by the test. It is not just that a student got these particular items correct, but rather that the score *generalizes* to some larger domain of knowledge or skill and tells us something important about what students know and can do—in the current context, the content and performance standards that have been established. We want to infer how well students have achieved the standards from their performance on the particular sample of items included on the test.

However, if teaching and learning focus, in the extreme, only on what is tested and on the formats in which it is tested, the test ceases to be a sample of performance. The test becomes the domain, and the generalizability of the results—and what meaning can be drawn from students' test performance other than that they scored at a certain level on this particular set of items—becomes suspect.

This raises the question of whether the gains shown on state assessments represent real improvement in learning, or whether they reflect narrow test-preparation activities that do not generalize beyond the test itself and inflate actual improvement. Koretz and Barron (1998) posit that if improvements in learning are genuine and meaningful, one should expect the increases in performance on the high-profile state assessment to show up on other similar measures of student achievement. Using data from fourth- and eighth-grade mathematics in 1992 and 1996, they compare standardized gains on KIRIS with state performance on the National Assessment of Educational Progress (NAEP) (Koretz & Barron, 1998). Granted, one would expect to see higher growth on KIRIS, which was customized to Kentucky's learning objectives, than to the more general and thereby less curricularly sensitive NAEP measure, but still the magnitude of the difference at grade 4 gives pause: The KIRIS results show 3.6 times the growth shown by NAEP.

Klein, Hamilton, McCaffrey, and Stecher (2000) found similar disparities when they examined Texas students' performance on the Texas Assessment of Academic Skills (TAAS) and on NAEP for the period 1994 to 1998. For example, the NAEP analysis showed an increase in fourth graders' reading performance from 1994 and 1998, comparable to national trends and with effect sizes of .13 standard deviation units and .15 standard deviation units for students of color. However, TAAS results for fourth graders over this same period showed dramatically greater gains, with effect sizes ranging from .31 to .49 standard deviation units, and African American and Hispanic students showing substantially greater gains than White students. Thus, NAEP results confirmed neither the slope of the increase in TAAS scores nor the claim that the achievement gap between White students and those of color was closing.

Beyond these empirical data, it is interesting as well to note that teachers are skeptical about the broader meaning that should be ascribed to score increases. For example, teachers in Stecher and colleagues' (1998) survey study of Kentucky were much more likely to attribute changes in their students' test performance to test-taking skills and test-preparation practices than to broad improvements in students' knowledge and skills. These beliefs mirror those found in an earlier study by Koretz and colleagues (1996).

Is There a Relationship Between Intended Changes in Practice and Student Performance?

A parallel question to the meaningfulness of gains is the extent to which desired changes in practice are associated with the improvement of student learning—or at least with observed test score gains. If tests are intended to signal desirable content and pedagogy with which to engage students, does implementing such changes result in intended student effects? The picture here is mixed, but results seem promising.

The first example comes again from the work of Stecher and colleagues (1998) in Kentucky, where they compared teachers' reports of practices in high- and low-gain schools based on second biennium KIRIS gains. While the study reports few consistent findings across grades and subject areas, and some contradictory results, the bulk of the positive findings do show a relationship between the standards-based practices that KIRIS was intended to stimulate and performance—particularly at the middle school level. Teachers in high- versus low-gain schools reported greater use of standards-based practices such as integrating writing across subjects and incorporating calculators and extended investigations in mathematics. However, these teachers also reported greater attention to specific skills, including regular practice in grammar and English mechanics and in mathematics computation. Perhaps teachers in high-gain schools found ways to incorporate reform practices without neglecting the basic skills of traditional instruction.

Stone and Lane (2000) examined similar issues using data from the MSPAP. Their results indicate that instruction-related variables that assessed the extent to which practice was aligned with reform goals consistently explained differences in performance across subject areas, except for social studies. That is, more reform-oriented practices were associated with higher levels of performance in reading, writing, mathematics, and science. However, only in language arts (writing and reading) were these variables significantly related to improvements in performance over time, and even in these subjects, the practical impact was very small.

Are Instructional Changes Sufficient to Influence Performance?

That teachers' reports of their use of reform practices show limited relationship to student learning should be expected. Decades of research show the difficulty of changing practices and admonish that meaningful change takes time (Cuban, 1993; McLaughlin, 1990). Moreover, available research suggests that teachers' responses to standards and assessments initially may be fairly shallow. That is, teachers do indeed listen to the signals sent by standards and assessments and attempt to model them in their practices, but, understandably, their initial attempts may mimic the superficial features of the intended reform without incorporating deep understanding or quality implementation.

Results from a number of studies provide evidence of the superficial nature of instructional change compared with the broader goals set forth by standards. In their study of changes in classroom practices in Maryland and Maine following implementation of performance assessments, Firestone and colleagues (1998) note that superficial features of instructional tasks did match the state standards and assessment goals, but these tasks failed overall to achieve the broader goals of reform. The authors conclude: "Such assessments generate considerable activity focused on the test itself. This activity can promote certain changes, like aligning subjects taught with the test. It appears less successful, however, in changing basic instructional strategies" (p. 95). McDonnell and Choisser (1997) came to a similar conclusion based on evidence from their study of Kentucky and North California. Although teachers implemented new instructional approaches, the depth and complexity of their content and pedagogy did not change in meaningful ways. Yet additional confirmation comes from Goldberg and Rosewell's (2000) study of MSPAP effects, looking at effects on writing instruction. They followed up a sample of elementary and middle school teachers who had been involved in scoring state writing assessments to examine the effects of the experience on their instructional practice and to see how well these teachers were implementing the state's vision of standards-based writing reform. Results indicate that teachers did implement a number of standards-based instructional practices but the quality of their implementation was "incomplete and superficial" (p. 257).

WHAT FACTORS MAY INFLUENCE EFFECTS?

There, of course, are innumerable factors that may influence how statewide assessment and accountability systems affect classroom instruction and student learning. Here we are interested primarily in those factors that may be part of the accountability system itself—for example, stakes attached to performance, efforts to support low-performing schools, and district- and school-level leadership and support for improvement. More is known currently about the variation in these elements across states and localities than about their influence on schools, teaching, and student learning.

Stakes provide one example: By attaching consequences to performance, states hope to motivate additional effort and improved learning. However, the nature of the stakes varies from state to state—from publishing test results; to financial and other rewards for schools and/or teachers;

to sanctions for principals, teachers, and/or students who do not meet their targets. There is ample evidence to suggest that state assessment systems do create pressure for teachers and principals (see, e.g., Aschbacher, 1994; Koretz et al., 1996; Koretz, Stecher, Klein, McCaffrey, & Deibert, 1993), but little clear evidence on how various stakes have differential effects on teachers, their curriculum and instruction, or, ultimately, student learning. In general, studies of teachers' and principals' reactions in states with higher stakes for schools (e.g., Kentucky) show similar results to those in which there currently are no special consequences for schools associated with test performance (e.g., Washington). However, deeper qualitative studies show there may be differences in how teachers respond (Firestone et al., 1998). Given the sizeable investment by many states in rewards and sanctions, more must be known about whether and how these measures work, including their intended and unintended consequences, and how stakes for students interact with those for teachers and schools.

Similarly, states and districts differ in how they respond to low-performing schools, but evidence on whether and how their various responses influence classroom teaching, test performance, and student learning is limited. As Goertz and Duffy (2001) document, states are implementing a variety of strategies to help such schools, including support for school improvement or corrective action planning, financial assistance, expert assistance in curriculum planning and instruction, and state- or regionally sponsored professional development opportunities. States also vary in the resources they make available to aid in these processes, from support teams composed of state and/or local officials, to distinguished educators, to regional service centers and external providers. The degree to which these efforts result in real changes to the teaching and learning process will vary according to the nature and quality of the strategies employed as well as the resources and expertise available to support them.

Finally, local school and district leadership will have a significant effect on whether and how assessments influence teaching and learning. Spillane (2000), for example, has explored how various models of district support may differentially affect success and how structural constraints, local circumstances, and competing demands on teachers may lead to fragmentation and less than optimal improvement efforts. Further research is necessary, however, to identify optimal approaches. Needed, too, is additional research on how schools can best orchestrate their improvement efforts. For instance, Borko and Wolf's qualitative studies of exemplary sites in Kentucky identified the importance of professional development time and money, coupled with the development of curriculum and assessment activities strongly linked to standards (Borko, Elliott, & Uchiyama, 1999). Common themes characterizing these exemplary sites included a strong sense of identity as a school, a cooperative view of leadership, strong but reflective alignment with the Kentucky standards and reform agenda, and a commitment to dedicating all school decisions and actions to the benefit of children (Wolf, Borko, McIver, & Elliott, 1999). However, not all the sites identified as exemplary in the beginning of the study continued to be identified as exemplary during the term of the study.

CONCLUSIONS AND RECOMMENDATIONS

A consistent picture emerges from these collective findings: Accountability systems and standards-based assessments can serve to stimulate reform and encourage schools and teachers to focus on teaching specified content, but they are no panacea for the many challenges associated with ensuring that all children achieve high standards of learning. Furthermore, there are a variety of issues in the design of current assessment and accountability systems that will need continued attention.

It is good news that assessment systems encourage teachers to adopt new content and pedagogy and bring their classroom and instruction into alignment with valued knowledge and skills, assuming that the test reflects such valued knowledge and skills. Assessment appears instrumental in initiating change and movement from existing practices in schools toward new expectations, including desired standards and pedagogy. It should come as no surprise, however, that there are imperfections in the current systems and that simply modeling test content and pedagogy does not result in increased teaching expertise or high-quality implementation of new practices. In some cases, teachers respond to assessment systems by focusing instruction on tested subjects at the expense of others. Further, when teaching mirrors tests that are not aligned with standards, broader learning goals may be compromised.

Simply getting the system moving is, however, no mean feat, and we need to capitalize on the existing momentum and continue to move productively toward the vision of standards-based assessment. There are implications here for the types of assessment systems we need to design and the types of capacities we need to help teachers and schools to develop.

MULTIPLE MEASURES

First, from the assessment side, the findings underscore the importance of having assessment systems that are aligned with our standards and, as Resnick (1996) put it, "tests worth teaching to." The evidence is strong: Teachers respond to what we ask of them and teach what is tested. If we are serious about standards and want teachers to teach to them, our assessment systems simply must measure the depth and breadth of those standards.

As measurement experts, we know that a single measure cannot serve all purposes or fully cover a domain or discipline, nor can it be responsive to the reality of individual differences. Students and schools need multiple and diverse opportunities to demonstrate learning. Because multiple-choice measures can go only so far in tapping the complex thinking, communication, and problem-solving skills that students need for future success, such multiple measures need to incorporate different kinds of assessment formats. For example, one large-scale measure of language arts might focus primarily on reading comprehension through traditional, multiple-choice measures, while another could require students to write and interpret literature, analyze given arguments, or, working across disciplines, construct a historical argument. Multiple measures also could involve combinations of large-scale measures with classroom-based assessments such as portfolios, research projects, or presentations. School staff even should be provided with training on use of standardized scoring rubrics. Scoring of these assessments can be made more reliable with proper auditing and sampling procedures. This way, these more performance-oriented measures can yield reliable evidence of students' learning—or at least their learning opportunities (see Gearhart & Herman, 1998). Not all assessments need to be scored and aggregated at the state or district level to be valuable in the system. Portfolios, for example, can be a source of evidence for parents and the community in looking at student achievement and for state audit or credential teams evaluating school quality.

With multiple measures in the system, teachers are less likely to fixate on a narrow range of content. Multiple measures also might help to encourage rich school-based inquiry rather than a narrow focus on a curriculum of test preparation based on a single test. Multiple measures, assuming they reflected a coherent standards-referenced system, might encourage teachers and schools to reflect on what the standards really mean and to internalize an overall framework into which the multiple measures fit. The multiple measures themselves would help to communicate the range and complexity of expectations for student performance.

COORDINATED SYSTEMS OF LOCAL AND CLASSROOM ASSESSMENT

This is not to say that all "multiple measures" must emanate from the top down or be part of an annual state "test." There are limits, of course, to how much time and other resources can be devoted to such testing. There are limits as well to the depth of knowledge and information such tests can provide. No matter how well aligned and how sensitively crafted, these assessments can offer only a limited perspective on what children really know and can do relative to standards and what factors may be working against their progress. In order to understand why student performance is as it is and to get to the root of whatever teaching and learning issues may exist, schools and teachers must move to a more detailed level of assessment and analysis than annual state tests afford. Schools and teachers need to be able to supplement the external assessment results with other local data.

How do we ensure a picture closer to the vision of standards-based assessment as intended? The answer lies at least partially in coordinated systems of local assessments. District, school, and/or classroom assessments that are aligned with standards can provide educators with the diverse forms of evidence that they need to understand and improve their students' learning. Moreover, integrated with classroom curriculum and/or administered periodically over the course of the year, such local assessments also are necessary to provide teachers with essential ongoing information to gauge student progress and adjust teaching and learning opportunities accordingly. For example, teachers involved in California's Focus on Results project assess their primary students' reading abilities quarterly with a battery measure and then work together to analyze the results and make instructional changes. To support students' writing progress, teachers can create a variety of writing assignments throughout the quarter or year that are sensitive to the content of the local curriculum and their students' interests, and score them using the rubric from the state assessment. Involving students in the scoring processes reinforces even further the standards that are expected and involves students in their own learning.

Ultimately, these are the multiple measures that really can make a significant difference in student learning. Good teaching is a process of continual assessment and adjustment; annual or semiannual external results are not enough. Multiple measures also may provide a safeguard against simply "teaching to the test" and a potential wealth of data against which the validity of gains can be judged—by parents and students as well as by external authorities. Local and classroom assessments also should help to strengthen the credibility of teachers' professional judgments, as these assessments provide sound, visible evidence according to which instructional decisions can be made.

Capacity Building

The findings reported here have strong implications for building the capacity of teachers and schools. As indicated earlier, it should come as no surprise that the content and pedagogical signals sent by assessments are insufficient to support teachers' mastery of new approaches. Moreover, the vast majority of teachers, schools, or districts lack the capacity to engage in the vision of coordinated local and classroom assessments that has just been described.

Surely, most states provide some attention to professional development along with their assessment systems, but such professional development is likely to deal with the tests themselves and their administration, and/or the mechanics of understanding scoring and scoring reporting. These efforts are often of limited duration—the kind of one-shot opportunities that we know are of limited valued. Even more intensive involvement in state or district scoring, the professional development value of which has been highly touted (Aschbacher, 1994; Falk & Ort, 1997; Sheingold, Heller, & Storms, 1997), is insufficient for meaningful change. As Goldberg and Rosewell (2000) characterized the effects of such experiences, "Like Socrates, the wise man who knows that he does not know all, teachers report that the experience [of training and rubric-based scoring of state writing assessments] highlights for them the as yet unfulfilled need for resources and professional support to meet demands and expectations that only grow greater and more complex with their increased understanding of the issues and implications of performance-based instruction and assessment" (p. 286).

Generally absent are the types of sustained, intensive, and ongoing professional development opportunities that would enable teachers to engage in standards-based reform and use assessment effectively within that context. Ample research shows that such opportunities are embedded in and responsive to the local environment; permit teachers to gain, apply, and progressively appropriate new content and pedagogical knowledge in supportive circumstances; provide coaching and mentoring; and encourage active reflection and problem solving (see, e.g., Cohen & Ball, 1999; Darling-Hammond & Ball, 1998).

The instinct to simply "teach to the test" may in part be a survival instinct. Lacking alternative strategies or effective avenues for acquiring them, teachers do what they can and what they know how to do to reach targeted goals. Just as we need coordinated systems of assessment, so too do we need coordinated systems of professional development that align preservice and inservice professional development programs with a comprehensive and integrated understanding of the requirements of standards-based instruction and assessment.

ONGOING EVALUATION TO SUPPORT VALIDITY AND POSITIVE CONSEQUENCES

The fact that good intentions are insufficient to ensure good consequences from assessment is a lesson that has been learned repeatedly over the past century—whether the topic has been admissions testing, objective-referenced testing, minimum competency testing, or performance assessment. That the stakes associated with performance standards-based assessment systems are on the increase across the country further increases the likelihood of corruption of test results. That is, such stakes may create incentives for some schools and teachers to only teach to the test—or worse—and such actions, as described earlier, can invalidate the meaning of the results and the inferences about student learning and progress that can be drawn from such results. These possibilities underscore the importance of ongoing evaluation of standards-based systems, as advocated by current standards for accountability systems (see Baker, Linn, Herman, Koretz, & Elmore, 2001).

Validity of Scores. Questions about reliability and accuracy of scores (Linn & Haug, 2001; Rogosa, 2000) and the validity of gains—whether score increases truly signal increases in learning—coupled with the high stakes attached to test results, make it essential that safeguards are built into accountability and assessment systems. If we are not confident that substantial increases in test performance really mean meaningful improvement in student learning, it is difficult to justify delivering substantial rewards or meting out severe punishments based on test scores alone. Rather, there need to be additional checks and balances in the system to verify the quality or level of learning in identified schools and to ensure that schools get what they deserve. Evidence derived from coordinated systems of local assessment could be used in such a verification process, as could spot checks or monitoring of the quality and comprehensiveness of classroom curriculum and instruction. Qualified audit teams, for example, could conduct site visits to assemble evidence and/or observe practices in schools potentially subject to high rewards or severe sanctions. Accountability systems also could incorporate promising and psychometrically sound approaches to assessing the quality of classroom practice that currently exist on a periodic, if not routine, basis. For example, existing approaches feature the collection of a limited number of classroom assignments and samples of student work (see, e.g., Aschbacher, 1999; Clare, 2000) to gauge the quality of classroom practice. If focused on challenging and academically rigorous types of assignments, the approach could encourage attention to these dimensions in classroom practice. Such checks not only could ensure the fairness of rewards and sanctions—they could mitigate against teaching solely to the test.

Similarly, at the state level, there need to be ongoing studies of the validity of state assessment results and convincing evidence mounted that increases in test scores translate into meaningful improvements in student learning for all students. The validity of gains for traditionally underperforming subgroups deserves special scrutiny, as closing the gap is a prime goal of standards-based reform, and disadvantaged subgroups are the ones who are at most risk of curricular corruption. Studies cited in this review provide possible models for looking at the relationship between gains on a particular state assessment and those on NAEP and/or other measures of performance that may be better aligned with that state's standards. One also would want to ensure that test scores were sensitive to quality instruction and well-honed improvements in standards-based classroom practice.

Consequences of Assessment Systems. Beyond issues of the validity of gains, the findings cited in this chapter make clear that there are gaps between the vision of standards-based assessment and current practice. It is therefore essential that we continue to evaluate the claims supporting standards-based assessment systems and regularly examine the actual consequences of such systems. The accountability standards advocate regularly assessing system effects on capacity building, resource allocation, instruction, equity and access to education, teacher quality, recruitment and retention, and unanticipated outcomes (see Chapter 3, this volume). For example, is there sufficient capacity at the district, school, and classroom levels to support standards-based reform? How or to what extent are the accountability systems and their results being used to marshal capacity to support improvement? How and to what extent are results used for resource allocation and to ensure that resources and attention get to the children and standards that are most in need of attention? Equity in resources and capacity to deliver effective standards-based programs should be an important, continuing issue, based on findings cited in this chapter (Firestone et al., 2000; Herman & Golan, 1993; Smith & Rottenberg, 1991).

The function of accountability systems in focusing teachers' and schools' attention on teaching to the standards and improving instructional practice has been the prime focus of this chapter; indeed, the research on instructional effects shows both good news and bad news. There needs to be continuing study, particularly of schools serving students at risk. We need to check our assumptions about the effects of accountability systems on equity and providing all children access to opportunity. Both history and specific studies cited in this chapter provide cause for concern. Despite intended consequences, is the gap increasing or decreasing between economically advantaged and disadvantaged groups or between White children and children of color? How are English-language learners and students with disabilities faring? What of equity in the curriculum and instruction offered in schools serving traditionally underperforming groups and other students? Are curriculum and instruction devolving into test preparation, while schools serving wealthier students benefit from more varied instructional resources and a richer curriculum that provides better opportunities to develop the complex thinking and communication skills students will need for future success?

The evaluation questions are complex and varied and deserve continuing inquiry. Just as standards-based assessment is intended to improve the quality of the educational system, so too should the evaluation of assessment and accountability systems lead to their continued improvement. Building on the current momentum, such improvement should support refinement of systems that can better deliver the promise of standards-based reform.

REFERENCES

Aschbacher, P. R. (1994). Helping educators to develop and use alternative assessments: Barriers and facilitators. *Educational Policy, 8*(2), 202–223.

Aschbacher, P. R. (1999). *Developing indictors of classroom practice to monitor and support school reform* (CSE Technical Report No. 513). Los Angeles: National Center for Research on Evaluation, Standards, and Student Testing, University of California.

Baker, E. L., Linn, R. L., Herman, J. L., Koretz, D., & Elmore, R. F. (2001, April). *Holding accountability systems accountable: Research-based standards*. Symposium presented at the annual meeting of the American Educational Research Association, Seattle.

Borko, H., & Elliott, R. (1998). *Tensions between competing pedagogical and accountability commitments for exemplary teachers of mathematics in Kentucky* (CSE Technical Report No. 495). Los Angeles: National Center for Research on Evaluation, Standards, and Student Testing, University of California.

Borko, H., Elliott, R., & Uchiyama, K. (1999). *Professional development: A key to Kentucky's reform effort* (CSE Technical Report No. 512. From Technical Report No. 514). Los Angeles: National Center for Research on Evaluation, Standards, and Student Testing, University of California.

Borko, H., & Stecher, B. M. (2001, April). *Looking at reform through different methodological lenses: Survey and case studies of the Washington State education reform*. Paper presented as part of a symposium at the annual meeting of the American Educational Research Association, Seattle.

Chapman, C. (1991, June). *What have we learned from writing assessment that can be applied to performance assessment?* Presentation at ECS/CDE Alternative Assessment Conference, Breckenridge, CO.

Clare, L. (2000). *Using teachers' assignments as an indicator of classroom practice* (CSE Technical Report No. 532). Los Angeles: National Center for Research on Evaluation, Standards, and Student Testing, University of California.

Cohen, D. K., & Ball, D. L. (1999). *Instruction, capacity, and improvement* (CPRE Research Report No. RR-043). Philadelphia: Consortium for Policy Research in Education, University of Pennsylvania.

Corbett, H. D., & Wilson, B. L. (1991). *Testing, reform, and rebellion*. Norwood, NJ: Ablex.

Cuban, L. (1993). *How teachers taught: Constancy and change in American classrooms, 1890–1980* (2nd ed.). New York: Teachers College Press.

Darling-Hammond, L., & Ball, D. L. (1998). *Teaching for high standards: What policymakers need to know and be able to do* (CPRE Joint Report No. JRE-04). Philadelphia: Consortium for Policy Research in Education, University of Pennsylvania, and New York: National Commission on Teaching and America's Future, Teachers College, Columbia University.

Darling-Hammond, L., & Wise, A. E. (1988). *The evolution of teacher policy*. Santa Monica, CA: RAND.

Dorr-Bremme, D., & Herman, J. L. (1986). *Assessing student achievement: A profile of classroom practices* (CSE Monograph Series in Evaluation No. 11). Los Angeles: Center for the Study of Evaluation, University of California.

Falk, B., & Ort, S. (1997, April). *Sitting down to score: Teacher learning through assessment*. Presentation at the annual meeting of the American Educational Research Association, Chicago.

Firestone, W. A., Camilli, G., Yurecko, M., Monfils, L., & Mayrowetz, D. (2000). State standards, socio-fiscal context and opportunity to learn in New Jersey. *Educational Policy Analysis Archives, 8*(35). http://epaa.asu.edu/epaav8n35

Firestone, W. A., Mayrowetz, D., & Fairman, J. (1998). Performance-based assessment and instructional change: The effects of testing in Maine and Maryland. *Educational Evaluation and Policy Analysis, 20*(2), 95–114.

Gearhart, M., & Herman, J. L. (1998). Portfolio assessment: Whose work is it? Issues in the use of classroom assignments for accountability. *Educational Assessment, 5*(1), 41–55.

Goertz, M. E., & Duffy, M. C., with Le Floch, K. C. (2001). *Assessment and accountability systems in the 50 states: 1999–2000* (CPRE Research Report No. RR-046). Philadelphia: Consortium for Policy Research in Education, University of Pennsylvania.

Goldberg, G. L., & Rosewell, B. S. (2000). From perception to practice: The impact of teachers' scoring experience on performance-based instruction and classroom practice. *Educational Assessment, 6*(4), 257–290.

Herman, J. L., & Golan, S. (1993). Effects of standardized testing on teaching and schools. *Educational Measurement: Issues and Practices, 12*(4), 20–25, 41–42.

Herman, J. L., & Klein, D. (1996). Evaluating equity in alternative assessment: An illustration of opportunity to learn issues. *Journal of Educational Research, 89*(9), 246–256.

Herman, J. L., Klein, D., Heath, T. M., & Wakai, S. T. (1995). *A first look: Are claims for alternative assessment holding up?* (Technical Report 391). Los Angeles: National Center for Research on Evaluation, Standards, and Student Testing, University of California.

Kellaghan, T., & Madaus, G. (1991). National testing: Lessons for America from Europe. *Educational Leadership, 49*, 87–93.

Klein, S. P., Hamilton, L. S., McCaffrey, D. F., & Stecher, B. M. (2000). *What do test scores in Texas tell us?* Santa Monica, CA: RAND.

Koretz, D., & Barron, S. (1998). *The validity of gains in scores on the Kentucky Instructional Results Information System (KIRIS).* Santa Monica, CA: RAND.

Koretz, D., Barron, S., Mitchell, K. J., & Stecher, B. M. (1996). *Perceived effects of the Kentucky Instructional Results Information System (KIRIS).* Santa Monica, CA: RAND.

Koretz, D., McCaffrey, D., Klein, S., Bell, R., & Stecher, B. M. (1993). *The reliability of scores from the 1992 Vermont Portfolio Assessment Program* (CSE Technical Report No. 355). Los Angeles: National Center for Research on Evaluation, Standards, and Student Testing, University of California.

Koretz, D., Mitchell, K. J., Barron, S., & Keith, S. (1996). *Perceived effects of the Maryland State Assessment Program* (CSE Technical Report No. 406). Los Angeles: National Center for Research on Evaluation, Standards, and Student Testing, University of California.

Koretz, D., Stecher, B. M., & Deibert, E. (1992). *The Vermont Portfolio Assessment Program: Interim report on implementation and impact, 1991–1992 school year* (CSE Technical Report No. 350). Los Angeles: National Center for Research on Evaluation, Standards, and Student Testing, University of California.

Koretz, D., Stecher, B. M., Klein, S., McCaffrey, D., & Deibert, E. (1993). *Can portfolios assess student performance and influence instruction? The 1991–1992 Vermont experience* (CSE Technical Report No. 371). Los Angeles: National Center for Research on Evaluation, Standards, and Student Testing, University of California.

Lane, S., Stone, C. A., Parke, C. S., Hansen, M. A., & Cerrillo, T. L. (2000, April). *Consequential evidence for MSPAP from the teacher, principal, and student perspective.* Paper presented at the annual meeting of the National Council of Measurement in Education, New Orleans.

Linn, R. L., & Haug, C. (2001). *Stability of school building accountability scores and gains* (Draft Deliverable to OERI, Contract No. R305B960002). Los Angeles: National Center for Research on Evaluation, Standards, and Student Testing, University of California.

Linn, R. L., & Herman, J. L. (1997). *Standards-led assessment: Technical and policy issues in measuring school performances* (CSE Technical Report 426). Los Angeles: National Center for Research on Evaluation, Standards, and Student Testing, University of California, and Denver: Education Commission of the States.

McDonnell, L. M., & Choisser, C. (1997). *Testing and teaching: Local implementation of new state assessments.* Los Angeles: Center for the Study of Evaluation, University of California.

McLaughlin, M. W. (1990). The RAND change agent study revisited: Macro perspectives and macro realities. *Educational Researcher, 19*(9), 11–16.

Orlofsky, G. F., & Olson, L. (2001, January 11). The state of the states. Gaining ground. 2001: A better balance. Quality counts. Retrieved September 24, 2001, from http://www.edweek.org/sreports/qc01/articles/qc01story.cfm?slug=17 states.h20

Quellmalz, E., & Burry, J. (1983). *Analytic scales for assessing students' expository and narrative writing skills* (CSE Resource Paper No. 5). Los Angeles: Center for the Study of Evaluation, University of California.

Resnick, L. B. (1996). *Performance puzzles: Issues in measuring capabilities and certifying accomplishments* (CSE Technical Report No. 415). Los Angeles: National Center for Research on Evaluation, Standards, and Student Testing, University of California.

Resnick, L. B., & Resnick, D. P. (1992). Assessing the thinking curriculum: New tools for educational reform. In B. G. Gifford & M. C. O'Conner (Eds.), *Changing assessments: Alternative views of aptitude, achievement, and instruction* (pp. 37–75). Boston: Kluwer.

Rogosa, D. (2000). *Accuracy of year-1, year-2 comparisons using individual percentile rank scores: Classical test theory calculations* (CSE Technical Report No. 510). Los Angeles: National Center for Research on Evaluation, Standards, and Student Testing, University of California.

Rothman, R., Slattery, J. B., Vranek, J. L., & Resnick, L. B. (2000). *Benchmarking and alignment of standards and testing* (Draft Deliverable to OERI, Contract No. R305B960002). Los Angeles: National Center for Research on Evaluation, Standards, and Student Testing, University of California.

Sheingold, K., Heller, J., & Storms, B. (1997, April). *On the mutual influence of teachers' professional development and assessment quality in curricular reform*. Presentation at the annual meeting of the American Educational Research Association, Chicago.

Shepard, L. (1991). Psychometricians' beliefs about learning. *Educational Researcher, 20*, 2–16.

Smith, M. L., Edelsky, C., Draper, K., Rottenberg, C., & Cherland, M. (1990). *The role of testing in elementary schools* (CSE Technical Report No. 321). Los Angeles: National Center for Research on Evaluation, Standards, and Student Testing, University of California.

Smith, M. L., & Rottenberg, C. (1991). Unintended consequences of external testing in elementary schools. *Educational Measurement: Issues and Practice, 10*(4), 7–11.

Spillane, J. (2000). *District leaders' perceptions of teacher learning* (CPRE Occasional Paper No. OP-05). Philadelphia: Consortium for Policy Research in Education, University of Pennsylvania.

Stecher, B. M., & Barron, S. (1999). *Quadrennial milepost accountability testing in Kentucky* (CSE Technical Report No. 505). Los Angeles: National Center for Research on Evaluation, Standards, and Student Testing, University of California.

Stecher, B. M., Barron, S. L., Chun, T., & Ross, K. (2000). *The effects of the Washington State education reform on schools and classrooms* (CSE Technical Report No. 525). Los Angeles: National Center for Research on Evaluation, Standards, and Student Testing, University of California.

Stecher, B. M., Barron, S. L., Kaganoff, T., & Goodwin, J. (1998). *The effects of standards-based assessment on classroom practices: Results of the 1996–1997 RAND survey of Kentucky teachers of mathematics and writing* (CSE Technical Report No. 482). Los Angeles: National Center for Research on Evaluation, Standards, and Student Testing, University of California.

Stecher, B. M., & Borko, H. (2001). *Combining surveys and case studies to examine standards-based educational reform*. Los Angeles: National Center for Research on Evaluation, Standards, and Student Testing, University of California.

Stone, C., & Lane, S. (2000, April). *Consequences of a state accountability program: Relationships between school performance gains and teacher, student, and school variables*. Paper presented at the annual meeting of the National Council on Measurement in Education, New Orleans.

Wolf, S. A., Borko, H., McIver, M., & Elliott, R. (1999). *No excuses: School reform in exemplary schools of Kentucky* (CSE Technical Report No. 514). Los Angeles: National Center for Research on Evaluation, Standards, and Student Testing, University of California.

Wolf, S. A., & McIver, M. C. (1999). When process becomes policy: The paradox of Kentucky state reform for exemplary teachers of writing. *Phi Delta Kappan, 80*, 401–406.

Chapter 8

The Challenge of the High Schools

Leslie Santee Siskin

What happens when an irresistible force meets an immovable object? When a movement with the force and fervor of standards-based accountability reform hits the massive, highly stable, and reputedly reform-resistant form of the American high school? Something, the song lyrics tell us, has to give. But after more than a decade of focused and forceful reform effort, it is not at all clear what that something will be. Will high school structures finally give way before the mounting pressure of high-stakes tests? Or will standards-based accountability advocates have to give up, and see this attempt, like so many before it, relegated to the long list of faded reform efforts?

Standards-based accountability swept through the country during the late 1980s and 1990s with profound force, in a more concerted and coordinated effort than many earlier reforms. It provided a *powerful* logic, dominating education policy and reform discourse with irresistible calls for high standards for all students, in which equity, excellence, and economic success could combine (Smith & O'Day, 1991). It has been *persistent*, drawing initial momentum from a slumping economy tied to the "rising tide of mediocrity" in public schooling, then maintaining and even accelerating its pace when the economy soared in the 1990s. It has survived legal contests and union conflicts, massive scoring errors, and math wars. And it has been remarkably *pervasive*. Across party lines and administrative turnovers, government officials and candidates have kept education reform high on the public agenda and have made accountability the cornerstone of reform. By

2001, 49 states had adopted some form of standards-based reform, and 33 had established the central components of an accountability system (Goertz & Duffy, 2001). While no state had yet fully met the ambitious standards set by federal agencies and national advocacy groups, each state was working to demonstrate high content and performance standards, to develop and align an assessment system, and to hold someone accountable for ensuring that students met those standards.

High schools figured prominently in the early calls for standards-based reform; indeed, much of the evidence that gave the movement momentum came from a set of damning reports about the failure of high schools and of high school graduates (Boyer, 1983). The low standards and skills of graduates were heavily implicated in the argument that the United States was a "nation at risk" (National Commission on Excellence in Education, 1983). Graduates were lacking the "new basic skills" demanded in the new global economy (Murnane & Levy, 1996). Too few students took challenging coursework, either because they were "tracked" into dead-end curricula (Oakes, 1985) or because they chose poorly from the vastly varied array of courses in the "shopping mall high schools" (Powell, Farrar, & Cohen, 1985). And although the percentages of graduates were rising, too many adolescents still dropped out or were pushed out before gaining diplomas (Fine, 1991). Meanwhile, high school teachers were seen as isolated in classrooms, trapped with resistant students within a rampant bureaucracy, and forced to "compromise" their own academic standards (Sizer, 1984).

As standards-based reform took hold, however, high schools faded from the foreground as reformers and researchers shifted their emphasis to, and drew their evidence of progress from, the elementary grades (Haycock & Huang, 2001). The Consortium for Policy Research in Education (CPRE) project on Accountability and the High Schools, and the Consortium on Chicago School Research are among the few research efforts to have focused systematic attention on the effects of these new policies at the high school level. But by 2001, a pattern as persistent and pervasive as accountability reform itself was becoming apparent and demanding renewed attention: High schools were showing little, if any, progress toward meeting the state standards (Consortium on Chicago School Research, 2001; "Gaining ground," 2001; National Commission on the High School Senior Year, 2001). There was no compelling evidence of sustained or systemic change; even the scattered claims of success were explained away as artifacts of gains in earlier grades (Haycock & Huang, 2001; Hess & Cytrynbaum, 2001; Miller & Allensworth, 2001) or called into question, as in the "myth of the Texas miracle" (Haney, 2000). Still more discouraging were reports that on other national and international tests, if high school scores were moving at all, they were moving down. The 1997 international TIMSS tests showed

U.S. fourth graders in the top tier, eighth graders at the average, but twelfth graders ranking among the bottom four countries. According to the U.S. Department of Education's 2001 results, both fourth- and eighth-grade NAEP scores showed a rising trend, but twelfth-grade scores, after a brief gain, were lower than they had been in 1996. From state to state, TIMSS to NAEP, across studies and across tests, the pattern is strikingly similar: Elementary school scores were up; middle school scores made some, although smaller, gains; high schools stayed steady or even lost ground. Reformers and reporters began talking about high-stakes testing and high schools as the coming "train wreck" (Olson, 2001a), the "quiet crisis," or the "collision course" that might derail reform altogether (Olson, 2001b). Despite the steady force of accountability reform, moving the high school remains a formidable challenge.

What makes high schools so different—and so difficult? What happens when the new demands of accountability policies meet the complex structures and deeply embedded purposes and practices of the high school? My purpose in this chapter is to examine that challenge, to map the intersection of accountability and the high school by marshalling what we know—and what we still need to know—about the organizational particularities of those schools and the pressures of these policies.

To do so, I draw heavily on data from the 3-year CPRE study on Accountability and the High Schools. In this project, we selected four states (Kentucky, New York, Texas, and Vermont) that were all active in the testing movement, but had taken quite different strategic approaches to standards-based accountability (see Rhoten, Carnoy, Chabran, & Elmore, 2000). In each state, we worked with three high schools within an urban—or at least metropolitan—region. In three states, these schools are all within a single district: "Tate County" in Kentucky, "River City" in New York, and "Yaleo" in Texas (all district and school names are pseudonyms). The three schools were "positioned" somewhat differently with respect to accountability policies: One we selected as the "target" of the reform (a school that had not been performing well by traditional measures, but that had not been declared failing or selected for reconstitution), one was somewhat "better positioned" (not a highly selective exam school, but one that traditionally performed well on standardized achievement tests), and the third fell into a category we called "orthogonal" (a school, often a small school, with an articulated and distinctive mission, whose standards might not be congruent with state standards or assessments). Finally, while we interviewed administrators and teachers across the schools, we focused most intensively on four subjects—two that commonly are tested (math and English) and two that are not (music and technology).

From these data, the challenge of the high school—for both policy makers and practitioners—emerges in terms of (1) the magnitude of change, (2) the difficulty of setting standards, (3) the higher stakes, (4) the problem of timing, (5) the differences among high schools, (6) the contexts of teachers, and finally, and most important, (7) the high school students themselves.

THE MAGNITUDE OF CHANGE DEMANDED FROM HIGH SCHOOLS—AS ORGANIZATIONS—IS DRAMATICALLY DIFFERENT FROM WHAT IS DEMANDED OF ELEMENTARY SCHOOLS

The demands of standards-based reform call for a clarification and articulation of goals in elementary schools, for focused attention on instruction, and for improvement and intensification of effort at what they were already designed to do—to prepare third graders to enter fourth grade, and fourth graders to enter fifth grade. High schools, on the other hand, are being asked to do what they have never done before—something they were not designed to do—to prepare all students for the same academic endpoint. We have only in recent history expected all students to graduate from high school; we certainly have not organized high schools so all students would take the same content, or meet the same standards to graduate. In fact, comprehensive high schools historically have been designed to do precisely the opposite; since the highly influential Conant report (1959), their design imperative has been to serve democratic purposes and accommodate diverse student populations by creating a wide range of programs and a differentiated curriculum.

That idea of differentiation, of the "bell curve" of abilities in high schools, has been central to the organizational design of the comprehensive high school, to the tracks that accommodate the large bulge of students in the general courses and the small number of students along the right tail in advanced placement (AP) classes. It remains powerful even when challenged by the concept of standards that *all* students should meet. So, just as it resurfaces in the state comparisons of school scores, it surfaces in a teacher's explanation of how the school has "changed" to meet the new standards, how all students now encounter the same content and take the same test.

> Then we compare them, and it would make sense to us that the honors kids should have a lot of high grades, and then accelerated have some high grades; they should spread themselves out. If we are assessing them correctly, that's the way it should be. That shouldn't reflect badly on the [lower-level] teacher.

At worst, that strong differentiation devolved to large-scale tracking, with differential access to resources that was less the result of careful diagnosis of students' individual interests than of placements tied to the color of their skin, the accent of their speech, or the appearances of social class (Anyon, 1995; Lee, Bryk, & Smith, 1993; Metz, 1990; Oakes, 1985).

Teachers across our schools, like educators in national opinion polls, embraced the ideal of high standards for all students as means of reducing those inequities, both within and across schools, as "the right thing to do," as "mak[ing] the system more fair" (Siskin, 2001a). Many "applauded" the state for stepping in not only to set common standards, but also to establish common assessments and accountability that would force the issue of equity across schools.

Although teachers might applaud the ideal of common denominators and equal access, they did not equate this with narrowing the curriculum to provide one common experience, or to achieve a common outcome, for all students. Instead many worried that too much emphasis on the common core of academic subjects would betray the ideals of the comprehensive high school and the values of the school community: individual choices for students, preparation for diverse career paths, accommodation for different talents, opportunities for extracurricular activities, and room for social growth. In particular, educators expressed frequent concern that the emphasis on academic tests was undermining the value of vocational skills.

Teachers, students, and communities have developed a number of different, and sometimes competing, expectations of what is important for a high school to provide—and to be accountable for: safety, vocational counseling and training, extracurricular activities as well as academic programs. And they have come to expect that students will, and should, participate in different activities suited to their own individual needs and interests (Lee, 2001; Little, 1999; Lucas, 1999; Wasley, Hampel, & Clark, 1997; Wilson & Corbett, 2001). Holding all students, within and across schools, to the same high academic standards without sacrificing the advantages of that diversity would be a radical reform indeed: a formidable challenge for both policy makers and high schools.

HIGH SCHOOL IS A FUNDAMENTALLY DIFFERENT ARENA FOR DECIDING WHAT KNOWLEDGE COUNTS AND HOW TO COUNT IT

In the first efforts toward standards-based education, policy makers, educators, national subject associations, and public panels engaged in long and often heated debates about what high school graduates should know and be able to do. Over time, they produced long lists of valued content in each traditional subject area and new skills seen as suited to the needs of the twenty-first century (see Murnane & Levy, 1996). While this effort generally is framed as a shift from inputs to outcomes, from counting seat time or Carnegie units to rewarding achievement, the shift from a comprehensive curriculum to a more narrowly academic one is profound. The reflex response has been remarkably similar across states: the reassertion of the traditional categories of "core" academic subjects. Math and English always appear, science and social studies appear quite often, the arts, woodworking, or problem solving are increasingly rare. Yet agreement on the specifics of what will be on the short list, the essential knowledge and skills without which no high school student can graduate, still poses tremendous difficulties for policy makers and practitioners.

There is wide agreement, for example, that all students need literacy and numeracy, and relative agreement on the content and skill levels that all *elementary* school students should achieve. But at the high school level, where curriculum and faculty are officially and organizationally divided along subject lines, the questions are far more complicated, and states are struggling with the question of which subjects will count in their accountability systems. Does *every* student need to appreciate music or to be able to play an instrument? Should they be required to demonstrate mastery of world history, or U.S. government, or both? How well does *every* student actually need to perform on a chemistry test?

The question of "What subjects count?" highlights perhaps the most far-reaching, and largely unanticipated, consequences of the turn to high-stakes testing: It does not just measure knowledge; it changes the nature of knowledge itself by specifying its proper subjects. As one New York teacher put it, "If the standards are not on the test, they're not real" (Hartocollis, 1999). This effect is most evident and problematic in the organization of the high school, in its subject-specific departments and interdisciplinary teams. Accountability reforms heighten the stakes for both in unprecedented fashion, as states reassert the traditional subject disciplines, but reconfigure the resources and status they command. Subjects not tested risk becoming "not real," losing staff and time in the schedule, and thus their very footholds in the schools (Siskin, 2001b). Those that are tested assume extraordinary importance: If passing *all* tested subjects is the requirement for a diploma, then passing *each* one of those subjects becomes a single measure that determines whether students will graduate.

The "real" standards and test pressures affect what happens within subjects as well: Evolution disappeared from the science standards in three states; within our own sample, several English teachers lamented the demise of literature as they shifted their focus to the five-paragraph essays on which students will be assessed. In the most extreme example, music teachers in Kentucky, who worried that under that state's new accountability system "music teachers are not real teachers," put pressure on the state to include music among the tested subjects. What they won instead was a compromise that "backfired." The state created a new composite subject that *would* count: visual/performing arts and humanities, which no teacher had ever taught and no student had taken. At the same time, the policy brought about a change in how it would be counted—from actual performance assessments to paper and pencil tests (Siskin, 2001b). For our target schools, this requires new knowledge, new textbooks, new curriculum, and new teaching assignments—and student schedules that preclude electives like band. At schools like our better-positioned, more middle-class ones, however, the new content can be added on the side, downloaded from a CD the students have created, or simply brought in from home . . . while the band course plays on.

The possibility that schools, particularly low-performing schools, will be pressed to narrow curriculum to match what is asked on high-stakes tests raises concern among critics of standards-based accountability at all grade levels (Haycock & Huang, 2001; McNeil, 2000). The concern at the high school level, however, is particularly pointed, for it calls into question the very purpose of the comprehensive high school: to bring and keep large numbers of students by offering a broad range of curricular offerings suited to their tastes and talents. To some degree, this is precisely what reformers had in mind: "Gut" courses that had become holding tanks with little substance would be eliminated, and all students would have access to the more advanced and rigorous academic core. Recent studies suggest that to some degree high school course options are narrowing as prescribed, at least on paper: more algebra classes, more AP courses, and, as Chicago observers attest, a more general shift "from warehousing and managing student behavior to focusing on serious student learning" (Hess & Cytrynbaum, 2001, p. 4; see also Gutiérrez & Morales, 2001; Lee, 2001; Lucas, 1999; Miller & Allensworth, 2001; Porter, 1998).

What happens inside schools, however, may not be what reformers envisioned. In some cases, teachers take on the challenge, finding new materials or devising new approaches to reach students who would not have had access before (see DeBray, Parson, & Woodworth, 2001; Gutiérrez & Morales, 2001). In other schools, students who had been remanded to "basic" math are now assigned to classes *called* algebra, but since those classes have the same teachers, the same students, and the same textbooks, it's not clear what actually has changed. In still others, while curricular offerings have not changed, the schedule and the experiences of students have. In one Texas school, for example, the pressure of the math test is high, but so is the number of low-scoring students. In response, the school has provided intensive intervention: Selected students take one period of math, one of remedial math, and another of test-prep math. There is little time for other subjects and none for electives, and it is difficult to imagine a more perverse incentive for preparing well-educated high school graduates. Under such pressures, what happens to untested subjects—and to the students who found intellectual and social homes there? In which subjects, and in how many subjects, can high schools reasonably prepare students? And for what? Questions about what knowledge high schools do and should offer to all students, and what kinds of knowledge might be locally, socially, or culturally situated, take on new importance in this climate.

Some states are returning to the idea of a two- or even three-tiered system, in which all students must pass a set of tests to earn a high school diploma, but a subset who pass more subjects, or at higher levels, qualify for an honors diploma or special endorsement. Few states have given serious consideration to the question of whether all students actually need to— or, if given the chance, would choose to—perform to the same high level in all subjects, or whether they might achieve at high standards in different subjects—selecting the exam areas as they do with SAT-II tests, AP exams, or as students traditionally have done with the A levels and O levels in the United Kingdom. The issues of selectivity and what counts do not disappear even when there is general agreement about the need to test a particular subject. Testing math, for example, opens up the question of what kinds of math deserve attention. So far the tests have moved fairly quickly toward demanding higher-level skills of algebra and geometry; the states, however, have been slower to require that all students actually be taught those subjects before they take the tests (Grimes, 2001).

While the standards movement intended, at least in part, to ensure that students would be equipped for the economy of the twenty-first century, accountability systems have had to rely on the measurement tools, and the knowledge base, of the twentieth century. States are still working to develop consensus and precision around standards, and to devise adequate and reliable assessments to match (see Rothman, this volume). The pressure is mounting, for if what we want *all* high school students to know and what we know how to assess are not clearly and compellingly linked, the imposition of high stakes for students seems not only inappropriate but counterproductive.

THE STAKES ARE HIGHER IN HIGH SCHOOLS

High schools—to name a powerful, obvious, but largely ignored difference—are the end of the line for students in the public schooling system, a fact that magnifies the consequences of accountability and the meaning of "high stakes." While elementary and middle schools receive school-level sanctions, or see their rankings published in the newspaper (and I don't want to underestimate the power, or the fear, of public humiliation), it is at the high school that high stakes attach most directly and dramatically to students. In increasing numbers, state accountability policies are moving to make diplomas contingent on externally set exams, or on demonstrated competencies in externally set performance reviews (Goertz & Duffy, 2001). As an English teacher in New York reminded us, when scoring a high-stakes test, "You're looking at a paper; that's a human being. That's a kid reading or trying his best to get through state requirements." Ironically, in a system theoretically designed to benefit students, high school students may be the only people held directly accountable *as individuals* for achievement scores.

That makes the stakes higher for accountability systems as well, for while states and districts may be willing to embrace the idea of ending social promotion, or of remanding students to summer schools, the actual denial of a diploma is a consequence of a different kind, with political and legal complications, as well as financial and logistical ones. (See Heubert, this volume; and Fuhrman, Goertz, & Duffy, this volume.)

Teachers in our Accountability and the High Schools study made a sharp distinction between the standards, which they applaud, and the standardized high-stakes tests, which they deplore. Positive statements about raising standards were often followed with a pause, or a "but"—and a prediction of negative consequences, of rising failure rates and increasing numbers of dropouts. Here practitioners depart from the sentiments and expectations of policy makers, for they are much more worried that there will be what one calls "a lost generation"—students who have not been prepared to meet the standards, but will not be able to graduate without passing the tests. That pessimism, reported one New York teacher in the first year of the test, was widespread: "The general feeling amongst teachers is, this is going to be our last graduating class of any sizeable proportion, that next year it's going to be really bad."

State policy makers are caught in a dilemma around how high to set the bar for high school standards: If too many students fail, they risk a "lost generation" and a loss of public support; if too many pass, they risk not being taken seriously. The risk of high stakes and bars set too high seems more likely as many states introduced their new tests to low passing rates. In state after state, despite variation in policy particulars and in particular tests, results consistently pointed to high schools, especially urban high schools, as an ongoing site of crisis—the weakest link. More than half of California's high school students failed in their first round of testing; in Arizona, only 12% passed the 1999 math test. When Massachusetts first administered its new MCAS exams, only 27% of Boston's tenth graders passed the English section, and 16% the math.

Such numbers are numbing for any level of schooling, but when nearly insurmountable bars are set at the endpoint of high school, violence enters the vocabulary of policy. New York's Commissioner for Education, for example, acknowledged that under the newly reformed Regents policy, which he proudly proclaimed one of the hardest tests of any state's, there would be "casualties." Lorrie Shepard, an authority on assessment, compared high-stakes testing to "Darth Vader and the Death Star" (Jehlen, 2001). Across these state policies, where graduation becomes dependent on meeting the standard, and meeting the standard becomes equated with passing a particular test, high casualty counts indeed seemed likely.

Faced with low scores, and with stakes so high for students and for the system, the policy force that seemed so irresistible itself gave in, at least a little, or for a little while. Federal legislation continued to press for increasing accountability, and for more tests, but in 2001 specified annual testing only from third to eighth grade. Several states, while not quite silenced on high school accountability, moved to soften the pressure, to delay deadlines, or to narrow the scope of their testing systems. While 24 states had made passing a test a graduation requirement, many had created what were, in effect, time-release systems—where students would take the tests now, but not feel the full effects until later. (See Fuhrman, Goertz, & Duffy, this volume, for more on states' responses.) At best, these strategies buy time, while policy makers struggle to find incentives or levers sufficient to move high schools.

TIMING IS A DIFFERENT PROBLEM FOR HIGH SCHOOLS

For many teachers and administrators, buying time is the only action that makes sense for high schools, because unless the standards are phased in, grade by grade, reaching them seems impossible. They talk frequently, and intensely, about what we came to call "behindedness"—the huge gap between what the standards demand and the skills too many of their students have (Siskin & Lemons, 2000). While elementary schools may have students scoring 2 or 3 years below grade level, high schools have students who may be as many as 9 or 10 years behind. As one high school English teacher lamented: "You can't make up for a 9-year lack in 3 years; it's not possible."

In New York, where high-stakes testing hit the high schools very rapidly, a teacher complained that "they really hit kids over the head very hard with it. I think it was not phased in." Another explained it as a problem of social promotion, of underpreparation, that the standards movement actually is intended to fix.

> That's why they're changing the standards. And they *should* be making them higher, but they've got to start at the very bottom, with kids in kindergarten, and they are now. But then, they're going and giving us the tests in high school. If the kids haven't been prepared . . . haven't come up through the system getting prepared for it . . . .

The problem here is what teachers describe as the long-term absence of standards and accountability in the system, a system that historically has promoted students to high school without providing them with the education they need to succeed in academic work. In the most optimistic view, gradually phasing in standards-based education would create a self-correcting system: Students taught to standards at "the very bottom," in kindergarten or third grade, would carry the reform with them, raising skills as they rise through the grades.

But the hope of teachers in new systems like New York's are challenged by the more skeptical comments of teachers in Kentucky and Texas, for in those states the high school students now *are* the students who have been participating in standards-based accountability systems since they were in kindergarten (see also Haycock & Huang, 2001; Marks, 2000). At our target school in Kentucky, the principal reminded us, several times, of the challenge of teaching in a high school where "75% of our ninth graders are scoring in the first, second, or third stanines." A math teacher told us of helping his sixth-grade niece with her math and realizing that most of his tenth-grade students were not performing at that level. Another estimated that several of his students were working at a second-grade level.

That problem is compounded by the question of just what grade level means at the high school, and *when* an accountability system should assess whether students have reached it. If the purpose is to measure what students are expected to learn in high school, should an exit exam be given at the end of high school—when they have had the full opportunity to learn it? What would schools do with twelfth, or fourteenth graders, who did not pass? Would high school seniors remember what they had learned in ninth-grade biology to take a high school science test? Alternatively, should they instead choose, as most states have, to test in tenth grade (even if students haven't yet taken the geometry class)—so they have more opportunities to retake the test? Is it a problem of premature evaluation to test students before they have taken the coursework, or to assess schools when they have had students for less than half of their allotted time? What would schools then do with their juniors and seniors who passed and had officially filled the "requirement" for high school graduation? The risk of 2, or even 3, years of "senioritis" in students who had officially met graduation standards as sophomores, may seem like a relatively small problem, but for some schools it seems risky indeed. To address the challenges of timing, we need to rethink the very terms of the encounter between force and object—a rethinking that would confront the *specific* challenges of high schools as organizations, and high school curriculum as course-specific.

HIGH SCHOOLS ARE DIFFERENT FROM EACH OTHER; THEY RECEIVE AND RESPOND TO THE POLICIES IN RADICALLY DIFFERENT WAYS

Some high schools, of course, are more likely than others to confront large numbers of sophomores who have passed the state tests; others are more worried about large numbers of seniors who have not. While high schools differ in substantial ways from elementary schools, they also differ significantly from one another. They range from small schools of 200 to large, and even huge schools of 5,000 students, from comprehensives to career academies, magnets for science, and schools for the performing arts. Some responded to the early rounds of reform by restructuring, creating interdisciplinary houses, even breaking up large schools into small ones; some hold on to their traditional ways with pride, others in despair. The amount of variation in the high school system is tremendous—in terms of size, purpose, organizational structure, culture, and capacity, as well as achievement level. Although state policy may require the same standards for all schools and students, the specific contexts are quite different, and context matters (McLaughlin & Talbert, 2001).

Within the Accountability and the High Schools study, the most dramatic differences between schools lie in how the schools are positioned relative to the policy—contrasts that often were more evident than the differences between states, although the four states were selected for their diverse approaches to accountability (DeBray, Parson, & Woodworth, 2001). While all of our sampled schools were actively responding to the policy, and working hard to meet the challenge, in many ways they were trying to solve different problems. In the challenge of standards-based accountability, the problem that each school has to confront, and the capacity it can draw on to confront it, are largely a matter of how the school was positioned in the first place.

The primary challenge in what we called "better-positioned" schools was to extend—to provide the academic programs they were offering *most* students to *all* students. In our large districts, each of which offered some choice at the high school level, these better-positioned schools were not the most selective exam schools, but were considered "pretty good" to start with and often were chosen by academically oriented students. They were organized to prepare students for college, with a traditional core academic curriculum and subject departments with certified teachers, most of whom had taught high-level courses. So for an English teacher here, neither the content nor the testing was really new: "I think that if you had been teaching English the way you should have been teaching English, there is no reason why this exam should be difficult or you should be bent out of shape." But teachers had been able to forget, or ignore, that not everyone had been teaching "the way you should have been" and not all students had been reaching the standards. Although the starting point may be easier to find in these schools, their challenge is not small: Ensuring that the last 10% or 20% are prepared to pass the new exams is a difficult task. At the River City school, "a third of the kids had failures" in one or more courses, but with the pressures of the new policy, these failures now lead to redeployment of their most qualified faculty, to tutoring and after-school programs, and sometimes—although they say not often—to counseling students, and their families, to try another school.

For the "target" schools, which are often the schools low-achieving students are counseled into, the problem to be solved is more how to *invent*: They don't have the academic structures and strategies in place to prepare their students for these new standards. That may mean creating new classes or taking on new teaching assignments, but these schools find little in the way of new resources or even guidance to help them. As one principal laments, looking at her school's report card, "How do you even know where to begin?" These are not the lowest-scoring schools in their states—in our Vermont target, they celebrated when the newspaper published the list of the very bottom-ranking schools and they weren't on it. But typically the majority of their students are not reaching the standards, and although teachers speak of "working hard" and "overload," they see little reason to expect that to improve, and turnover is high. Qualified math teachers are hard to find, so teachers have been conscripted from Title I and business programs; in one year four teachers were hired for, but then left, the physics class. Many attribute that to "a lot of extenuating circumstances, things that are beyond our control within the building that affect our test scores. And we feel like those concerns fall on deaf ears." In Tate County, an English teacher described hers as "a school for the disenfranchised parent and student. Parents who weren't successful in school themselves don't know how to play this system, and so, therefore, their kids aren't successful. And I think that's what's happened here." To some degree, this may be a problem of low, or self-fulfilling, expectations, but the contrast between two schools in the same district is striking: At the target school, 70% of the students qualify for the free lunch program; at its better-positioned neighbor, the figure is 12%. In the target, 20% qualify for special education services, and another 20% for English as a Second Language; at the better-positioned school, they "don't offer any remedial classes" so special-needs students are discouraged from applying.

Our target school in River City is a comprehensive high school, where students for many years have performed poorly on standardized tests; before they were a graduation requirement, fewer than 10% of students had qualified for Regents diplomas. Like the Tate County target, the school has organized around improving safety and order with interdisciplinary programs devised to attract students to school and attach them to a faculty team. The school can point to substantial improvement: Applications are up, as is attendance; suspension and violent incidents are down. Those may be necessary first steps, but they are not sufficient to improve test scores. So, for schools like this one, the problem is a broad one, and they worry that many, or even most, of their students will be unable to pass the new test: "I think we're going to graduate many fewer kids . . . we're supposed to have 400 or 500 kids graduating; we're probably going to find ourselves with 150 or possibly 200." While the task of preparing students seems in general daunting, the challenge of preparing those students they see as most at risk seems almost impossible (see also Thurlow, this volume). The lack of adequate safety nets or additional resources seems, to some teachers, almost unconscionable: "There's no safety net for immigrant students; there's no safety net for special ed. students."

For the schools we have called "orthogonal," the policy presents a different problem: how to survive, to maintain a specialized mission under the pressure of high-stakes, standardized testing. One orthogonal school, for example, traditionally had provided special focus on African American studies, community service, and career preparation, but dramatically shifted its programs to center the standardized academic core demanded in its new policy context, while struggling to hold on to its historical pride and sense of providing something "special" and especially valuable to its constituents.

The concern takes on special intensity in the case of our River City orthogonal school, a small school where an administrator called the new policy "threatening. Not to my job, but to our philosophy. And philosophy is everything." This is a school that by design operates outside the "mainstream" of district high schools and by choice serves only immigrant students. The school, like the better-positioned school, has some capacity to select students, but has chosen students whose scores on the English-language battery lie in the lowest quartile. The students, in turn, have chosen this particular school instead of a comprehensive; their incoming tests scores may be low, but teachers describe them as "motivated," as "oriented" toward their particular focus, and as filled with "a lot of school pride." This school is organized around not traditional department lines, but an innovative—and nationally renowned—program for teaching English and subject-based content at the same time. The ideal of high standards is not seen as a problem: The school expects students to attend regularly, work hard, and graduate, and well over 90% of students do. It has developed a demanding performance-based assessment system and annually sends more than 90% of graduates to college. But standardizing course content and standardized tests lead many here to a profoundly pessimistic view about the potential failure rate of their students, and about the future survival of their school.

The idea of "no exceptions" and no excuses has been a central element of standards-based reform since its inception. But in cases like New York, the potential conflict between *high* standards for all students and the *same* standards, as measured by standardized assessment of all schools and students, has come into sharp focus and into an ongoing court case. When the standards and the stakes are so high, and the schools are starting—or aiming to continue—in such different positions, policies that don't take account of the differences between high schools, risk unintended and undesired consequences.

Ironically, standards-based accountability actually may exacerbate the very inequities it was designed to alleviate. The pattern is clear, although the sample is small. Schools that started out better-positioned relative to the new standards have extended what they were doing, making adaptive improvements. They have been able to employ their own internal accountability systems, to draw on staff capacity, to reduce the "general" tracks of nonacademic courses, and to provide additional time and focused curriculum to students at risk. But at the same time they have been able to reduce the numbers of at-risk students they admit and retain, and to attract more academic students and teachers as their "higher-scoring school" status becomes more public. The "targets" of the reform, on the other hand, suffer the consequences of public statements of their "low-scoring school" status—their ability to recruit and retain is severely constrained in the new "accountability markets" (Siskin & Lemons, 2000). At the edges of the system, the small schools, the special mission schools, the "orthogonal" outliers that had provided some of the few existence-proofs that high schools could be "transformed" and successful in urban contexts, are pulled back from what made them distinctive.

IN THE HIGH SCHOOLS, ENGAGING—OR EVEN REACHING—TEACHERS ENTAILS DIFFERENT STRATEGIES AND DIFFERENT STRUCTURES

High bars and looming graduations create a daunting set of unfamiliar demands for secondary school staffs, since accountability reform demands not only that all students be expected to meet high standards, but that *teachers* be expected to adequately prepare them to do that. Many teachers argue that policy makers are out of touch with local realities, particularly the harsh realities of underfunded, and underperforming, urban schools. At a hearing where state policy makers talked of "raising the standards for all students," a teacher asked incredulously, "Do you not understand that there are some schools where not one student will be able to graduate?" For reformers to reach an understanding with those who must implement reforms in the classroom, they need to recognize the demands that standards-based accountability imposes not just on teachers in general, but on those who teach in high schools in particular. Teachers are very aware of this call to change; unlike many previous reform efforts, they generally agree with its ideals, but, as noted earlier, their agreement insists on the distinction between the standards they support and the tests they deplore.

Teachers' agreement and engagement are essential elements of the reform, particularly since teachers are quite forthcoming about the fact that they themselves will not be held directly accountable for the academic achievement of their students. As one teacher said, "What I'm not accountable for, I think sometimes—facetiously I say it—if every kid failed math in this school, I would still have a job." If anything is going to happen, then, it will be because teachers look at the new demands and see them as possible to achieve and worth their support and effort.

To capitalize on that support and allay the fears, reformers must work through the specific barriers posed by the particular organizational structure of high schools. The lever they must pull is long, extending from the state through many layers of bureaucracy into the classroom, where, finally, the change has to take place. To communicate even straightforward information is difficult from that distance; at River City, for example, teachers who applauded the standards movement could not always tell what the policy actually required, when it would take effect, or what the consequences really would be.

Reaching teachers with professional development support for changes in instruction is even more complicated; in high schools instruction is subject-specific, so teachers need to be addressed not just as teachers but as math teachers or English teachers or music teachers (Siskin, 2001b). In many cases, high school teachers are being asked to teach what they have not taught before, what they are not certified to teach, or, quite simply, what they do not have the capacity to provide. U.S. Department of Education figures for 1998 show that 28% of math teachers and 55% of physics teachers have neither a major nor minor in their subject; another analysis estimates the figures at one in three math teachers, and one in four English teachers, who are teaching "out-of-field" (Ingersoll, 2001). Those shortages are more critical factors in the schools that are the very target of the reform, where an administrator asks, "Who is going to teach this stuff?" Each high school teacher who either cannot or does not provide sufficient "opportunities to learn" the new standards translates into approximately 150 students who don't receive them. Not only are teachers faced with new courses (like the humanities), but many teachers, after years of teaching general classes, suddenly find themselves teaching what had been the honors track.

Where we did find teachers engaged in substantive and sustained conversations about teaching to the new standards was in their own departments, but few departments were organized to facilitate these conversations. Without the time to engage in these conversations on a regular basis, teachers had little opportunity to work on the standards, to learn what the standards entailed, or even to become knowledgeable about the new policies. This is not, I would argue, because these are unmotivated or resistant teachers; it is more a result of the relative absence of departmental mechanisms around information sharing, standards-based work, and talk about teaching and learning.

The professional development and capacity-building endeavors of many districts and states, however, seem to assume that principals are the key agents of instructional leadership and support. As one principal explained:

> In terms of assisting us, and that's what it is, it's a support and assist to the schools, providing us with expertise in the areas, doing staff development with [the principals] so we can then turnkey it with our staff. We meet monthly. . . . Last month's principals' meeting was focusing all on social studies, and we had some people come in and do presentations, and then we as principals worked together on stuff that's going to be on the new exam for social studies.

The idea of having principals get together and work on the "stuff" that's going to be on the tests is probably quite valuable, but the probability of high school principals going back to "turnkey" meaningful changes, given the size of their faculties and the complexity of the changes entailed in standards-based work, seems quite low.

In the absence of serious investments of time and support to change what is taught and how it is taught, the impact of standards-based accountability on student achievement in high schools is likely to be disappointing. In high schools, that investment has to take place subject by subject, addressing the level of particular content materials, expectations for students, and teaching strategies, which generally means it has to take place in subject departments (Aguirre, 2000; Gutiérrez & Morales, 2001; Siskin & Little, 1995; Stodolsky & Grossman, 2001; Wetterstein, 1993). Otherwise, schools that are better positioned to start with, and whose internal structures correspond to the external demands of the subject-specific standards, may be even further advantaged in the educational marketplace. There is a growing body of research, for example, that links subject expertise to student performance, but finds that, as in our sample, shortages of academically prepared teachers are higher in poorer schools and high-stakes testing encourages teachers with higher qualifications to move to higher-scoring schools (Hanushek, Kain, & Rifkin, 2001; Haycock & Huang, 2001; Ingersoll, 2001). So as the curriculum narrows (or rises, depending on your point of view), the questions of who will teach these courses, and how they themselves will be prepared to prepare students, take on new salience.

IN HIGH SCHOOLS, STUDENTS PLAY A CENTRAL AND ACTIVE ROLE IN THE REFORM

Finally, but foremost in teachers' minds, students themselves are a central element in the particular challenge of high schools. They play multiple roles in the process and products of standards-based accountability: They are the bottom line and the intended beneficiaries, a resource and a result.

High schools differ in critical ways from elementary schools, not simply in the early hour at which the school day begins, or the larger size of physical and organizational structures; they are full of adolescents, and the interactions between teachers and teenagers are quite different from those with younger children. High school students are not like younger students who "can be compelled to perform," explained a music teacher, who splits his time between teaching elementary and high school classes. Instead, as young adults they see a teacher as "more like a peer," so that "[teachers] have to earn their respect," and students have to be "convinced" that there is a reason to engage in schoolwork. Nor, a principal observed, are high school students quite like adults: "They don't react like us."

Yet high school students are making—and see themselves as old enough to make—important choices about what they need to know and what they are willing to do: They decide which schools to attend, which days to come (or cut), whether to stay in school or drop out, what courses they will take, and how much effort to put into an exhausting battery of state tests. Some, perhaps aspiring lawyers, elect to study English and social studies, but plan to hire accountants to deal with the math problems in their lives. Others know, or think they know, that they will be musicians or mechanics and not need academic courses at all. Some even organize boycotts, or create websites, in opposition to high-stakes tests. They are old enough to ask why, and to demand and deserve a meaningful answer.

With remarkable consistency across the states and types of schools, whether or not the stakes are high, teachers and administrators struggle with ways to convince and connect to adolescents, with what we have called the "mystery of motivation" (Siskin & Lemons, 2000). How to motivate high school students to engage in academic work has always been difficult to some degree, but it poses a particular challenge under the demands of standards-based accountability, when all students are expected to achieve high standards in all tested subjects, and teachers search for convincing answers to why everyone needs to know the quadratic formula or how to write a five-paragraph essay.

At its core, the design of an effective accountability system depends heavily on the answers it can provide, on the motivation of students and the meaning they attach to what they are expected to achieve. The assessments rely on a set of critical conditions: that students actively engage in the effort, attend their classes, show up to take the exams, and take the tests seriously. Achieving those conditions, in turn, depends on convincing students they have reason to participate, and a reasonable chance of success, which entails schools that are organized to prepare them, qualified and committed teachers to educate them, community consensus on what the next generation needs to know, and the political will to provide the particular resources to make that possible in every school. As standards-based accountability reform enters the era of second-generation revisions, those conditions remain a challenge for high schools, and the high school remains a challenge to the reform movement.

REFERENCES

Aguirre, J. M. (2000, October). *Examining teacher beliefs related to algebra competency in the context of "algebra for all" mathematics reform debate*. Paper presented at the meeting of Psychology of Mathematics Education, Tucson, AZ.

Anyon, J. (1995). Inner city school reform: Toward useful theory. *Urban Education, 30*(1), 56–70.

Boyer, E. (1983). *High school: A report on secondary education in America*. New York: Harper & Row.

Conant, J. B. (1959). *The American high school today: A first report to interested citizens*. New York: McGraw-Hill.

Consortium on Chicago School Research. (2001). *Research on high school reform efforts in Chicago: Summary of presentations*. Chicago: Author.

DeBray, E., Parson, G., & Woodworth, K. (2001). Patterns of response in four high schools under state accountability policies in Vermont and New York. In S. H. Fuhrman (Ed.), *From the capitol to the classroom: Standards-based reform in the states* (pp. 170–192). Chicago: University of Chicago Press.

Fine, M. (1991). *Framing dropouts: Notes on the politics of an urban public high school.* Albany: State University of New York Press.

Gaining ground. Quality counts 2001: A better balance. (2001, January 11). Education Week, *20*(17), 33–40.

Goertz, M. E., & Duffy, M. C., with Le Floch, K. C. (2001). *Assessment and accountability systems in the 50 states: 1999–2000* (CPRE Research Report No. RR-046). Philadelphia: Consortium for Policy Research in Education, University of Pennsylvania.

Grimes, M. (2001, June 24). California confronts algebra anxiety. *Boston Globe/Los Angeles Times,* p. A22.

Gutiérrez, R., & Morales, H. (2001, March). *Developing a teacher community that advances Latina/Latino students in mathematics: Exploring the origins of a successful high school department.* Paper presented at the meeting of the Consortium on Chicago School Research on Research on High School Reform Efforts in Chicago, Chicago.

Haney, W. (2000). The myth of the Texas miracle in education. *Education Policy Analysis Archives.* Retrieved from http://epaa.asu.edu/epaa/v8n41/

Hanushek, E., Kain, J. F., & Rifkin, S. G. (2001). *Why public schools lose teachers.* Washington, DC: National Bureau of Economic Research. Retrieved from http://www.nber.org

Hartocollis, A. (1999, April 1). The man behind the exams: New York's education chief pushes agenda of change. *The New York Times,* Section B, p. 1.

Haycock, K., & Huang, S. (2001). Are today's high school graduates ready? *Thinking K-16: Publication of the Education Trust, 5*(1), 3–17.

Hess, G. A., & Cytrynbaum, S. (2001). The effort to redesign Chicago high schools: Effects on schools and achievement. In *Research on high school reform efforts in Chicago* (pp. 19–49). Chicago: Consortium on Chicago School Research.

Ingersoll, R. M. (2001). The realities of out-of-field teaching. *Educational Leadership, 58*(8), 42–45.

Jehlen, A. (2001). Interview with Lorrie Shepard: How to fight a "death star." *NEA Today Online.* Retrieved from http://www.nea.org/neatoday/0101/intrvw.html

Lee, V. (2001). *Restructuring high schools for equity and excellence: What works.* New York: Teachers College Press.

Lee, V., Bryk, A. S., & Smith, J. B. (1993). The organization of effective secondary schools. In L. Darling-Hammond (Ed.), *Review of research in education* (Vol. 19, pp. 171–267). Washington, DC: American Educational Research Association.

Little, J. W. (1999). *Teachers' professional development in the context of high school reform: Findings from a three-year study of restructuring schools.* Unpublished manuscript.

Lucas, S. R. (1999). *Tracking inequality: Stratification and mobility in American high schools.* New York: Teachers College Press.

Marks, H. M. (2000). Student engagement in instructional activity: Patterns in the elementary, middle, and high school years. *American Educational Research Journal, 37*(1), 153–184.

McLaughlin, M. W., & Talbert, J. E. (2001). *Professional communities and the work of high school teaching.* Chicago: University of Chicago Press.

McNeil, L. (2000). *Contradictions of school reform: Educational costs of standardized testing.* New York: Routledge.

Metz, M. H. (1990). How social class differences shape teachers' work. In M. McLaughlin, J. Talbert, & N. Bascia (Eds.), *The contexts of teaching in secondary schools* (pp. 40–107). New York: Teachers College Press.

Miller, S. R., & Allensworth, E. A. (2001, March). *Who attends Chicago high schools and how are they doing? Changes between 1994 and 2000.* Paper presented at the meeting of the Consortium on Chicago School Research on Research on High School Reform Efforts in Chicago, Chicago.

Murnane, R., & Levy, F. (1996). *Teaching the new basic skills: Principles for educating children to thrive in a changing economy.* New York: Free Press.

National Commission on Excellence in Education. (1983). *A nation at risk: The imperative for educational reform.* Washington, DC: Author.

National Commission on the High School Senior Year. (2001). *The lost opportunity of senior year: Finding a better way.* Washington, DC: U.S. Department of Education.

Oakes, J. (1985). *Keeping track: How schools structure inequality.* New Haven, CT: Yale University Press.

Olson, L. (2001a). States adjust high-stakes testing plans. *Education Week on the Web.* Retrieved from http://www.edweek.org/January 24, 2001

Olson, L. (2001b). A quiet crisis: Unprepared for high stakes. *Education Week on the Web.* Retrieved from http://www.edweek.org/April 18, 2001

Porter, A. C. (1998). The effects of upgrading policies on high school mathematics and science. In D. Ravitch (Ed.), *Brookings papers on education policy, 1998* (pp. 123–164). Washington, DC: Brookings Institution.

Powell, A., Farrar, E., & Cohen, D. K. (1985). *The shopping mall high school: Winners and losers in the academic marketplace.* Boston: Houghton Mifflin.

Rhoten, D., Carnoy, M., Chabran, M., & Elmore, R. F. (2000, April). *Conditions and characteristics of assessment and accountability: The case of four states.* Paper presented at the annual meeting of the American Educational Research Association, New Orleans.

Siskin, L. S. (2001a, April). *Daydreams and nightmares: Implementing the new Regents exam in New York.* Paper presented at the annual meeting of the American Educational Research Association, Seattle.

Siskin, L. S. (2001b, April). *Outside the core: Tested and untested subjects in high-stakes accountability systems.* Paper presented at the annual meeting of the American Educational Research Association, Seattle.

Siskin, L. S., & Lemons, R. (2000, April). *Internal and external accountability: The challenge of the high school.* Paper presented at the annual meeting of the American Educational Research Association, New Orleans.

Siskin, L. S., & Little, J. W. (1995). *The subjects in question: Departmental organization and the high school.* New York: Teachers College Press.

Sizer, T. R. (1984). *Horace's compromise: The dilemma of the American high school.* Boston: Houghton Mifflin.

Smith, M., & O'Day, J. (1991). Systemic school reform. In S. H. Fuhrman & B. Malen (Eds.), *The politics of curriculum and testing* (pp. 233–267). New York: Falmer Press.

Stodolsky, S., & Grossman, P. (2001). Changing students, changing teaching. *Teachers College Record, 102*(1), 125–172.

Wasley, P. A., Hampel, R. L., & Clark, R. C. (1997). *Kids and school reform.* San Francisco: Jossey-Bass.

Wetterstein, J. A. (1993, April). *Leadership strategies of exemplary high school department chairs: Four cases of successful "middle managers."* Paper presented at the annual meeting of the American Educational Research Association, Atlanta.

Wilson, B., & Corbett, H. D. (2001). *Listening to urban kids: School reform and the teachers they want.* Albany: State University of New York Press.

Chapter 9

Does External Accountability Affect Student Outcomes? A Cross-State Analysis

Martin Carnoy
Susanna Loeb

The current wave of assessment-based school accountability reforms combines two traditions in American education—public accountability and student testing. The combination seems to be changing what schools do and how they do it. Strong accountability increases centralized state control, even as other reforms, such as charter schools, strive to decentralize educational decision making. This chapter asks whether the stronger statewide approaches to accountability achieve their stated goal of improving student achievement.

In the past, accountability and assessment were only loosely connected. Assessment was used mainly to divide students into academic tracks or for diagnostic purposes, helping school administrators and teachers see whether students were learning loosely defined state curricula. Accountability traditionally has been based in community participation and parental control, as represented by local school boards. Schools have been accountable to district administrators, who, in turn, answer to elected boards. Parents also have been able to influence schools directly. School test results enter into parental decisions on where to live and fuel parental criticisms of school board actions, especially in higher-income neighborhoods. The link between traditional local accountability and traditional student assessment has

Redesigning Accountability Systems for Education. ISBN 0-8077-4425-5 (cloth). Prior to photocopying items for classroom use, please contact the Copyright Clearance Center, Customer Service, 222 Rosewood Drive, Danvers, MA, 01923, USA, telephone (978) 750-8400.

long been important in neighborhoods with high parental participation. In the majority of schools, however, this link has been either indirect, acting through family residential choice, or practically nonexistent. It has been especially weak in low-income communities and large urban school districts.

States' initial accountability efforts generally entailed judging schools on the basis of the amount and kinds of inputs they had—library books, lab equipment, building conditions, percent certified teachers, and class size, for example. Although schools with greater resources often had higher test scores, the causal link between student outcomes and such inputs was not clear once neighborhood income was accounted for. Partially in response to such weak links, reformers questioned the benefits of focusing policy solely on improving school inputs and moved to restructure accountability systems. Some states already had considerable centralized control over education policy; in others, the shift occurred gradually over the past 3 decades. Now many states with little tradition of state-level accountability have legislated or are in the process of legislating school accountability systems that focus on student outcomes and judge school quality in terms of these outcomes (Elmore, Abelmann, & Fuhrman, 1996).

In making average student scores on state tests a main gauge of school performance, state school officials also have shifted influence over teacher and principal behavior from local school boards and district offices to the statehouse. The new accountability reforms ratchet up the degree of central state power over schools and reduce local control over school policy. In this context, it is important to ask what effect these new accountability systems are having on student performance. Does this new accountability improve student learning and educational attainment? Are low-income and other traditionally low-performing students the main beneficiaries of the reforms?

Evaluations of recent accountability reforms are marked by controversy. RAND Corporation's Grissmer and Flanagan (1998) made headlines when they released a study showing that Texas and North Carolina, two states that had implemented "strong" accountability systems early (Texas in the mid-1980s and North Carolina in the early 1990s), made much larger gains than other states in the math portion of the National Assessment of Educational Progress (NAEP) between 1992 and 1996. The study supported claims by the Texas Education Agency that minority students made the largest gains, at least in primary school mathematics. These results suggested that state accountability systems could help lift academic achievement substantially and that low-performing students could be the primary beneficiaries of the new accountability reforms.

Later studies disagreed with the Grissmer and Flanagan conclusions.

For example, RAND's Stephen Klein claimed that the Texas NAEP reading scores made only average increases and that minorities actually lost ground (Klein, Hamilton, McCaffrey, & Stecher, 2000). Haney (2000) went beyond test scores in his critique of the "Texas miracle." He argued that the Texas school assessment system motivates high schools to retain an increasing proportion of students in ninth grade and increases high school dropout rates, particularly for minority students. Haney's and other studies suggest that additional important indicators of educational improvement, such as graduation and college enrollment rates, have not improved in these high-stakes accountability states (Carnoy, Loeb, & Smith, 2001; Haney, 2000).

Now that more states have implemented Texas- and North Carolina-type state accountability systems, we are in a better position to test the effect of accountability on student outcomes. A difficulty with this assessment is finding appropriate outcomes that are measured consistently across states. The recent availability of 2000 math NAEP scores by state allows us to relate math score increases from 1996 to 2000 to the strength of a state's accountability system. Other outcomes we examine are student retention in ninth grade and progression through high school. These are also important, albeit more indirect, educational outcome measures that may be linked to implementing higher standards and statewide assessment (Carnoy, Loeb, & Smith, 2001).

STANDARDS-BASED REFORM AND THE ROLE OF TESTING

The use of student testing at the state level with consequences for students, and even as a measure of school performance, is not new. New York has used Regent examinations to test students' command of high school curriculum since the nineteenth century. The Iowa Test of Basic Skills (ITBS) has been given to eighth graders in Iowa since 1935. It subsequently has been applied in many other states for students in many grades. However, the purpose of the ITBS was (and, in Iowa, continues to be) diagnostic. How well students, classes, or schools performed on ITBS-type tests had few consequences. Schools stored the data, and school results often were published in local newspapers, but few administrators were compelled to take action because of declines in scores or continued low performance. High-stakes testing, such as the Regents, the Scholastic Aptitude Test, or advanced placement (AP) tests, were mainly related to college entrance and focused on individual student performance, not school performance.

Texas was a pioneer in using a state assessment test to measure school performance directly and to both sanction those schools not meeting improvement norms and reward schools exceeding norms. Other states, such as South Carolina and North Carolina, began implementing such systems a few years later.

Based on these new types of state accountability systems, educators developed the notion of *standards-based reform* in the late 1980s. They incorporated two main concepts: alignment and capacity building (O'Day & Smith, 1993; Smith, O'Day, & Cohen, 1990). Alignment means that, in order to focus on improving outcomes, school systems need to set clear standards and align curriculum and accountability mechanisms with those standards. However, standards-based reform does *not* necessarily assume that alignment alone can improve education. Education reform may need to improve the capacity of teachers and administrators to deliver better education. Much of the policy literature on building capacity focuses on organizational change (Cohen & Ball, 1999; Elmore, 1995; Talbert, McLaughlin, & Rowan, 1993). But, capacity is not just embedded in organization. "Quality" teachers need to know the subject matter they are teaching and be effective pedagogues. Principals and superintendents need to know how to manage schools and school districts (Darling-Hammond, 1997).

In the standards-based reform movement, testing is one component of a broader and deeper set of sustained changes necessary for educational improvement to occur. Testing can be used in several ways. It can be an indicator to tell administrators and teachers whether they are reaching the organization's goals and to provide information on which elements of the curriculum are reaching students and which are not. It can be used as a measure of success or failure in an incentive system. It can be used as a gauge to increase standards, to assess curricula, or to provide technical assistance. It can be used as a mechanism to allocate additional resources in order to improve outcomes for groups having difficulty reaching the standards.

Testing in the states that implemented accountability systems has been used in several of these ways. But, in contrast with the 1984 Texas reform, which addressed a number of different facets of standards-based reform, including raising teacher salaries from very low levels to attract better-prepared individuals into teaching, testing has been *the* central element of most recently implemented accountability systems. Between 1980 and 1996, per-pupil spending in Texas rose 60%, adjusted for inflation—compared with a 37% increase in spending per pupil nationally. Accountability has not been accompanied by this increase in resources in most states.

With the focus on measurable and easily understood results, test scores are rapidly becoming the end-all of state accountability reforms. Our results suggest that there is considerable variation in the improvement of student outcomes in states with similar levels of outcome-based state accountability.

Although in this chapter we do not analyze why this variation occurs, some of it may be due to states' commitment and ability to build capacity.

EXPECTED OUTCOMES OF ACCOUNTABILITY

Across the states, accountability systems are aligning incentives toward raising test scores. States with such systems reward schools that perform well on tests and send negative signals to those that do not. A clear measure of the effect of accountability is, thus, whether accountability systems have a positive effect on test scores. The National Assessment of Educational Progress tests students every 4 years in mathematics and reading, in fourth and eighth grades. These tests, designed at the federal level and considered a reasonable assessment of student knowledge in these subjects, have been used by many analysts to gauge whether students have been learning more or less over time. Since 1990, NAEP scores also have been available by state, although not every state participates in the assessment. Some states participate in some years, and not in others. Since the NAEP math test was given in 1996 and 2000, it provides a good measure of whether state accountability systems—many of which came into being in the mid-1990s—are having a significant effect on student learning outcomes.

The stated objective of higher standards (for example, requiring all students to pass ninth-grade algebra or biology in order to graduate from high school) and statewide assessment, including high school exit tests, is to increase schools' focus on how much students learn. This new focus may have unintended consequences, at least in the short and medium run. Raising the bar on student learning in high school may make it more difficult for students to pass courses, hence increasing student retention and decreasing graduation rates. In his analysis of Texas data, for example, Haney (2000) found that the implicit retention rates in ninth grade (the ratio of ninth graders in year t to eighth graders in year $t-1$) of Texas high schools increased steadily after the early 1980s to the mid-1990s for all ethnic groups, but particularly for African Americans and Hispanics. He associated this trend with the implementation of statewide assessment and particularly with the Texas Assessment of Academic Skills (TAAS) high school exit testing, first implemented in 1991. We reanalyzed Texas enrollment data and confirmed Haney's ninth-grade retention finding. However, we were not as convinced that increased retention in ninth grade could be associated with the TAAS high school exit test because much of the change occurred before the TAAS was implemented. If there is a link between retention and state policies, it is likely to date back to the implementation of accountability in the 1980s and not to the current policy (Carnoy, Loeb, & Smith, 2001). The connection between accountability and ninth-grade retention requires more study—one of our objectives in this chapter.

Evidence of higher retention rates due to the new focus on assessment is important because, at the individual level, retention is a strong predictor of dropping out. For example, Rumberger (1995) shows that retained students are four times more likely than other students to drop out, even after controlling for a host of background and school measures. In the 1980s in Texas, increased ninth-grade retention rates were clearly associated with declining high school completion rates for all ethnic groups (as measured by the ratio of the number of students graduating to the number of students in eighth grade 4 years earlier). Yet, graduation rates stopped declining in the early 1990s, just as the tenth-grade TAAS exit test was implemented across the state; by the end of the 1990s, the graduation rate was rising. Thus, a few years after the implementation of the high school exit test, retention rates had leveled off and graduation rates had begun to climb (Carnoy, Loeb, & Smith, 2001).

There are several possible explanations for these Texas trends. One is that the exit test has been easy enough or graded easily enough, so that it has not affected the decision of students who would not have dropped out anyway. A second is that retention rates may have affected dropout rates but the implementation of a stronger accountability system may not have had much effect on retention. A third is that it has taken some years for the positive effects of the accountability system to be felt in Texas high schools, so that the initial impact of stronger accountability through assessment was to increase retention rates, and hence increase dropouts, but by the mid-1990s, student performance had improved sufficiently to increase graduation rates. Finally, financial resources may have played a role. The courts also mandated more-equal distribution of spending across districts, and Texas began to implement the court order in the early 1990s. We test some of these possibilities by examining data across states.

THE MODEL

States implement accountability systems to improve educational outcomes. Students' performance on tests is the main measure states use for gauging educational improvement. However, improvements on state tests may not be an accurate measure of educational gains, since schools may substitute important learning for strategies to increase performance on the particular testing instrument. Because of this, it is important to use alternative measures to gauge the success of these policies. In this chapter, we use a variety of measures, including NAEP scores, ninth-grade retention rates, and high school survival rates (the proportion of students who reach twelfth grade).

We are interested in four questions:

- Do states with strong accountability systems see larger increases in national assessment test results? Since states with strong accountability systems put the most pressure on low-scoring schools, we posit that the influence of strong accountability is greater on the proportion of students succeeding at the basic skills level than on the proportion of students scoring at the "proficient" level.
- Do states with strong accountability see increases in their retention rates in ninth grade relative to states with weak accountability? Once these systems are implemented, they are supposed to improve the likelihood that students will finish high school. But according to some analysts, the pressure on schools to do well on high school minimum competency tests pushes administrators and teachers to increase retention rates in the first year of high school (Haney, 2000).
- Do high school progression rates in states with strong accountability increase or decrease relative to progression rates in states with weak accountability? If accountability raises student performance in the earlier grades, this ultimately should raise the proportion completing high school; if, however, strong accountability increases retention rates in earlier grades, it could well reduce survival rates.
- Does the relationship between accountability and student outcomes differ between minority students and White students?

We first look at the impact of accountability on student achievement, testing whether the proportion of eighth graders or fourth graders achieving at the basic skills level or better, and at the proficient level or better, on the NAEP math test increased more between 1996 and 2000 in states with "strong" outcome-based accountability than in states with "weak" accountability. We control for the 1996 test score to test whether lower-scoring states in 1996 had a significantly higher gain in the next 4 years independent of the accountability index. Similarly, we allow states in the South or with a high proportion of African American and Hispanic students to have done significantly better or worse than other states, independent of the accountability index.

$$G_i = \phi_0 + \phi_1 A_i + \phi_2 M_i + \phi_3 T_i \text{ (or } H_i) + \phi_4 S_i + \varepsilon; \tag{1}$$

where

G = the change in the proportion of eighth-grade students in state i who demonstrate basic skills or better on the mathematics NAEP between 1996 and 2000;

M = the proportion of African American and Hispanic (public school) students in state i;

T = the average percentage of eighth-grade students in state i demonstrating basic math skills or better or demonstrating proficient level or better on the mathematics NAEP in 1996;

H = the change in the average percentage of eighth-grade students in state i demonstrating basic math skills or better on the mathematics NAEP between 1992 and 1996; and

S = a dichotomous variable indicating whether state is in the South.

We run a number of specification checks on this basic model. One specification focuses on scale scores, but we are more interested in the percent of students passing at different skill levels (basic skills or better and proficient or better) because that allows us to test whether stronger accountability affects gains just in basic skills or also in higher-level skills. We run another model including the change in average revenue per pupil from 1990 to 1998. As described in more detail below, we also check the estimated coefficient for accountability for possible bias due to those excluded from the NAEP math test because they were special education (SD) or limited English proficient (LEP) students.

We also test whether ninth-grade retention (the number of students in ninth grade divided by the number of students in eighth grade the year before) rose more in the late 1990s in states with strong accountability than in states with weak accountability. Finally, we test whether tenth- to twelfth-grade survival rates increase more in states with strong accountability than in states with weak accountability, controlling for test score, higher proportion of minorities, and also ninth-grade retention rates.

$$Rt_i \text{ or } Pg_i = \alpha_0 + \alpha_1 A_i + \alpha_2 T_i + \alpha_3 M_i + \alpha_4 P_i + \alpha_5 S_i + \varepsilon; \qquad (2)$$

where

Rt = ninth-grade retention rate in state i;
Pg = the high school progression rate in state i; and
T = NAEP eighth-grade math test scores in 1996.

We run a number of specification checks on this basic model as well.

THE DATA

We use four sets of data. For test scores, we use the posted NAEP math results by state from *The Nation's Report Card* (http://nces.ed.gov/nations

reportcard/states). We use a number of different test scores to estimate Equations (1) and (2). In Equation (1), the outcome measure is the latest one available, the gain in score on the NAEP math test compared from 1996 to 2000. We estimate the effect of the accountability index and other variables on both eighth-grade results and fourth-grade results. We also compare the effect of the accountability index on the proportion of students demonstrating proficiency at the basic skills level or above and the proficient level or above. In Equation (2), the most relevant measure of test score is the 1996 eighth-grade math results, since these directly precede in time the changing ninth-grade retention rates and student survival rates in high school. In checking for possible bias from exclusion, we use an alternative set of gain scores provided by Don McLaughlin (2001) as the dependent variable in one set of alternative estimates and two exclusion adjustments provided to us by the National Center for Educational Statistics (NCES) as control variables in another set of alternative estimates of Equation (2).

Unfortunately, not all states took part in the NAEP in each year. For the 1992 NAEP reading exam, the following states do not have data: Alaska, Idaho, Illinois, Indiana, Kansas, Montana, Nevada, Ohio, Oklahoma, Oregon, South Dakota, Vermont, and Washington. For the 1994 NAEP reading exam, the same states are missing, with the exception of Montana and Washington. For the 1992 NAEP mathematics exam, Alaska, Idaho, Illinois, Kansas, Montana, Nevada, Oregon, South Dakota, Vermont, and Washington are missing for White students, and the same states plus Hawaii, Iowa, Minnesota, New Mexico, Utah, and Wyoming are missing for African American students. Thirteen states do not have both the 2000 math NAEP and an earlier comparison year (1996, 1992, or 1990) for eighth graders: Alaska, Colorado, Delaware, Florida, Iowa, Kansas, Nevada, New Hampshire, New Jersey, Pennsylvania, South Dakota, Washington, and Wisconsin. Of the 37 states with NAEP 2000 scores, all but Illinois, Ohio, and Oklahoma had 1996 scores. For those three states, we interpolated between 1992 and 2000 to get a 1996 score for Illinois, and between 1990 and 2000 to get a 1996 score for Ohio and Oklahoma. The situation was identical for the fourth-grade math NAEP except for Illinois, which had no 1992 score, so was left out of the fourth-grade regression estimates. Of the 37 states, Arkansas, Kentucky, Maine, and Vermont are not in the estimates for Hispanic students, and Hawaii, Idaho, Maine, Minnesota, Montana, New Mexico, North Dakota, Oregon, Utah, Vermont, and Wyoming are not in the estimates for African American students.

For retention rate and survival rate student outcome measures, we use enrollment figures that we gathered from a number of different sources, including state department of education web pages and NCES. Using data on eighth-, ninth-, tenth-, and twelfth-grade enrollment for the years 1987–1988 through 1998–1999, we calculate (1) the ratio of students in ninth grade in year t to the number of students in eighth grade in year $t-1$, (2) the ratio of the number of students in twelfth grade in year t to the number in tenth grade in year $t-2$, and (3) the ratio of the number of students in twelfth grade in year t to the number in eighth grade in year $t-4$. We were unable to obtain sufficient enrollment data for Idaho, North Dakota, and Utah.

For accountability strength, we use the database developed by the Consortium for Policy Research in Education (CPRE), available on the CPRE website (http://www.cpre.org/Publications/Publications_Accountability.htm). From the database, we constructed a scale of accountability levels 0 to 5, with states such as Iowa and Nebraska at 0 and states such as Texas, North Carolina, Alabama, Florida, and Massachusetts at 5. States receiving a zero do not test students statewide or set any statewide standards. States that require testing to state standards in lower grades but have no school sanctions or rewards (weak repercussions) get a 1, those that test at all grades and at the high school level but have no school sanctions or rewards get a 2, those that test at the lower grades and high school and the tests have moderate repercussions for schools get a 3 (or, in some cases, weak or no repercussions for schools but a high school exit exam—"+HS"), and those that test at all levels and the tests have strong repercussions for schools (threat of reconstitution, principal transfer, loss of students) but no high school exit test get a 4. States receiving a 5 have students tested in many different grades, schools strongly sanctioned or rewarded based on student test scores, and a high school minimum competency exit test required for graduation ("+HS"). Most states had some of these elements, but not others. Table 9.1 reports our index, state by state. We also run specification checks using an alternative categorization, which is noted in the table.

THE RESULTS

Descriptions of our variables appear in Table 9.2. We see that average math test scores rose in 1996 to 2000 for all three racial/ethnic groups in both fourth and eighth grades. This was not the case in all states, however (see maximum and minimum score changes). A much lower proportion of African Americans and Hispanics than Whites achieve at the basic skills level or better and at the proficient level or better. In the worst-performing state, Mississippi, only 1% of African Americans score at the proficient level or above. In the states in which African American students perform best, such as New York, about 8 to 10% of African Americans score at the proficient level or above. In the states where Whites perform best, such as Connecti-

Table 9.1. State Accountability Programs (with alternative index in parentheses)

State	Index	Exit Exam in 2000	Grade	Grad. Class	Repercussions
Alabama	4	Yes	10	2001	Strong
Alaska	1	Yes	10	2002	Weak
Arizona	2	Yes	10	2002	Weak
Arkansas	1	No			Weak
California	4 (2)	No	10	2004	Strong
Colorado	1	No			Weak
Connecticut	1	No			Weak
Delaware	1	No	10	2004	Weak
Florida	5	Yes	10	1988	Strong (+HS)
Georgia	3	Yes	11	1995	Weak
Hawaii	1	No			Weak (None)
Idaho	1	No			Weak
Illinois	3.5	No	11	2000	Medium
Indiana	3	Yes	10	1999	Weak
Iowa	0	No			Weak (None)
Kansas	1	No			Weak
Kentucky	4	No			Strong (+HS)
Louisiana	3	Yes	10	1991	Weak
Maine	1	No			Weak (None)
Maryland	4 (5)	No	10,11,12	2001	Strong
Massachusetts	4 (2)	Yes	10	2003	Strong
Michigan	1	No			Weak
Minnesota	2	Yes	10		Weak
Mississippi	3	Yes	11	1994	Weak
Missouri	1	No			Weak
Montana	1	No			Weak
Nebraska	0	No			Weak

Table 9.1. (*continued*)

State	Index	Exit Exam in 2000	Grade	Grad. Class	Repercussions
Nevada	3	Yes	11	1999	Weak
New Hampshire	1	No			Weak (None)
New Jersey	5	Yes	11		Strong (+HS)
New Mexico	4	Yes	10	1990	Strong (+HS)
New York	5 (2)	Yes	10	1998	Strong (+HS)
North Carolina	5	Yes	9	1994	Strong (+HS)
North Dakota	1	No			Weak
Ohio	3	Yes	9		Weak
Oklahoma	1	No			Weak
Oregon	3	Yes	10	1991	Medium (+HS)
Pennsylvania	1	No			Weak
Rhode Island	4 (1)	No			Strong
South Carolina	3	Yes	10	1990	Weak
South Dakota	1	No			Weak
Tennessee	3	Yes	9		Weak
Texas	5	Yes	10		Strong (+HS)
Utah	1	No	10	2007	Weak
Vermont	1	No			Weak
Virginia	1	No			Weak
Washington	1	No	10	2008	Weak
West Virginia	3.5	No			Medium/strong
Wisconsin	1	No	11	2004	Weak
Wyoming	1	No			Weak

Table 9.2. Descriptive Statistics for Analysis Variables

Variable	Sample Size	Mean	Std. Dev.	Min	Max
Accountability Index	50	2.28	1.52	0.00	5.00
Ninth-Grade Enrollment/Eighth-Grade Enrollment 1 Year Earlier					
All 1998–1999	50	1.10	0.07	0.97	1.26
Whites 1998–1999	46	1.07	0.06	0.96	1.32
African Americans 1998–1999	46	1.18	0.16	0.73	1.67
All 1994–1995	50	1.09	0.06	0.97	1.21
Whites 1994–1995	47	1.06	0.03	0.98	1.14
African Americans 1994–1995	47	1.16	0.15	0.58	1.50
Twelfth-Grade Enrollment/Tenth-Grade Enrollment 2 Years Earlier					
All 1998–1999	50	0.84	0.06	0.70	0.98
Whites 1998–1999	47	0.86	0.14	0.66	0.94
African Americans 1998–1999	47	0.74	0.13	0.48	1.39
All 1994–1995	50	0.86	0.07	0.73	1.04
White 1994–1995	47	0.87	0.06	0.74	1.03
African Americans 1994–1995	47	0.77	0.11	0.50	1.11
Twelfth-Grade Enrollment/Eighth-Grade Enrollment 4 Years Earlier					
All 1998–1999	50	0.83	0.08	0.66	1.01
Whites 1998–1999	45	0.84	0.07	0.68	1.02
African Americans 1998–1999	45	0.76	0.16	0.50	1.58
All 1994–1995	50	0.86	0.08	0.69	1.03
All 1996–1997	50	0.84	0.08	0.67	1.01
White 1994–1995	44	0.85	0.05	0.74	1.03
African Americans 1994–1995	43	0.76	0.10	0.56	0.99
State Characteristics					
Population	49	5529	6037	480	33145
Southern State	50	0.24		0.00	1.00
% African American population	49	0.11	0.10	0.004	0.36
% Hispanic population	49	0.07	0.09	0.006	0.41
% African American H.S. Students 1994	47	0.14	0.13	0.004	0.50
% Hispanic H.S. Students 1994	47	0.07	0.10	0.002	0.45
NAEP 1992 Reading	41	61.8	8.69	41.3	75.9
NAEP 1992 Reading Whites	37	70.4	5.50	61.0	80.7
NAEP 1992 Reading African Americans	37	39.9	12.3	25.5	75.0
NAEP 1994 Reading	40	59.1	8.69	40.3	75.2

Table 9.2. (*continued*)

Variable	Sample Size	Mean	Std. Dev.	Min	Max
NAEP 1994 Reading Whites	39	68.5	5.48	58.1	80.0
NAEP 1994 Reading African Americans	39	35.4	9.44	21.1	62.9
NAEP 1996 Fourth-Grade Math	36	62.4	9.47	76	42
NAEP 1996 Fourth-Grade Whites	36	71.9	6.25	86	63
NAEP 1996 Fourth-Grade African Americans	27	30.9	6.63	47	18
NAEP 1996 Fourth-Grade Hispanics	32	42.6	9.87	66	24
NAEP 2000 Fourth-Grade Math	36	66.6	8.96	79	45
NAEP 2000 Fourth-Grade Whites	36	77.0	6.48	89	66
NAEP 2000 Fourth-Grade African Americans	27	38.7	9.04	60	25
NAEP 2000 Fourth-Grade Hispanics	32	48.2	8.77	68	30
NAEP 1996 Eighth-Grade Math	37	60.7	10.55	77	36
NAEP 1996 Eighth-Grade Whites	37	70.5	6.95	80	56
NAEP 1996 Eighth-Grade African Americans	26	27.5	6.13	40	16
NAEP 1996 Eighth-Grade Hispanics	33	37.4	9.41	55	11
NAEP 2000 Eighth-Grade Math	37	65.1	10.02	80	41
NAEP 2000 Eighth-Grade Whites	37	75.2	6.94	86	59
NAEP 2000 Eighth-Grade African Americans	26	33.2	8.21	48	18
NAEP 2000 Eighth-Grade Hispanics	33	43.5	11.50	68	15
NAEP 1996 Eighth-Grade Math Prof.	37	21.4	7.04	34	7
NAEP 1996 Eighth-Grade Whites	37	26.4	6.80	37	12
NAEP 1996 Eighth-Grade African Americans	25	3.8	1.86	8	1
NAEP 1996 Eighth-Grade Hispanics	33	8.2	3.6	19	2
NAEP 2000 Eighth-Grade Math Prof.	37	24.5	7.55	40	8
NAEP 2000 Eighth-Grade Whites	37	30.4	7.27	44	14
NAEP 2000 Eighth-Grade African Americans	26	5.3	2.30	10	1
NAEP 2000 Eighth-Grade Hispanics	33	10.7	5.00	23	1
Gain in Fourth Grade 2000/1996 Basic	36	4.2	3.82	13	−3
Gain in Fourth Grade 2000/1996 White	36	5.1	6.25	13	−2
Gain in Fourth Grade 2000/1996 African Americans	27	7.7	6.60	21	−11
Gain in Fourth Grade 2000/1996 Hispanics	32	5.6	6.32	19	−13
Gain in Eighth Grade 2000/1996 Basic	37	4.4	3.82	14	−2
Gain in Eighth Grade 2000/1996 White	37	4.8	3.62	15	−1
Gain in Eighth Grade 2000/1996 African Americans	26	5.7	6.32	17	−9
Gain in Eighth Grade 2000/1996 Hispanics	33	8.5	6.12	23	−9

cut, more than 40% of White students scored at the proficient level or better on the 2000 test.

We also see that the ratio of ninth graders in 1998–1999 to eighth graders in 1997–1998 averaged approximately 1.10 across the states. With no population growth, this would indicate an approximately 10% retention of students in ninth grade. In 1994–1995 the corresponding rate was 9%. There are large differences between African American and White students. In 1998–1999 the retention ratio averaged 18% for African American students and 7% for White students. The ratio of twelfth-grade enrollment in 1998–1999 to eighth-grade enrollment in 1994–1995 captures students' progression through high school. We see that on average this ratio is 0.83. With no population growth, this would indicate that 83% of eighth graders in 1994–1995 progressed to twelfth grade 4 years later. Again, the numbers are different for African American and White students, 76% and 84%, respectively.

Does Stronger Accountability Improve Test Scores? The results of our estimates suggest a statistically significant relationship between the degree to which states hold schools accountable for student outcomes and their gains in NAEP math scores at the end of the 1990s. We estimated gains in the percentage of students scoring at the basic skills level or better and at the proficient level or better in the 1996–2000 period. We also estimated gains in scale scores for the three racial/ethnic groups as a check on our other estimates. We do not report these results here, but the results using scale scores confirmed the other estimates. We estimated gains for the fourth- and eighth-grade tests by ethnic group across states, correcting in all equations for the initial score on the test in order to check whether gains were related to the initial test score. A negative coefficient of the 1996 score implies declining returns as scores increase.

A potentially serious bias in the NAEP math gains may arise because some students are eligible for exclusion from the test because they are designated as SD or LEP. The proportion of SD plus LEP varies greatly among states. All states have some of these students take the standard NAEP test without accommodation and exclude others. A potential bias in gains arises because the proportion of students designated SD plus LEP increased in most states administering the math NAEP from 1996 to 2000, and in some states the percentage assessed increased, whereas in others it decreased (state-level data for SD and LEP proportions and the proportion assessed and excluded, by year, are available from the National Center for Educational Statistics in Washington, DC). Some analyses have claimed that changing exclusion rates can account for a substantial proportion of NAEP math and reading gains in the late 1990s in states with strong accountability systems (Amrein & Berliner, 2002).

Since our analysis focuses on the relationship between the accountability index and math NAEP gains, it is important to adjust for the possible exclusion bias in the gains. There are several possible ways to do this given available data. Don McLaughlin of the American Institutes for Research estimated an imputed set of fourth- and eighth-grade math NAEP scale scores for 1996 and 2000 by state, assuming that all excluded students took the test without accommodation (McLaughlin, 2001). He was kind enough to make a special calculation for us of scale scores by racial/ethnic group and state. We use his imputed math scores to re-estimate the regression equations for each, compared with those from the adjusted results reported in NAEP publications.

Since McLaughlin's estimates rely on imputed scores, they may over- or undercorrect for changing exclusion rates. We made our own adjustments to the estimate regression equations that include control variables measuring the change in inclusion and assessment rates by state from 1996 to 2000. These rates are unpublished, but were provided to us by NCES. One variable we use as a control is the ratio of the percent of identified SD and LEP students of each racial/ethnic group who took the NAEP math test without accommodations in 2000 and in 1996 in each state. Some states included a higher percentage of identified SD and LEP students in 2000 than in 1996, and others, a lower percentage. If states with a stronger accountability system have had a propensity to exclude a greater proportion of their identified SD/LEP students from the NAEP test from 1996 to 2000, this should reduce the estimated coefficient of accountability in the test score gain equation. However, the change in the percent included does not capture the fact that the percent identified also might have risen substantially between 1996 and 2000. Thus, we estimate the accountability index effect using an alternative control variable: the absolute difference in percent of identified SD plus LEP students assessed between 1996 and 2000.

Results Using Published NAEP Scores. Table 9.3 shows that for the percent scoring at the basic skills level or better, the effect of a two-step move in the accountability index (from, say, 1 to 3) implies a considerable increase in gains in the percentage of those students who score at this level. For White eighth graders, for example, a two-step move means 2.6 percentage points more gain in the proportion scoring at the basic skills level or better. With a mean gain of 4.8 percentage points and a standard deviation of 3.6 in average state proportions scoring at or above the basic skills level, the increase in gain from raising the external pressure on schools by the state appears to be substantial. Figure 9.1 shows how gains of White eighth graders vary from state to state across accountability levels.

Additional gains for other groups from greater emphasis on student out-

Table 9.3. Gain in Percent of Students at Basic Skills Level or Better, NAEP Eighth-Grade Math, 1996–2000, as Function of 1996 Level and Accountability, Across States, by Race/Ethnicity (*t*-values in parentheses)

Independent Variables	White Gain		African American Gain *		Hispanic Gain	
	I	II	I	II	I	II
Accountability Index	1.07 (2.81)	1.32 (2.93)	1.26 (1.92)	0.98 (1.41)	3.49 (3.54)	4.35 (3.97)
1996 Eighth-Grade Math	−0.082 (−1.02)	.0089 (0.10)	0.19 (1.23)	0.41 (1.78)	0.081 (0.53)	0.080 (0.51)
Proportion African American		6.25 (1.02)		7.75 (0.77)		
Proportion Hispanic		−9.67 (−1.87)				−18.74 (−1.67)
South		−0.84 (−0.46)		1.48 (0.56)		2.56
Constant Term	7.85 (1.32)	0.97 (0.15)	−2.62 (−0.61)	−9.22 (−1.32)	−5.91 (−0.81)	−5.56 (−0.73)
R-2	0.200	0.289	0.160	0.148	0.272	0.293
Sample Size	37	37	25	25	33	33

* Nebraska omitted from African American regression because of unusually high negative gain in scores from 1996–2000. Omitting Nebraska lowers size of accountability coefficient and its statistical significance. With the alternative index, the coefficient and *t*-statistic on the index in columns II for Whites, African Americans, and Hispanics are 1.02 (2.12), 1.49 (2.17), and 4.04 (3.99), respectively. With the change in revenues per pupil from 1990 to 1998 included, the coefficient and *t*-statistic on the index in columns II for Whites, African Americans, and Hispanics are 1.43 (3.26), 0.99 (0.18), and 4.36 (3.91), respectively.

Figure 9.1. Accountability Index and NAEP Math Basic Skills Percentage Gain 1996–2000, by State (percentage point change)

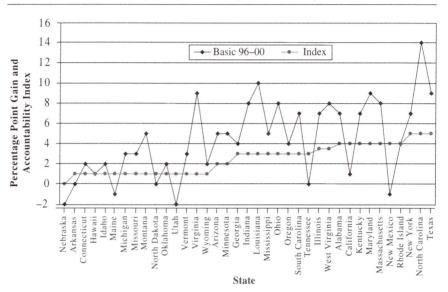

comes and accountability also appear to be substantial. For a two-step increase in the accountability index, the gain in the proportion of Hispanic eighth graders scoring at the basic skills level or better increases between 7 and 8 percentage points, depending on whether we control for the percentage of Hispanic students in the state. The mean of the gains is 6 percentage points, and the standard deviation of gains among states, 8.5 points, so a two-step increase again makes a large difference. For African Americans, the potential gains on the eighth-grade test from increased outcome-based accountability are smaller and not statistically significant. Figures 9.2 and 9.4 show how the gains of African American and Hispanic eighth graders, respectively, vary across states by level of state accountability.

We would expect the impact of stronger accountability on the proportion of White students scoring at the basic skills level or better to be lower on math tests in the lower grades, where the proportion at that level of proficiency was already high in 1996 (72%). As the estimates in Table 9.4 show, this may be the case. The coefficient of the accountability index is not significantly different from 0 in the estimated equation for the proportion of White fourth graders' gains achieving basic skills proficiency. We also would expect that, given the emphasis on basic skills in most state

Figure 9.2. Accountability Index and Gains on NAEP Mathematics Test, 1996–2000, African Americans, by State

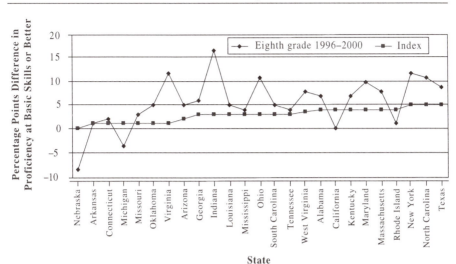

accountability testing, the impact on African American and Hispanic gains in the primary grades could be higher than for Whites. Since African Americans and Hispanics start out at lower levels of basic skills proficiency than Whites, it may be easier to raise their low basic skills in the primary grades. This is only partially borne out by our estimates. The increase in the proportion of Hispanic fourth graders scoring at basic skills proficiency or higher is not significantly related to the strength of state accountability, but the proportion of African American fourth graders is, and the coefficient of the effect size of the accountability index is greater than in the case of African Americans in eighth grade. A two-step gain in accountability implies a 3.4 percentage point increase in the proportion of African American fourth graders scoring at this level. With an average gain of about 7 points and a standard deviation of 6 points, this is a large gain. The gain tends to get smaller for African American students as the initial level of basic skills proficiency was higher (although not statistically significant), suggesting again that the effect may be higher in states with initially low levels of proficiency. Figure 9.3 shows how gains of African American fourth graders vary across states by level of state accountability.

The effect of strong accountability systems at higher skill proficiency levels on the NAEP test might be expected to be less, given the relatively "basic" nature most states used for accountability. Our estimates are not

Table 9.4. Gain in Percent of Students at Basic Skills Level or Better, NAEP Fourth-Grade Math, 1996–2000, as Function of 1996 Level and Accountability, Across States, by Race/Ethnicity (*t*-values in parentheses)

Independent Variables	White Gain		African American Gain *		Hispanic Gain *	
	I	II	I	II	I	II
Accountability Index	0.85 (1.98)	0.52 (1.11)	1.71 (2.25)	1.71 (2.26)	0.64 (0.95)	0.22 (0.31)
1996 Fourth-Grade Math	−0.15 (−1.48)	−0.096 (−0.93)	−0.076 (−0.49)	−0.12 (−0.73)	−0.17 (−1.58)	−0.11 (−1.01)
Percent African American		9.67 (1.30)		−15.55 (−1.37)		
Percent Hispanic		−1.77 (−0.30)				0.26 (0.03)
South		−0.040 (−0.02)		5.18 (1.67)		4.98 (2.20)
Constant Term	13.80 (1.84)	9.23 (1.22)	5.91 (1.14)	8.44 (1.40)	11.71 (2.17)	8.64 (1.63)
R-2	0.115	0.168	0.112	0.144	0.076	0.176
Sample Size	36	36	26	26	31	31

* North Dakota omitted from Hispanic regression because of unusually high negative gain in scores from 1996–2000. Omitting North Dakota lowers size of 1996 math score coefficient and its statistical significance. Nebraska is again omitted from the African American regressions. With the alternative index, the coefficient and *t*-statistic on the index in columns II for Whites, African Americans, and Hispanics are −0.20 (0.37), 1.92 (2.23), and 0.86 (1.12), respectively. With the change in revenues per pupil from 1990 to 1998 included, the coefficient and *t*-statistic on the index in columns II for Whites, African Americans, and Hispanics are 0.85 (1.69), 1.80 (2.40), and 0.25 (3.44), respectively.

Figure 9.3. African American Fourth-Grade NAEP Math Score Gains 2000/1996, by State Accountability Index

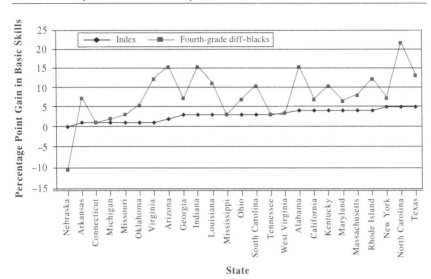

consistent with this hypothesis (Table 9.5). When compared with the estimates in Table 9.3, the coefficients of accountability for each ethnic group are smaller in the equation for the increase in the proportion of students scoring at the higher, proficient level than at the basic skills level or better. But a two-step increase in the accountability index implies a 0.7 standard deviation increase in the percent gain of White students scoring at proficient or better on the test. For African American students, a two-step increase in accountability implies almost doubling the small average 2-point gain across states. However, the gains are larger in states with lower percentages of African American students scoring at the proficient level in 1996. For Hispanic students, the coefficient of accountability is not significantly different from 0.

The inconsistent effect of stronger accountability on Hispanic student performance is in part due to the low gains in two states—California and New Mexico—with relatively strong accountability systems and large Hispanic populations but very low gains on the NAEP math test for all ethnic groups (Figure 9.4). It also may be due to large relative increases in the Hispanic population in some states. Such increases, mainly from new immigration, may have made it difficult to increase Hispanic scores. We tested this hypothesis by including as an independent variable the percentage in-

Table 9.5. Gain in Percent of Students at Proficient Level or Better, NAEP Eighth-Grade Math, 1996–2000, as Function of 1996 Level and Accountability, Across States, by Race/Ethnicity (*t*-values in parentheses)

Independent Variables	White Gain		African American Gain		Hispanic Gain	
	I	II	I	II	I	II
Accountability Index	0.82 (2.41)	1.18 (3.00)	0.64 (2.48)	0.73 (3.28)	0.34 (0.65)	0.51 (0.84)
1996 Eighth-Grade Math	−0.004 (−0.05)	0.073 (0.93)	−0.36 (−1.79)	−0.63 (3.28)	−0.16 (−0.76)	−0.16 (−0.73)
Percent African American		−0.071 (−0.01)		−3.56 (−1.03)		
Percent Hispanic		−11.38 (−2.50)				−0.12 (−0.02)
South		0.61 (−0.37)		−1.50 (−1.61)		
Constant Term	2.07 (0.91)	−0.019 (−0.01)	1.06 (0.92)	3.17 (2.52)	2.97 (1.17)	3.04 (1.14)
R-2	0.100	0.218	0.258	0.448	0.023	0.060
Sample Size	37	37	26	26	33	33

Note: With the alternative index, the coefficient and *t*-statistic on the index in columns II for Whites, African Americans, and Hispanics are 1.15 (2.81), 0.80 (3.28), and 0.29 (0.51), respectively. With the change in revenues per pupil from 1990 to 1998 included the coefficient and *t*-statistic on the index in columns II for Whites, African Americans, and Hispanics are 1.33 (3.44), 0.74 (3.28), and 0.57 (0.95), respectively.

Figure 9.4. Hispanic Eighth-Grade NAEP Math Score Gains, 2000/1996, by Accountability Index

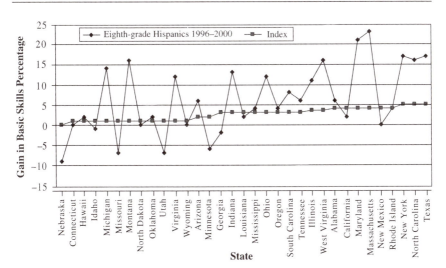

crease in the proportion of Hispanic students in each state between 1996 and 2000. The sign of the coefficient of the population increase variable is negative, suggesting that states with a more rapid rise in Hispanic students will see lower gains in Hispanic scores. But the estimated coefficient is not significantly different from zero. The coefficient of the accountability index is hardly changed by including the student population growth variable. Finally, inconsistency may be due to varying proportions of Hispanic students taking the NAEP test because of language difficulty. We were unable to test that possibility.

Even in the case of eighth-grade basic skills proficiency, where strong accountability is positively associated with higher gains, we observe considerable variation in how well students scored in states with the same level of accountability (Figures 9.1, 9.2, 9.3, and 9.4). This suggests that variables other than accountability also are important in explaining gains.

As a specification check, we run another model including the change in average revenue per pupil from 1990 to 1998. The results are noted at the bottoms of Tables 9.3, 9.4, and 9.5. Inclusion of the revenue measure did not qualitatively change the estimates.

Adjusting Results for Differential Exclusion and Inclusion Rates. As described above, we re-estimated Equation (2) using the McLaughlin imputed scale score gains for each racial/ethnic group. We also re-estimated Equation (2) using two different control variables constructed from the proportions of each racial/ethnic group's identified SD/LEP students included in the NAEP. These two separate estimates were made for three different sets of test score gains: the proportion of students scoring at the basic skills level or higher, the proportion scoring at proficient or higher, and the scale score. The results comparing the estimated coefficients of the accountability index using "unadjusted" test scores, McLaughlin's imputed scores, and adjustments for changing inclusion rates are shown in Table 9.6.

The results suggest that the positive relationship between test score gains and the strength of a state's accountability system hold up across racial/ethnic groups at eighth grade even when adjusted for changing inclusion rates. The relationship of accountability to gains is generally not statistically significant for fourth-grade students.

High School Progression Rates and Ninth-Grade Retention. As might be expected, tenth- to twelfth-grade progression rates are significantly related to retention rates. Table 9.7 shows that the progression rate in 1998–1999 for both African American and White students is negatively related to ninth-grade retention rate in 1995–1996 even when NAEP 1996 eighth-grade math score (percent scoring at or above basic skills) is accounted for. For every percentage point higher of ninth-grade retention, high school survival from tenth to twelfth grade falls 0.4 percentage point for White students and 1.0 percentage points for African American students.

White progression rates in high school are also significantly related to math test score in eighth grade, even when variation in retention rates is accounted for. If 10% more White students in a state are proficient at the basic level or higher on the NAEP test, the White progression rate increases by about 3%, from 86% to 89%. This improvement would occur, in theory, even if the ninth-grade retention rate remained at the average of 6%. Unlike for Whites, the state NAEP score for African American students in 1996 is not related to African American student survival rate and has little effect on the coefficient of retention rate. One explanation is that the percent of African Americans scoring at or above basic skills on the NAEP math test is so low (40% is a high state average for African Americans) that variation at this low level probably bears little relation to survival rate.

Does stronger accountability raise retention rates and/or improve survival rates in high school? We do not find a strong relationship between the accountability system in a state in the late 1990s and changes in the retention rate, although there is a weak indication that strong accountability may

Table 9.6. Coefficients of State Accountability Index from Regression Estimates Using Unadjusted NAEP Test Score Gains, 1996–2000, and Various Adjustments for Students Excluded from Taking the NAEP Test

Group/Grade and Dependent Variable	Coefficient of Accountability Index Using Unadjusted Gains on NAEP	Coefficient Using McLaughlin Scale Scores as Dependent Variable	Coefficient Using Growth in Inclusion as Control Variable	Adjusted Coefficient Using Change in % Assessed as Control
Eighth-Grade Basic Skills				
Whites	1.26**	NA	1.13**	1.31***
African Americans	0.98	NA	1.88**	1.90***
Hispanics	4.35***	NA	3.32***	3.36***
Eighth-Grade Proficient				
Whites	1.18***	NA	1.00**	1.19***
African Americans	0.73***	NA	0.78***	0.65***
Hispanics	0.51	NA	0.94*	0.81
Eighth-Grade Scale Score				
Whites	1.23***	1.08***	0.99**	1.14***
African Americans	1.46***	1.33	1.84***	1.87***
Hispanics	3.08***	1.97*	1.99*	1.91*
Fourth-Grade Basic Skills				
Whites	0.52	NA	0.45	0.52
African Americans	1.71	NA	2.41***	2.39***
Hispanics	0.22	NA	0.34	0.55
Fourth-Grade Scale Scores				
Whites	0.24	0.35	0.14	0.16
African Americans	0.88*	0.74	0.89*	0.82
Hispanics	0.51	0.15	0.11	0.4

Note: Coefficient of accountability index reported for regression estimates that include percent African American and/or Hispanic, score on 1996 NAEP math test, and South.

NA: not applicable.

Table 9.7. Tenth- to Twelfth-Grade Survival Rate, 1998–1999, Related to Ninth-Grade Retention and Eighth-Grade Math Score, Across States, by Race (*t*-ratios in parentheses)

Independent Variables	White Survival Rate	African American Survival Rate
Ninth-/Eighth-Grade Retention, 1995–1996	−0.40 (−2.35)	−1.00 (−3.05)
Percent African American and Hispanic	0.005 (0.06)	0.30 (1.79)
Eighth-Grade 1996 NAEP Math	3.35E-3 (2.58)	0.0010 (0.38)
Southern	−0.01 (−0.47)	0.02 (0.37)
Population	4.93E-07 (0.32)	−2.01E-06 (−0.80)
Constant	1.06 (4.99)	1.73 (4.89)
R-2	0.45	0.34
Sample Size	38	29

raise the retention of African American students. Table 9.8 gives these results. First consider the results for White students. Accountability is correlated with White student retention in the univariate model, but this relationship goes away once prior retention is included. Thus, strong accountability systems were implemented in states with high retention rates, but the accountability did not increase these rates. For African American students, we see a similar pattern, with slightly higher point estimates in the final model. Although the effect is not statistically significantly different from zero, states with one unit stronger accountability retained approximately 1% more African American students. This is not a big effect, especially considering that the standard deviation in retention rates across the states is 16%.

We also do not find evidence that stronger accountability has negatively impacted progression rates either from tenth to twelfth or eighth to twelfth grade. Table 9.9 shows that, on average, states with one unit stronger accountability systems had approximately one-half of 1% higher progression rates from tenth to twelfth grade. This result is, again, not statistically different from zero but does characterize the states. Similarly, Table 9.10 shows

Table 9.8. Ninth-Grade Retention, 1998–1999, as Function of Retention in 1995–1996 and Accountability, Across States, by Race (*t*-values in parentheses)

Independent Variables	White Retention Rate			African American Retention Rate		
	I	II	III	I	II	III
Accountability Index	0.010 (1.82)	0.003 (0.77)	0.005 (0.76)	0.030 (1.82)	0.01 (0.86)	0.013 (1.44)
Prior Retention Rate		1.22 (7.25)	1.24 (5.71)		0.65 (5.24)	0.85 (7.17)
Percent African American and Hispanic			−0.10 (−1.33)			(−2.28)
NAEP 1996 Eighth-Grade Math			1.84E-5 (0.01)			3.56E-3 (1.61)
South			0.02 (0.81)			0.05 (1.24)
Population			7.79E-7 (0.53)			2.34E-6 (1.09)
Constant	1.05 (70.78)	−0.23 (−1.28)	−0.24 (−0.98)	1.12 (25.40)	0.41 (2.89)	0.14 (0.89)
R-2	0.07	0.59	0.59	0.07	0.44	0.76
Sample Size	47	45	36	47	45	28

that, on average, states with one unit stronger accountability systems had approximately one-half of 1% higher progression rates from eighth to twelfth grade. In theory, eighth- to twelfth-grade progression is as important as in our prior two analyses, but in fact our data limit us so that we can look only at changes from 1996–1997 to 1998–1999.

CONCLUSIONS

Our results indicate a positive and significant relationship between the strength of states' accountability systems and their math achievement gains

Table 9.9. Tenth- to Twelfth-Grade Survival, 1998–1999, as Function of Survival in 1994–1995 and Accountability, Across States, by Race (*t*-values in parentheses)

Independent Variables	White Survival Rate		African American Survival Rate	
	I	II	I	II
Accountability Index	0.0060 (1.18)	0.0048 (0.71)	0.0066 (0.50)	0.0083 (1.32)
Prior Survival Rate	0.77 (5.44)	0.67 (2.65)	0.48 (2.66)	0.83 (7.65)
Percent African American and Hispanic		0.006 (0.07)		−0.12 (−1.25)
NAEP 1996 Eighth-Grade Math		1.48E3 (0.92)		−1.30E-3 (−0.78)
South		0.004 (0.17)		−0.008 (−0.33)
Population		4.43E-7 (0.26)		1.46E-6 (0.95)
Constant	0.17 (1.31)	0.15 (0.76)	0.36 (2.38)	0.17 (1.97)
R-2	0.45	0.45	0.15	0.80
Sample Size	45	37	45	26

at the eighth-grade level. Students in states with stronger accountability systems have had greater gains on the NAEP mathematics test at the basic skills level in the late 1990s. Surprisingly, White and African American students' achievement at higher levels of math skills also increases significantly more in states with stronger state accountability, suggesting that focusing on higher standards and how well schools do on tests also may improve higher-level skills. Since stronger accountability seems to target basic skills and low-income students, another surprise is that fourth-grade test gains generally are not significantly higher in states with stronger accountability. African American students may have had higher fourth-grade gains in such states,

Table 9.10. Eighth- to Twelfth-Grade Survival, 1998–1999, as Function of Survival in 1996–1997 and Accountability, Across States, by Race (*t*-values in parentheses)

Independent Variables	White Survival Rate			African American Survival Rate		
	I	II	III	I	II	III
Accountability Index	–0.019 (–2.76)	0.003 (0.39)	0.00071 (0.11)	–0.015 (–0.89)	–0.010 (–0.47)	0.018 (0.74)
Prior Survival Rate		0.75 (5.52)	0.77 (4.68)		0.17 (0.40)	0.91 (2.40)
Percent African American and Hispanic			–0.038 (–0.53)			–0.34 (–1.07)
NAEP 1996 Eighth Grade Math			1.19E-3 (0.89)			–4.59E-3 (–1.06)
South			0.013 (0.60)			–0.011 (–0.13)
Population			1.15E-6 (0.82)			8.46E-7 (0.16)
Constant	0.89 (47.13)	0.19 (1.54)	0.10 (0.73)	0.80 (17.57)	0.64 (1.60)	0.27 (0.78)
R-2	0.15	0.51	0.75	0.02	0.35	0.27
Sample Size	45	45	35	45	45	32

but this relationship is much less clear than in eighth grade. Furthermore, despite positive effects on math achievement of stronger accountability, we observe considerable variation among states with similarly weak or strong accountability systems.

The longer-term effects of stronger accountability are less clear. We find little effect of stronger accountability in lowering or raising the retention rate of students in the first year of high school, or decreasing or increasing the progression through high school. Why might we find positive test score effects but not positive attainment effects? There are a number of possible explanations. First, while the NAEP results suggest that students in states with strong accountability programs are learning more than simply how to score well on their own state tests, these programs may be improving test-taking skills but not changing factors that influence educational attainment and other outcomes of significance. An alternative explanation is that despite the positive effects of high-stakes accountability on math test scores, it simply may be too early to assess the long-term implications of this relatively new policy initiative on more important attainment outcomes. We may see attainment effects as the students who have spent more of their education under accountability systems move through high school. A third possibility is that outcomes for younger children are more easily influenced than those for high school students. Even though the current fourth- and eighth-grade students are performing better on the NAEP, other factors may affect them in high school and reverse the impact of accountability even on test performance. Our finding that states with stronger accountability systems have higher math gains on the eighth-grade NAEP may mean that students in those states will be more likely to do well in their ninth-grade courses and more likely to graduate and to reap the high rewards of a 4-year college education. On average, states with higher math scores do have lower ninth-grade retention rates, but this relationship is much weaker for African American students. African American students' average achievement may be sufficiently low in eighth grade that marginal increases in performance are not enough to improve high school course pass rates significantly, especially if standards for passing are being raised.

A final possible explanation is that higher scores even on the NAEP math test may not measure "real" learning—the kind of learning (or desire to learn) that converts into better grades in math, English, and social studies courses in high school and enables students to complete high school with their cohort and makes them successful in entering college.

ACKNOWLEDGMENTS

Funding for this research was provided by the Office of Education Research and Improvement (OERI), U.S. Department of Education, under a grant to the Consortium for Policy Research in Education (CPRE). The authors would like to thank Paula Razquin and Tiffany Smith for their invaluable help in developing the enrollment data used in the chapter. We also would like to thank Susan Fuhrman and Margaret Goertz for their helpful comments. The analysis of the data and interpretations expressed in this chapter are wholly those of the authors and should not be attributed either to OERI or CPRE.

REFERENCES

Amrein, A., & Berliner, D. (2002). High-stakes testing, uncertainty, and student learning. *Education Policy Analysis Archives, 10*(18). Retrieved from http://epaa. asu.edu/epaa/v10n18

Carnoy, M., Loeb, S., & Smith, T. (2001). *Do higher state test scores in Texas make for better high school outcomes?* (CPRE Research Report No. RR-047). Philadelphia: Consortium for Policy Research in Education, University of Pennsylvania.

Cohen, D. K., & Ball, D. L. (1999). *Instruction, capacity, and improvement* (CPRE Research Report No. RR-043). Philadelphia: Consortium for Policy Research in Education, University of Pennsylvania.

Darling-Hammond, L. (1997). The quality of teachers matters most. *The Journal of Staff Development, 18*(1).

Elmore, R. F. (1995). Teaching, learning, and school organization: Principles of practice and the regularities of schooling. *Educational Administration Quarterly, 31*(3).

Elmore, R. F., Abelmann, C. A., & Fuhrman, S. H. (1996). The new accountability in state education reform: From process to performance. In H. Ladd (Ed.), *Holding schools accountable: Performance-based reform in education* (pp. 65–98). Washington, DC: Brookings Institution.

Grissmer, D., & Flanagan, A. (1998). *Exploring rapid achievement gains in North Carolina and Texas*. Washington, DC: National Education Goals Panel.

Haney, W. (2000). *Report for testimony in G.I. Forum v. Texas Education Agency*. Boston College, School of Education, Boston, MA.

Klein, S. P., Hamilton, L. S., McCaffrey, D. F., & Stecher, B. M. (2000). *What do test scores in Texas tell us?* Santa Monica, CA: RAND.

McLaughlin, D. (2001). *Exclusions and accommodations affect state NAEP gain statistics: Mathematics, 1996 to 2000*. Washington, DC: American Institutes for Research.

O'Day, J. A., & Smith, M. S. (1993). School reform and equal opportunity: An introduction to the education symposium. *Stanford Law and Policy Review, 4*.

Rumberger, R. (1995). Dropping out of middle school: A multi-level analysis of students and schools. *American Educational Research Journal, 32*(3), 583–625.

Smith, M. S., O'Day, J. A., & Cohen, D. K. (1990). National curriculum, American style: What might it look like? *American Educator, 14*(4), 10–17, 40–47.

Talbert, J. E., McLaughlin, M., & Rowan, B. (1993). Understanding context effects on secondary school teaching. *Teachers College Record, 95*(1), 45–68.

Chapter 10

High-Stakes Testing in a Changing Environment: Disparate Impact, Opportunity to Learn, and Current Legal Protections

Jay P. Heubert

This chapter focuses on "high-stakes" tests, defined here as tests that states and school districts use in deciding whether individual students will receive high school diplomas or be promoted to the next grade. As most educators and policy makers know, large-scale assessment, including testing for high-stakes purposes, has changed in important ways since the "minimum competency test" (MCT) programs of the 1970s and 1980s; most tests embody much higher standards today, more low-achievers are assessed and there has been growth in graduation testing and especially promotion testing. Less well known to educators, federal law has changed recently in ways that weaken important civil-rights protections, even in situations where minority students, students with disabilities, and English-language learners (ELLs) fail high-stakes tests at rates far higher than in the 1970s and 1980s. Also, legal standards developed in older cases involving MCTs, although useful, do not take into account the current standards movement, which, in seeking to educate *all* students to *high* standards, places heavy new demands on assessments, schools, and students. The results are: (1) a changed legal climate in which to evaluate current graduation tests and promotion tests, and (2) a more complex educational context that educators and researchers may need to help courts understand, and that may call for refinement in the standards that courts developed decades ago in MCT cases.

The sections below (1) describe the current nature and scope of graduation and promotion testing in the United States; (2) examine empirical evidence of the current disparate effects of such testing on minority students, students with disabilities, and ELLs; (3) consider varied evidence now available about whether states, school districts, and schools are teaching all students the kinds of knowledge and skills they need to pass high-stakes tests; and (4) examine the current status of federal law concerning high-stakes testing, pointing out changes in the law, limitations in the law's current treatment of high-stakes tests, and shortcomings in existing mechanisms for enforcing broadly accepted norms of appropriate test use.

THE NATURE AND EXTENT OF HIGH-STAKES TESTING IN THE UNITED STATES

THE EXTENT OF GRADUATION TESTING

As part of the "back to the basics" movement in the 1970s and early 1980s, some 17 states adopted MCTs, which students had to pass to receive standard high school diplomas, even if they had completed satisfactorily all other requirements for graduation.

In the past few years, the number of states with graduation tests has remained fairly constant at about 18. This number is expected to rise in coming years.

Equally important is the changing *nature* of large-scale assessments. While earlier exit tests focused on *minimum* competencies, more than two-thirds of the current tests embody standards at the tenth-grade level or higher (American Federation of Teachers [AFT], 2001), and an increasing number reflect "world-class" standards such as those embodied in the National Assessment of Educational Progress (NAEP), a highly regarded assessment administered nationally to representative samples of students. This trend reflects the emphasis, in the standards movement and in state and federal laws, on helping all students reach *high* standards of achievement.

There is little debate over the desirability of teaching students high-level knowledge and skills; higher expectations and improved instruction lead to improved achievement (Elmore, 2000; Individuals with Disabilities Education Act [IDEA], 1997). At the same time, where standards are high, the gaps in teaching and learning that must be closed are greater than where standards reflect only basic skills. The gaps are greatest in schools where instruction is weak, resources are inadequate, and students start out at low achievement levels.

As discussed below, student failure rates on newer, more demanding exit tests are much higher, more persistent, and more persistently disparate for different groups than on MCTs, when failure rates and group disparities typically declined quickly to low levels. Even after initial test implementation, there are graduation tests that some groups fail at rates of 60 to 90%.

Persistently high and disparate failure rates could slow the growth in graduation testing. Two states have backed away from exit exam requirements and at least seven others have postponed them (see Fuhrman, Goertz, & Duffy, this volume). New York has delayed application of its exit test requirements to students with disabilities, and other states are considering similar measures.

Declining state revenues also could slow such growth. The budget situation also may explain the apparent decline in the number of states providing special funding to help low-achieving students meet state test standards (AFT, 2001), even as more states adopt demanding exit test requirements.

Two other developments have affected the scope of high-stakes testing: the rapid growth of promotion testing and the inclusion of students with disabilities and ELLs in large-scale assessments, some of them high-stakes tests.

THE EXTENT OF PROMOTION TESTING

Promotion testing has grown very rapidly in response to concerns about social promotion. In 2001, 17 states required or planned to require students to pass standardized tests as a condition of grade-to-grade promotion, compared with six in 1999. Thirteen states administer promotion tests at both the elementary and middle school levels or plan to do so (AFT, 2001). In addition, many urban school districts have adopted promotion test policies even where their states have not. Thus, many of the nation's minority students and immigrant students—and increasing numbers of all students— must pass promotion tests.

STUDENTS WITH DISABILITIES, ELLS, AND HIGH-STAKES TESTING

Since 1994, federal laws have required states and school districts to include students with disabilities and ELLs in their large-scale assessments, to report disaggregated scores for these and other groups, and to give all students access to high-quality instruction (Improving America's Schools Act [IASA],

1994; IDEA, 1997). Many such students had previously been exempted from testing (see Thurlow, this volume).

This chapter deals less with system accountability than with tests that have high-stakes consequences for individual students, and on this question federal laws are silent. Thus, federal law requires *system* accountability but leaves states and school districts to decide whether students with disabilities or ELLs who fail such tests will be subject to individual high-stakes consequences such as retention or denial of a standard diploma (Heubert, 2002).

This decision is a complex one, and states have approached it differently. Some authorize Individual Education Plan (IEP) teams to decide individually whether a student with disabilities who fails a promotion test will be promoted anyway. In other states, promotion test requirements apply fully to students with disabilities. States differ in similar ways on graduation testing.

In some states, students who fail state exit tests are eligible for alternative diplomas or certificates. Some, such as IEP diplomas, are available only to students with disabilities, while others, such as certificates of completion or attendance, may also be available to other students. Unfortunately, there is little research on the value of such certificates and alternative, nonstandard diplomas in terms of a student's future opportunities for education or employment. The only alternative certificate on which extensive research exists is the general equivalency diploma (GED), and evidence suggests that GED holders are more like high school dropouts in terms of future educational and employment opportunities than they are like individuals with standard diplomas. Students with disabilities who do not receive standard diplomas have a right to special education and related services until the age of 21 or 22. Policy makers therefore should proceed cautiously with alternatives to standard diplomas (Heubert, 2002).

FROM MINIMUM COMPETENCIES TO WORLD-CLASS STANDARDS: PASS RATES, DISPARATE IMPACT, AND OTHER EFFECTS OF HIGH-STAKES TESTING

A central objective of standards-based education reform is "to improve learning for students who have done poorly in the past," and to "reduce inequality in educational achievement" by helping *all* students reach high standards (see Baker & Linn, this volume). Indeed, many believe that "current versions of standards-based reforms will have their greatest impact on children at the bottom of the achievement distribution" (Murnane & Levy, 2001, p. 401).

Some believe that standards-based reform will *benefit* low-achieving students especially; as attorney William Taylor (2000) writes, "When schools and districts are held accountable for the achievement of all students, the means are at hand to force them to improve the quality of schooling provided for previously neglected students" (p. 56). Taylor speaks here of *system* accountability. There is broad agreement both that (1) accountability for improved educational achievement should be widely shared (Heubert & Hauser, 1999), and (2) accountability for improved educational achievement should be based on *school* performance (Elmore & Rothman, 1999; No Child Left Behind Act [NCLB], 2002).

Although "accountability for adults is only in its infancy" (see Fuhrman, Goertz, & Duffy, this chapter), accountability is expanding for individual students, who are increasingly subject to the serious and well-documented harms associated with being retained in grade or denied standard high school diplomas. There are concerns that low-achieving students—including many minority students, students with disabilities, and ELLs—may be failing increasingly demanding high-stakes tests because their schools do not yet expose them to the knowledge and skills that students need to pass the tests (see Elmore, this volume).

What is known, then, about the pass rates and group disparities on high-stakes tests? This section compares empirical evidence for early MCTs and for current tests that embody higher standards.

STATE PASS RATES AND DISPARATE IMPACT

Even on basic skills tests, minority students, students with disabilities, and ELLs typically fail at higher rates than other students, especially at first. For example, 20% of African American students, compared with 2% of White students, initially failed Florida's MCT (*Debra P.* v. *Turlington* [*Debra P.*], 1981). And while most students with disabilities and ELLs were exempted from early exit tests, those who were tested failed at higher rates than other students.

For a variety of reasons, failure rates typically decline among all groups in the years after a new graduation test is introduced (Linn, 2000). This was true of early MCTs; within a few years, failure rates declined substantially for all groups (Jacob, 2001).

This pattern—initial high failure rates that decline over time—apparently holds true for graduation tests adopted more recently, but with important qualifications. First, where high-stakes tests embody demanding standards, initial failure rates are much higher than for earlier tests. Second, group disparities on high-standards tests are typically quite large—well beyond the requirements for showing "disparate impact" under federal law, under which a test has adverse impact when a statistical analysis shows that one group's pass rate is significantly lower than another's (Office for Civil Rights [OCR], 2000), or when one group's pass rate is less than four-fifths of another's (*G.I. Forum* v. *Texas Education Agency* [*G.I. Forum*], 2000). Third, both failure rates and group disparities on high-standards tests typically decline more slowly. The following discussion illustrates how failure rates and group differences can change as tests become more demanding.

Texas's graduation test, the Texas Assessment of Academic Skills (TAAS), is set at the seventh- or eighth-grade level, higher than earlier MCTs but lower than current standards in most states. Texas reports that pass rates of African Americans and Hispanics roughly doubled between 1994 and 1998, and that the gap in failure rates between Whites, African Americans, and Hispanics narrowed considerably during that time—conclusions that scholars have since questioned (Klein, Hamilton, McCaffrey, & Stecher, 2000; Linn, 2001). Texas data for 1998 nonetheless show continuing disparities: cumulative failure rates of 17.6% for African American students, 17.4% for Hispanic students, and 6.7% for White students (Natriello & Pallas, 2001). Thus, even on fairly low-level exit tests, failure rates for African Americans and Hispanics remain higher in Texas than was true for early basic skills exit tests, and a court found that TAAS has an adverse impact (*G.I. Forum*, 2000). Moreover, these statistics substantially understate minority failure rates and group discrepancies since they do not account for students who were not tested because they had dropped out, been retained in grade, or been excluded improperly from the test-taking population—all categories in which minority students, students with disabilities, and ELLs are disproportionately represented (Natriello & Pallas, 2001).

California's new English and mathematics exit tests, first administered in spring 2001, reflect ninth-grade standards (see Fuhrman, Goertz, & Duffy, this volume). Initial failure rates were far higher than those of the early basic skills tests: Only 42.2% of all test takers passed both tests (Wise et al., 2002, Table 5.1, p. 80). Among African Americans and Hispanics, 22.8% passed compared with 61.4% of Whites. Students with disabilities and ELLs passed both tests at far lower rates: 10.3% and 11.9%, respectively (Wise et al., 2002, p. 81). Students will have additional opportunities to pass before graduation requirements take effect, but California has already been advised to consider alternative provisions for students with disabilities and ELLs (Heubert, 2002; Wise et al., 2002).

Failure rates are typically highest on exit exams that embody "world-class" standards such as those of NAEP assessments. About 38% of *all* students would fail tests that reflected such "world-class" standards, and failure rates would be about twice as high for minority students (Linn, 2000). Careful multistate studies show students with disabilities failing various state tests at rates 30–40 percentage points higher than for other students (Thurlow, Nelson, Teelucksingh, & Ysseldyke, 2000; Ysseldyke et al., 1998).

These predictions generally are borne out in several states with exit exams reflecting high standards. Alaska first administered its three present tests in 2000. In 2001, tenth graders had high and disproportionate failure rates: on one test, 46.5% for White students, 79.9% for African American students, 70% for Hispanic students, 91.1% for students with disabilities, and 84.1% for ELLs (Alaska Department of Education, 2001). The proportions of students passing all three graduation tests, while not available online, is presumably much lower than the proportions passing any one test. Alaska has postponed the effective date of its exit exam.

In Massachusetts, where current state graduation tests were first administered in 1999, the proportions of tenth graders passing both tests rose considerably between 2000 and spring 2001. For African Americans, Hispanics, and students with disabilities, the proportions passing both tests more than doubled. At the same time, 63% of African Americans, 71% of Hispanics, 71% of students with disabilities, and 93% of ELLs had not passed both tests, as they must to graduate in 2003. Group differences among tenth graders—by race and ethnicity, by disability, and by language proficiency—actually *increased* between spring 2000 and spring 2001: the African American–White gap by 3 percentage points; the Hispanic–White gap by 7 percentage points; the gap between students with and without disabilities by 3 percentage points; and the gap between ELLs and all students by 15 percentage points (Massachusetts Department of Education, 2001). Data for *eleventh*-grade members of the class of 2003 show improved pass rates for some groups but continuing high group disparities. The percentages of *eleventh*-grade members of the class of 2003 who had *not* passed both parts of the Massachusetts Comprehensive Assessment System were as follows: 84% of ELLs, 55% of students with disabilities, 17% of nondisabled students, 52% of African Americans, 59% of Hispanics, 25% of Asians, and 18% of Whites (Massachusetts Department of Education, 2002, p. 2). Moreover, pass rates do not account for students who dropped out or were retained and were therefore not tested with their original cohorts.

New York received national publicity when it reported that nearly twice as many students with disabilities passed the state's new Regents English exam in 1998–1999 as had taken the exam 2 years earlier (Keller, 2000). This information is factually correct, but the state's pass rate data suggest less dramatic improvement. Between 1997–1998 and 1999–2000, the percentages of twelfth-grade students with disabilities who passed New York's Regents English exam increased from 5.1% to 8% (New York Department of Education, 2000, 2001). In other words, the percentages of *twelfth graders* who had *not* passed the Regents exam declined from 94.9% to 92% over 2 years—not including dropouts, students previously retained, or students absent on test day. Koretz and Hamilton (2001) estimate that for a Regents exam administration they studied, only about half the students with disabilities were present.

These data, while limited, suggest that where high-stakes tests embody higher content and performance standards, (1) initial failure rates are higher than for earlier tests, (2) group disparities are typically quite high and legally "disparate," and (3) both failure rates and group disparities typically decline more slowly than for earlier MCTs.

EVALUATING STATE PASS RATE DATA

State data *understate* low achievement and group disparities, for two reasons. First, NAEP data, which researchers consider more reliable than state test reports, consistently show much less gain in student performance than do state test results. This was true during the 1980s—when most states reported sharply increased student achievement even as aggregate NAEP data showed little or no gain—and it remains true today.

As many states report higher pass rates on more demanding graduation tests, national NAEP results for 2000 show that the math achievement of twelfth graders has *declined* since 1996, with significantly more students in the "below basic" category and significantly fewer students demonstrating "basic mastery" ("NAEP Achievement," 2001). While NAEP scores have improved for fourth- and eighth-grade students, nationally and especially in some states, twelfth-grade students are more likely to be affected by state graduation test policies.

A study of the Texas achievement gap (Klein et al., 2000) is noteworthy. A court there placed heavy emphasis on state data showing that the achievement gap between White students, African American students, and Hispanic students had closed dramatically between 1994 and 1998 (*G.I. Forum*, 2000). Using NAEP data, however, Klein and colleagues (2000) showed that the achievement gap between White students and other groups in Texas actually had *increased* slightly during this period. For Robert Linn (2001), this evidence "raises serious questions about the trustworthiness of the TAAS result for making inferences about improvements in achievement in Texas or about the relative size of the gains for different segments of the student population" (p. 28).

National NAEP math results for 2000 also suggest a widening *racial* achievement gap among 13- and 17-year-olds (National Center for Education Statistics, 2001). The racial gap is widening most at higher performance levels (Lee, 2002), an obvious concern as more states' tests emphasize high-level skills. NAEP does not yet include enough students with disabilities (or ELLs) in its samples to provide meaningful state-level performance scores for these groups, but future NAEP results should help assess state data suggesting improvements for these groups.

Second, as discussed earlier, the meaning of state pass rate data depends on what proportion of all students took the test. Apparently good news—that 100% of eleventh graders passed a graduation test, for example—means something quite different if three-fourths of all students dropped out before eleventh grade, or if many students with disabilities or ELLs did not take the test. Since the standards movement is concerned with *all* students, an assessment of the disproportionate impact of high-stakes testing should consider the many individuals who do not take such tests with other students their age.

As noted earlier, state test data rarely include information on dropouts, students previously retained in grade, students improperly exempted or excluded from testing, or students absent on test days. Even NAEP results do not account for these students. At the grade levels where states administer exit tests, however, these students often represent a substantial portion of the cohort. If these students were included in the denominator when states calculated pass rates, those rates would be much lower, especially for minority students, students with disabilities, and ELLs.

A closely related question is whether exit testing or promotion testing *causes* increased dropout rates or retention in grade.

The effects of graduation testing are debated. Walt Haney argues that the Texas graduation test does increase retention and dropout rates, especially for African Americans and Hispanics, while Martin Carnoy and colleagues claim that high retention and dropout rates for these groups are not due to TAAS (Murnane & Levy, 2001). A 2001 California survey indicates that 80% of principals and 61% of teachers in the state *believe* that graduation tests there will have "a strongly negative or negative impact on student dropout rates," and that 55% of principals and 32% of teachers think the tests will have "a strongly negative or negative impact on student retention rates" (Wise et al., 2002, p. 45). The most carefully designed *national* longitudinal study of high school students to date (Jacob, 2001)—students who were eighth graders in 1988 and seniors in 1992—finds no general relationship between basic skills graduation tests and dropout rates, but concludes that students in the lowest quintile are "25% more likely to drop out of high school than comparable peers in non-test states" (p. 116).

There is less debate about failing *promotion* tests. Students retained in elementary or secondary school are much more likely to drop out later, and effects are even greater for students retained more than once (Heubert &

Hauser, 1999). Retention is the single strongest predictor of who will drop out. Thus, unless schools rely on early intervention rather than retention to improve achievement, the proliferation of promotion testing is likely to increase, perhaps significantly, the numbers of minority students, students with disabilities, and ELLs who suffer the serious economic, educational, and other harms associated with dropping out (Heubert & Hauser, 1999). It would be unfortunate—and hardly evidence of success—if states, school districts, or schools achieved high graduation test pass rates because large numbers of low achievers had already left school and were no longer among the test takers.

EVIDENCE THAT STUDENTS ARE BEING TAUGHT THE REQUISITE KNOWLEDGE AND SKILLS

The standards movement rests on the premise that virtually all students can reach high levels of achievement if they receive high-quality curriculum and instruction. This premise rests, in turn, on dramatic recent research findings in such areas as brain development, early childhood education, and effective pedagogy. In three federal statutes (IASA, 1994; IDEA, 1997; NCLB, 2002), Congress has accepted this premise and the research supporting it.

Standards on the appropriate use of high-stakes tests are consistent with the standards movement's central premise. Under applicable legal standards and psychometric norms, states may administer tests that all students must pass as a condition of receiving standard high school diplomas—*if* states and schools first give students an adequate opportunity to acquire the knowledge and skills that such tests measure. Courts have ruled for 2 decades that graduation tests must be a fair measure of what students have been taught (*Debra P.*, 1981; *G.I. Forum*, 2000). The measurement profession, the National Research Council, and the American Educational Research Association all say that results of large-scale tests may be used in making individual promotion or graduation decisions only *after* students have had an adequate opportunity to acquire the knowledge and skills that such tests measure. These standards apply to all students, including ELLs and students with disabilities. This "prior opportunity to learn" requirement does not apply to the use of student test information to improve *schools*.

It is far harder today than in the MCT days to ensure that all students have had a meaningful opportunity to learn the knowledge and skills that tests measure. Standards have gotten much higher and they now apply to many more low-achieving students, who start out behind and often must also overcome barriers related to disability, English proficiency, or poverty.

Moreover, the school districts and schools that serve large numbers of needy students often must operate with less money and fewer certified teachers than other school districts and schools.

CRITERIA BY WHICH TO EVALUATE "OPPORTUNITY TO LEARN"

There are different types of evidence by which to determine whether students are being taught the knowledge and skills that tests measure.

Perhaps the most straightforward approach is to examine actual indicators of student achievement, such as test scores and grades. As Lauress Wise and colleagues (2002) suggest in evaluating California test results, "*the best evidence that a school system is providing its students adequate opportunity to learn the required material is whether most students do, in fact, learn the material*" (p. 93, emphasis in original). And even if "most students" are learning well, there may be *groups* of students for whom achievement is low and who may not have received an adequate opportunity to learn. Indeed, what is adequate opportunity to learn for some students may be inadequate for others; that is why we need Title I, IDEA, and programs for ELLs.

A second broad approach, which federal law employs, is to see whether states have met system accountability standards that are intended to gauge how well schools are serving different kinds of students and to ensure that states and school districts set high standards for all students.

A third broad approach focuses on whether states have adopted demanding content and performance standards; on whether curriculum, instruction, and large-scale assessments are properly aligned with those standards; and on whether schools and teachers possess the capacity to deliver high-quality instruction to all students. This approach is based on the logic of the standards movement, under which improved capacity and alignment are the principal means to improved student achievement (Elmore & Rothman, 1999; Fuhrman, 2001).

EVIDENCE THAT SCHOOLS ARE TEACHING STUDENTS THE KNOWLEDGE AND SKILLS THAT TESTS MEASURE

There is research evidence that achievement, especially for younger students, has improved in some states and schools. There is also evidence, however, that many schools are not yet giving all students an opportunity to acquire the knowledge and skills they need to pass increasingly demanding high-stakes tests.

Consider state pass rate data of the kind discussed above. While pass rates continue to rise, there are many states, especially those with more demanding exit tests, that continue to show failure rates for minority students, students with disabilities, and ELLs that are disproportionate and extremely high. If virtually all children can learn to high standards, such high failure rates must be due at least partly to insufficient high-quality instruction.

In terms of state compliance with current federal system accountability requirements, the good news is that more states meet current federal system accountability requirements than before (see Thurlow, this volume). But the ambitious federal education reforms adopted in 1994 "are . . . still a work in progress in the field" (Elmore & Rothman, 1999, p. 6). Many states do not yet include all students with disabilities or ELLs in their assessment systems, and many do not yet disaggregate achievement information properly for various student populations (Citizens' Commission on Civil Rights, 2001; Cohen, 2001; Robelin, 2001). Without such data, states and school districts lack basic information about how well low-achieving groups are performing and how they might be served more effectively. Such information is a *precondition* to improved achievement.

And what is the evidence that curriculum and instruction *are* aligned with high-stakes assessments? Once again, there is evidence that such alignment is increasing (McLaughlin, 2000; Wise et al., 2002) but also evidence that alignment—and the improved capacity that alignment requires—are still more aspiration than reality in many schools.

Eva Baker and Robert Linn (2000) describe alignment as "the linchpin of standards-based accountability systems" (p. 1) and express the view that "in many parts of the country . . . alignment is weak" (p. 3).

Empirical research supports such expressions of concern. One line of research, by Andrew Porter, John Smithson, and others, studies 11 states and finds only modest overlap between a state's tests and what teachers in that state say they teach. For example, in fourth-grade mathematics, reports from five states showed overlaps ranging from a high of 45% to a low of 23%; in eighth-grade mathematics, reports from six states showed overlaps ranging from a high of 35% to a low of 5% (Porter & Smithson, 2000, tables 5–6). In other subjects overlap was comparable or even lower. Other studies find low overlap and "instructional content . . . not very well aligned with . . . the state test" (Blank, Porter, & Smithson, 2001, p. 26).

Despite limitations, these studies suggest that many states and schools have not yet reached the point where they are teaching students all or even most of what state tests measure. This is a serious problem where tests are used to make high-stakes decisions about individual students, as is true in some states Porter and Smithson studied. In such circumstances, close alignment should *precede* the use of test scores for high-stakes purposes.

Alignment is closely linked with capacity. According to Richard Elmore

(2002), "The work of turning a school around entails improving the knowledge and skills of teachers—changing their knowledge of content and how to teach it—and helping them to understand where their students are in their academic development." In many places, the necessary investments have yet to be made: "Low-performing schools, and the people who work in them, don't know what to do. If they did, they would be doing it already. . . . Without substantial investments in capacity, [the increased pressure of test-based accountability] is likely to aggravate the existing inequalities between low-performing and high-performing schools and students" (pp. 13–14).

Indeed, a central objective of education reform efforts since at least the 1950s has been to attract strong teachers to schools that serve large numbers of low-achieving students. Reversing traditional teacher mobility patterns, in which experienced, well-regarded teachers gravitate toward wealthier suburban schools, "is a necessary condition for standards-based reform to improve educational outcomes for children of color" (Murnane & Levy, 2001, p. 411). According to those authors, however, current standards and accountability mechanisms may already be creating conditions in which teachers have incentives to avoid schools with high proportions of low-achieving students.

There are also long-standing problems of alignment and capacity between "general education" and programs for students with disabilities or ELLs, both of which also serve large minority populations. For example, while some studies document real progress reducing barriers between general education and special education (McLaughlin, 2000; Thurlow, this volume), others raise serious concerns. Case studies at high schools in three states (Dailey, Zantal-Wiener, & Roach, 2000) found that many special education teachers "lacked guidance about how to align IEPs with the standards," that they were "by and large . . . not involved in school-wide discussions about standards," that special education teachers "tended to use the IEPs rather than the standards as a guide for instruction," that "most IEPs were not aligned with the standards," and that many special education and general education teachers "tended to have a 'wait and see' attitude about exposing students with disabilities to and engaging them in standards-based instruction" (Dailey et al., 2000, pp. 8–9).

Taken together, such studies suggest improvement coupled with major continuing problems of capacity and alignment. State test score data, studies of system accountability under federal law, state-specific studies of alignment, and studies of standards-based reform for students with disabilities all indicate that many schools are not yet teaching students the full range of subject matter and skills that high-stakes tests measure. It therefore seems problematic that so many states and school districts are already administering or moving forward with high-stakes graduation and/or promotion tests.

FEDERAL LAW ON HIGH-STAKES TESTING

In what circumstances will the federal government or other entities intervene where some student groups fail high-stakes tests at substantially higher rates than other students, or where there is evidence that states and schools do not yet teach students the knowledge and skills that graduation or promotion tests measure? (Other legal issues, while important, are beyond the scope of this chapter.)

Despite clear "opportunity to learn" language in the standards of the measurement profession, covering both promotion tests and graduation tests (American Educational Research Association, American Psychological Association, & National Council on Measurement in Education, 1999), the measurement profession itself will not intervene. There is no mechanism by which the testing profession investigates complaints or enforces its own standards (Heubert & Hauser, 1999). Thus, legal action is often the only mechanism for challenging inappropriate use of high-stakes tests.

Legal protections, however, may be less extensive than many educators, parents, and students think. In 2001, the U.S. Supreme Court held that private individuals could no longer bring "disparate impact" cases under Title VI of the Civil Rights Act of 1964, the federal civil-rights statute that most strongly protects minority groups and ELLs. Similarly, most graduation test cases were decided in the days of minimum competency testing and suggest a judicial reluctance to probe deeply into whether schools actually are teaching what exit tests measure. And in the relatively few cases involving promotion test policies, courts have tended to assume that students *benefit* from retention in grade and have no legal interest in avoiding it.

Changed conditions in education argue for more sensitive judicial inquiry. Even if it was appropriate to assume that most schools taught students basic skills, recent research suggests that there are problems in assuming that all students are being taught the knowledge and skills that current "high-standards" exit tests measure, especially as students with disabilities and ELLs increasingly take part and as researchers document continuing problems of alignment and school capacity. Similarly, court opinions on promotion testing do not refer to strong research on grade retention's harmful effects.

It may be possible to resolve concerns over high-stakes testing through the policy process. But if judges are to play a role in protecting equality of opportunity, they will need help from educators, researchers, and lawyers in understanding the current policy context, the current educational realities, and the complex issues surrounding high-stakes testing.

DISPARATE IMPACT CLAIMS

Since the early 1970s, most cases alleging discrimination in education have been brought under federal civil-rights statutes and the regulations that accompany them. The regulations forbid federal fund recipients from engaging in policies or practices that, while not overtly discriminatory, produce disparate impact and have the *effect* of discriminating—unless the defendant can show that the policies or practices advance a substantial, legitimate objective.

Thus, in *Lau* v. *Nichols* (1974), a case brought by parents of children who recently had arrived from China, the U.S. Supreme Court ruled that San Francisco's failure to make any provision for the students' language needs had the effect of discriminating against them, in violation of Title VI regulations. Similarly, when private citizens challenged the Texas graduation test, the court explored whether TAAS had disproportionate, adverse impact on African American and Hispanic students. Concluding that it did, the court nonetheless ruled for Texas because the court accepted the state's asserted justifications: that TAAS provided a uniform, objective standard for high school diplomas in Texas, and that group disparities were being reduced.

In 2001, however, in *Alexander* v. *Sandoval*, the U.S. Supreme Court ruled, 5-4, that only the federal government, and not private individuals, may invoke the Title VI regulations that allow "disparate impact" claims. If *Sandoval* had been decided 30 years earlier, hundreds of discrimination cases—many successful—could never have been brought, including the famous *Lau* case and the Title VI part of the 2000 TAAS case. Since *Sandoval*, numerous discrimination cases have been dismissed.

What can private individuals do? They can file complaints with the U.S. Department of Education or the U.S. Department of Justice, which may still bring disparate impact cases, administratively or in court. In the current climate, however, these agencies are probably less likely than private individuals to challenge testing programs.

Private individuals also can file their own lawsuits, but they must prove that education policies or practices having adverse impact were motivated, at least partly, by *intent to discriminate*. This standard is very hard to meet, and "intent" claims consistently have been rejected in cases challenging exit tests. Thus, unless Congress overrules *Sandoval*, which is unlikely in the present climate, this decision substantially reduces the likelihood of successful discrimination cases against high-stakes testing programs.

GRADUATION TESTING AND OPPORTUNITY TO LEARN

Relying on due-process provisions in the U.S. Constitution, federal courts have ruled that students have a legally protected "property interest" in receiving standard high school diplomas if they have completed their other graduation requirements. Where this property interest exists, courts then examine (1) whether students received sufficient advance notice of the exit test requirements, and (2) whether the exit test is a fair measure of what students actually have been taught.

In the early graduation test cases, which involved basic skills tests, most courts did not inquire deeply into whether students were being taught the requisite knowledge and skills. In *Anderson* v. *Banks* (1981), where a school official acknowledged that there had been no effort to determine whether students were being taught what the district's exit test measured, the court ruled without discussion that the district could rectify the situation within 2 years, given the availability of remedial programs and multiple test-taking opportunities. In *Debra P.* (1981), a statewide case in Florida, the court concluded after 4 years that the test was a fair measure of what students were taught based on (1) evidence that the test measured skills included in the state curriculum, (2) a survey showing that most teachers considered the skills ones they should teach, and (3) evidence that teachers were *actually* teaching the requisite knowledge and skills.

It would be problematic today, however, for judges to assume that the gaps could be closed so quickly when the gaps are often far greater, when historically excluded groups are increasingly included in high-stakes testing, when numerous indicators show that many states are not yet providing adequate opportunities for students to learn the knowledge and skills they need, and when profound "capacity" problems have been well defined and documented. And while courts usually are inclined to defer to educators' judgments, some high-stakes testing programs appear to lack a firm foundation in educational research or practice. As Richard Elmore, this volume, points out, "State policies require proficiency levels for grade promotion and graduation for students . . . without any empirical evidence or any defensible theory about how much it is feasible to expect students to learn over a given period of time or what types of instruction have to be in place in order for students to meet expected rates of improvement." These are matters that call for careful scrutiny.

It is therefore noteworthy that two recent court decisions, both involving students with disabilities, did not explore more thoroughly the issues surrounding whether students had been taught what a state exit test measures.

Rene v. *Reed* (2001) arose in Indiana, which announced in 1997 that most learning-disabled (LD) students would have to pass the state's exit exam in spring 2000 to receive standard diplomas. Previously, students with disabilities had received diplomas if they met their IEP requirements, which often did not track the state standards. In spring 2000, over 1,000 LD students failed the test. The students sued in state court, arguing that their IEPs had not been modified in time for them to learn the knowledge and skills on the graduation test, particularly since they had been behind in 1997. The state argued that students had had sufficient time to prepare in light of remedial programs, opportunities to retake the exam, and the option to remain in school for further instruction after the senior year.

While recognizing Indiana's legal duty to test only what students had been taught, the judge found it "implausible" that the learning-disabled students had not been exposed to the subjects on the exit test. In reaching this conclusion, the court showed little evidence that it had considered the difficulty of the exit test, students' prior achievement levels, or whether schools had the capacity to provide students with the instruction they needed. The court encouraged students to remain in school after the senior year to receive additional instruction and retake the test. (Since this litigation involved a request for a preliminary injunction—a court order issued *before* a full hearing in court—the Indiana courts could still reach a different result after trial, although that is unlikely given the strong language in which the courts rejected students' due-process claims. An Indiana appeals court affirmed the decision.)

In California, students with disabilities filed a lawsuit challenging the state exit test, which was first administered in spring 2001 and which all students in the class of 2004 must pass to graduate (*Chapman* v. *California Department of Education* [*Chapman*], 2002). Before the trial began, the students sought a preliminary injunction, an emergency court order, on several matters that they said could not wait until after the trial. One claim was that students with disabilities would not have sufficient time before spring 2004 to learn what the exit test measures.

In February 2002, the court issued detailed orders on issues of testing accommodations and alternative assessments. The court declined, however, to act immediately on the opportunity to learn claim, saying only that "the present state of the evidence does not reveal an asymmetry between what students are taught and [the exit test]" (*Chapman*, 2002, p. 9).

The students' claims will be heard at trial, but the court's brief ruling on this issue raises questions. Since only 10.3% of all students with disabilities who took both state tests in spring 2001 passed (Wise et al., 2002), there appears to have been some evidence of "asymmetry" between what students had been taught and what the exit test required them to know.

More thorough consideration of "opportunity to learn" issues would not be without precedent. Early cases held that students with disabilities, like their nondisabled peers, could be denied standard high school diplomas if they failed exit exams—as long as they had received sufficient advance notice and as long as they had already been taught the knowledge and skills that the exam measured (*Board of Education* v. *Ambach*, 1981; *Brookhart* v. *Illinois State Board of Education* [*Brookhart*], 1983). These courts also recognized that students with disabilities probably would need more time than other students to master the requisite knowledge, both because some "learn at a slower rate than regular division students" (*Brookhart*, 1983, p. 187) and because students whose IEPs did not yet reflect the content of the state exit test would have to be taught a substantially different curriculum before they could be expected to pass the state test.

In other words, these courts saw even in the early 1980s that for students with disabilities, "opportunity to learn" issues could be complex, requiring an inquiry into how far behind students were at the outset, what measures would be needed to align IEPs and instruction with state standards and tests, and how much time these students would need to master the requisite knowledge and skill once schools were equipped to provide the necessary instruction. Similar logic would apply to ELLs and low-SES students, who also must acquire increasingly high-level knowledge and skill while overcoming different barriers, and whose schools often have limited capacity to provide high-quality instruction to these students.

PROMOTION TESTING AND OPPORTUNITY TO LEARN

According to the standards of the testing profession, promotion tests (like graduation tests) should cover only the "content and skills that students have had an opportunity to learn" (AERA et al., 1999, p. 146). AERA (2000) agrees, as does the U.S. Department of Education's Office for Civil Rights (2000, p. 20).

Nonetheless, most courts that have evaluated promotion tests under the Constitution's due-process clause have taken a different view. As noted above, the due-process claims recognized in *Debra P.* and other cases rest on the view that students have a property interest in receiving a high school diploma. Without this property interest, students would have no claim to remedies such as advance notice of testing or a test that measures only what students actually have been taught.

There have been few reported federal cases involving promotion test policies, and in each the court has upheld promotion testing. Courts have drawn a distinction between graduation testing and promotion testing, declining to recognize a property interest in being promoted. As one federal appeals court said about a classroom-based promotion test, "We conclude that *Debra P.* is distinguishable and hold that plaintiffs had no property right [that would justify judicial intervention]" (*Bester* v. *Tuscaloosa Board of Education* [*Bester*], 1984, p. 7). The decision rested, in part, on the court's view that retention in grade is *beneficial* for low achievers: "A program of retention for students who do not perform satisfactory work is both acceptable and desirable" (*Bester,* 1984, p. 7). A more recent decision used similar language in upholding a statewide retention test policy: "[The policy] is designed to help the retained students: a student who is not promoted is given what is, in effect, a remedial year which should allow the student to catch up on the skills that he is lacking and perform better in the future" (*Erik V.* v. *Causby*, 1997, pp. 388–389). (Another circuit court, apparently in an unpublished opinion, recently rejected due-process claims in connection with a Louisiana state promotion test [Thevenot, 2001].)

Such views are understandable, particularly considering the bipartisan calls to end social promotion. There is, however, powerful social science evidence on the *harmful* effects of retention. It shows that students who are retained—compared with similar low-performing students who are promoted—are likely to have lower academic achievement, impaired social development, and a substantially increased likelihood of dropping out (Hauser, 2001; Heubert & Hauser, 1999). Moreover, some critics of social promotion are equally critical of retention in grade, finding early intervention strategies preferable to both.

Courts presented with this research might conclude that a student does have a property interest in avoiding retention. A student's interest in avoiding retention is certainly greater than the interest in avoiding a short-term suspension from school, in which courts have long recognized a property interest. If such a property interest in avoiding retention were recognized, presumably students also would have a right to advance notice and a test that measures only what they have been taught.

At present, however, students probably cannot count on courts to support them in opportunity to learn cases involving promotion tests.

CONCLUSION

Evidence presented here shows that minority students, students with disabilities, and ELLs are failing some state tests, especially those that reflect high standards, at rates as high as 60–90%, that "disparate impact" often declines slowly, and that failure rates would be higher if states took into account students who have dropped out, been retained, or been excluded improperly from testing. This chapter also presents powerful evidence from leading scholars that many students are not yet being taught the knowledge and skills that current high-stakes tests measure.

Low-achieving students need high-quality instruction more than anyone else, and there is little question that data from large-scale assessments, if used properly, can help improve instruction, hold schools accountable for improved achievement, and identify and address students' learning needs. It is a tragedy that so many of these students have been ill-served by their schools for so long, and a welcome change when states and schools aspire to educate all students to high standards.

At the same time, where demanding tests have high stakes for individual students, minority students, students with disabilities, ELLs, and low-SES students are at heightened risk of suffering the serious, well-documented harms associated with grade retention and denial of high school diplomas. It would be a great loss if high-stakes testing policies operated to deny diplomas to large numbers of these students, or to subject them to the serious harms of retention. It would be unfortunate if states and schools used high-stakes tests in ways that punished students for not knowing what their schools had never taught them.

Principles of law and measurement hold that high-stakes tests should measure only what students have already been taught, and there should be ways of ensuring that high-stakes tests are used properly.

But the measurement profession does not enforce its own rules of appropriate test use, and the law is limited in the protections it affords. The U.S. Supreme Court has closed off for now the chief route by which individuals have challenged education policies and practices that have adverse impact by race, national origin, and language. Federal courts thus far have been unsympathetic to lawsuits challenging promotion testing, perhaps because they are unfamiliar with powerful research, now widely accepted, on the negative effects of grade retention.

In reviewing future legal challenges, courts will have to evaluate circumstances markedly different from those associated with early minimum competency tests. Fortunately, much more is understood today about the human and social consequences of inappropriate test use, about what school improvement requires, and about how educators can help all students acquire high-level knowledge and skills. Educators and researchers who understand these complex issues well can help judges as they attempt to apply and modify legal precedents and principles in light of dramatically changed educational objectives and of realities that have been slower to change.

ACKNOWLEDGMENTS

The author is grateful to the Carnegie Scholars Program of the Carnegie Corporation of New York, which supported this research. The views expressed are the author's.

REFERENCES

Alaska Department of Education. (2001). *Statewide spring 2001 HSGQE student test results*. Juneau: Author.

Alexander v. *Sandoval*, 532 U.S. 275 (2001).

American Education Research Association. (2000). *AERA position statement concerning high-stakes testing in pre-K–12 education*. Washington, DC: Author. Retrieved from http://www.aera.net.about/policy/stakes.htm

American Educational Research Association, American Psychological Association, & National Council on Measurement in Education. (1999). *Standards for educational and psychological testing*. Washington, DC: Authors.

American Federation of Teachers. (2001). *Making standards matter 2001: A 50-state report on efforts to implement a standards system*. Washington, DC: Author.

Anderson v. *Banks*, 540 F. Supp. 472 (S.D. Ga. 1981).

Baker, E., & Linn, R. (2000). Alignment: Policy goals, policy strategies, and policy outcomes. *The CRESST Line*, pp. 1–3.

Bester v. *Tuscaloosa Board of Education*, 722 F.2d 1514 (11th Cir. 1984).

Blank, R., Porter, A., & Smithson, J. (2001). *New tools for analyzing teaching, curriculum, and standards in mathematics and science: Results from survey of enacted curriculum project*. Washington, DC: Council of Chief State School Officers.

Board of Education v. *Ambach*, 436 N.Y.S.2d 564 (N.Y. 1981).

Brookhart v. *Illinois State Board of Education*, 697 F.2d 179 (7th Cir. 1983).

Chapman v. *California Department of Education*, No C. 01–01780 CRB, Preliminary Injunction (N.D. Cal. February 21, 2002).

Citizens' Commission on Civil Rights. (2001). *Closing the deal: A preliminary report on state compliance with final assessment and accountability requirements under the Improving America's Schools Act of 1994*. Washington, DC: Author.

Cohen, M. (2001, January 19). *Review of state assessment systems for Title I*. Memorandum to Chief State School Officers from the Assistant Secretary for Elementary and Secondary Education, U.S. Department of Education.

Dailey, D., Zantal-Wiener, K., & Roach, V. (2000). *Reforming high school learning: The effect of the standards movement on secondary students with disabilities*. Alexandria, VA: Center for Policy Research on the Impact of General and Special Education Reform.

Debra P. v. *Turlington*, 474 F. Supp. 244 (M.D. Fla. 1979); *aff'd in part and rev'd*

in part, 644 F.2d 397 6775 (5th Cir. 1981); *rem'd*, 564 F. Supp. 177 (M.D. Fla. 1983); *aff'd*, 730 F.2d 1405 (11th Cir. 1984).

Elmore, R. F. (2000). *Building a new structure for school leadership*. Washington, DC: Albert Shanker Institute.

Elmore, R. F. (2002). Unwarranted intrusion. *Education Next*. Palo Alto, CA: Hoover Institution. Retrieved from http://www.educationnext.org/20021/30.html

Elmore, R. F., & Rothman, R. (Eds.). (1999). *Testing, teaching, and learning: A guide for states and school districts*. Washington, DC: National Academy Press.

Erik V. v. Causby, 977 F. Supp. 384 (E.D.N.C. 1997).

Fuhrman, S. H. (2001). Conclusion. In S. H. Fuhrman (Ed.), *From the capitol to the classroom: Standards-based reform in the states* (pp. 263–278). Chicago: University of Chicago Press.

G.I. Forum v. *Texas Education Agency*, 87 F. Supp. 2d 667, 675n.7 (W.D. Tex. 2000).

Hauser, R. (2001). Should we end social promotion? Truth and consequences. In G. Orfield & M. Kornhaber (Eds.), *Raising standards or raising barriers? Inequality and high-stakes testing in education* (pp. 151–178). New York: Century Fund.

Heubert, J. (2002). Disability, race, and high-stakes testing of students. In D. Losen & G. Orfield (Eds.), *Racial inequity in special education* (pp. 123–152). New York: Century Fund. Retrieved from http://www.cast.org/ncac/index.cfm?i=387

Heubert, J. P., & Hauser, R. M. (Eds.). (1999). *High stakes: Testing for tracking, promotion, and graduation*. Washington, DC: National Academy Press.

Improving America's Schools Act, 20 U.S.C. sections 6301 *et seq.* (1994).

Individuals with Disabilities Education Act, 20 U.S.C. section 1401 *et. seq.* (1997).

Jacob, B. (2001). Getting tough? The impact of high school graduation exams. *Educational Evaluation and Policy Analysis*, *23*(3), 99–122.

Keller, B. (2000, April 12). More New York special education students passing state tests. *Education Week*, *2*(97), 33.

Klein, S., Hamilton, L., McCaffrey, D., & Stecher, B. (2000). *What do tests scores in Texas tell us?* Santa Monica, CA: RAND.

Koretz, D., & Hamilton, L. (2001). *The performance of students with disabilities on New York's revised Regents examination in English*. Los Angeles: National Center for Research on Evaluation, Standards, and Student Testing, University of California.

Lau v. *Nichols*, 414 U.S. 563 (1974).

Lee, J. (2002). Racial and ethnic achievement gap trends: Reversing the progress toward equity? *Educational Researcher*, *31*(1), 3–12.

Linn, R. (2000). Assessments and accountability. *Educational Researcher*, *29*(2), 4–16.

Linn, R. (2001). *The design and evaluation of educational assessment and accountability systems*. Los Angeles: National Center for Research on Evaluation, Standards, and Student Testing, University of California.

Massachusetts Department of Education. (2001). *Spring 2001 MCAS tests: State results by race/ethnicity and student status*. Boston: Author.

Massachusetts Department of Education. (2002). *Progress report on the class of 2002: Percentages of students who have earned a competency determination, statewide, and by district.* Boston: Author.

McLaughlin, M. (2000). *Reform for every learner: Teachers' views on standards and students with disabilities.* Alexandria, VA: Center for Policy Research on the Impact of General and Special Education Reform.

Murnane, R., & Levy, F. (2001). Will standards-based reforms improve the education of children of color? *National Tax Journal, 54*(2), 401–416.

NAEP achievement. (2001, August 8). *Education Week, 20*(45), 24.

National Center for Education Statistics. (2001). *The condition of education 2001.* Washington, DC: Author.

Natriello, G., & Pallas, A. (2001). The development and impact of high-stakes testing. In G. Orfield & M. Kornhaber (Eds.), *Raising standards or raising barriers: Inequality and high-stakes testing in public education* (pp. 19–38). New York: Century Foundation.

New York Department of Education, Office of Vocational and Educational Services for Students with Disabilities (2000). *2000 pocket book of goals and results for individuals with disabilities.* Albany: Author.

New York Department of Education, Office of Vocational and Educational Services for Students with Disabilities. (2001). *2001 pocket book of goals and results for individuals with disabilities.* Albany: Author.

No Child Left Behind Act, Public Law 107–110 (January 8, 2002).

Office for Civil Rights. (2000). *The use of tests when making high-stakes decisions for students: A resource guide for educators and policymakers.* Washington, DC: U.S. Department of Education.

Porter, A. C., & Smithson, J. (2000, April). *Alignment of state testing programs, NAEP, and reports of teacher practice in grades 4 and 8.* Paper presented at the annual meeting of the American Educational Research Association, New Orleans.

Rene v. Reed, 751 N.E.2d 736 (Ind. App. 2001).

Robelin, E. (2001, November 28). States sluggish on execution of 1994 ESEA. *Education Week, 21*(13), 1, 26, 27.

Taylor, W. (2000, November 15). Standards, tests, and civil rights. *Education Week, 20*(11), 56, 40, 41.

Thevenot, B. (2001, September 18). Students who fail LEAP can be held back: Court rules in favor of high-stakes testing. *Times Picayune.*

Thurlow, M., Nelson, J., Teelucksingh, E., & Ysseldyke, J. (2000). *Where's Waldo: A third search for students with disabilities in state accountability reports.* Minneapolis: National Center on Educational Outcomes.

Title VI, Civil Rights Act of 1964, 42 U.S.C. section 2000(d).

Wise, L., Sipes, D. E., Harris, C., George, C., Ford, J., & Sun, S. (2002). *Independent evaluation of the California high school exit examination (CAHSEE): Analysis of the 2001 administration.* Sacramento, CA: California Department of Education.

Ysseldyke, J., Thurlow, M., Langenfeld, M., Nelson, J., Teelucksingh, E., & Seyfarth, A. (1998). *Educational results for students with disabilities: What do the data tell us?* Minneapolis: National Center on Educational Outcomes.

PART IV

MOVING FORWARD: REFINING ACCOUNTABILITY SYSTEMS

"Slow Down, You Move Too Fast": The Politics of Making Changes in High-Stakes Accountability Policies for Students

Susan H. Fuhrman
Margaret E. Goertz
Mark C. Duffy

Over the past decade, the concept of standards-based reform has become equated to a set of ideas and policies focused on accountability. The accountability movement has swept across the United States in the form of statewide assessment and accountability systems based on performance outcomes. Changes in state policy have been influenced by policy initiatives at the federal level. Under the Clinton administration, states were expected to establish challenging content and performance standards, implement assessments that measured students' performance against those standards, and hold schools and school systems accountable for the achievement of all students as required in the Improving America's Schools Act of 1994 and supported by Goals 2000. In the first year of his presidency, George W. Bush requested and Congress enacted even stronger accountability legislation. The No Child Left Behind Act (NCLB) of 2001 calls for states to administer comparable assessments every year in grades 3–8 and to establish sanctions for schools that fail to educate students and rewards for schools that improve overall student performance.

While policies in a number of states initially focused on institutional accountability, more and more states have developed high-stakes accountability systems for students as well as schools. Eight states have enacted promotion policies for students in the elementary and middle grades that incorporate state test scores. By 2008, high school students in 35 states will have to take a high school exit examination (HSEE). In 26 of these states, students will have to pass a state-administered test in order to graduate from high school, an increase of 10 since 1996–1997. Two states will require that students either pass the state or a local high school assessment. In the other seven states, student performance on a state assessment may be noted on a student's transcript or diploma, but passing a state test will not be required for high school graduation.

Most state high school tests assess a student's general knowledge of English/language arts and mathematics and often of science and social studies as well. Eleven states have or are developing end-of-course examinations for their high school students, although only six of these states—Georgia, Maryland, Mississippi, New York, Tennessee, and Virginia—will require students to pass these examinations to graduate from high school. Most of the older graduation tests focus on basic skills, and many of these states are in the process of revising their high school assessments so they will measure more rigorous content.

Public opposition to high-stakes accountability has been directed more at student than at institutional accountability policies. Prior to the enactment of the NCLB Act, only a few states had changed their school accountability policies. Kentucky, for example, revised its policies in the late 1990s to accommodate high-scoring schools, drop the use of the term "sanctions," and account for measurement error. The state superintendent of schools in Michigan postponed the implementation of that state's new school accreditation system so that it did not rely solely on measures of tested achievement. Many more states have made, or are considering, revisions to their promotion and graduation policies in the face of growing parental, educator, and community concerns. Michigan, for example, used to require students to pass the state assessment in order to graduate from high school. Now students who score at the top levels on the test receive a state endorsement on their diploma and are eligible for a college scholarship. Other states, like Alaska, Arizona, and Maryland, have delayed when students must pass a test to receive a high school diploma. States have revised or postponed promotion policies as well. For example, Ohio eliminated its fourth-grade "reading guarantee" before this policy was implemented in spring 2002.

This chapter looks at four states that have made changes to their high school exit examination systems: Arizona, California, Maryland, and Massachusetts. We first present brief summaries of each state's assessment and accountability policies and recent changes in and challenges to the states' high school assessment programs. We then explore the problems, proposals, and politics that are common across these states and offer recommendations for adjusting accountability policies to address these issues. We are interested in the circumstances and political alignments that permitted the adjustments and in the implications for other states facing the need for mid-course corrections. In general, states implementing HSEEs are finding that they have to slow down and fine-tune these policies, as indicated by the title of this chapter. Our findings are based on document reviews and interviews with policy makers and representatives from business and education groups. (Information on state assessment and accountability policies and changes was drawn from state department of education websites, local and national newspapers, and pertinent reports from external evaluators and research organizations. We conducted telephone interviews with at least six respondents in each state, including state department of education officials, members of the state board of education, representatives of stakeholder groups, external evaluators, and legislators.)

ARIZONA

ASSESSMENT AND ACCOUNTABILITY POLICIES

Arizona has a long history of assessment, but limited experience with education accountability. In the 1980s, the state tested all students annually in grades 3–12 using a norm-referenced standardized test focused on basic skills. In 1990, the legislature required the State Board of Education (SBE) to develop new assessments aligned with the state's new and more constructivist Essential Skills, while ensuring that the assessment program would continue to yield national comparisons. State Superintendent of Public Instruction Lisa Graham Keegan suspended the resulting Arizona Student Assessment Program in January 1995, calling for revisions to the state's standards, assessments, and accountability policies. The legislature enacted a high school graduation requirement later in 1995.

The SBE adopted the more traditional Arizona Academic Standards in 1996, and the legislature enacted a new testing program, the Arizona Instrument to Measure Standards (AIMS), in 1998. Designed to measure the degree to which students are learning the content outlined in the Arizona Academic Standards, AIMS assesses students in grades 3, 5, 8, and 10. Students in grades 2–8 also take the SAT-9, a standardized, norm-referenced test. The tenth-grade AIMS serves as the high school graduation test mandated by the legislature. Students are given up to five opportunities to pass the reading, writing, and mathematics sections of the test: once in sophomore year, and twice in both junior and senior years. The high school graduation test initially applied to the class of 2002. It now applies to the class of 2006. School and district accountability was limited to public reporting of student test scores until 2002, when the state enacted Arizona LEARNS. This new accountability system designates underperforming and failing schools, specifies school improvement activities for these schools, and outlines consequences for schools that do not show progress over time. The state identified 227, or 14%, of Arizona's schools as underperforming in October 2002 (Arizona Department of Education, 2002d).

CHANGES AND CHALLENGES TO THE HIGH SCHOOL ASSESSMENT

From the outset, using AIMS as a graduation requirement created controversy in the state, and low student test scores helped to fuel community concerns. When the majority of sophomores failed the initial round of testing in 1999, the SBE and Superintendent Keegan reinforced the 2002 deadline (Kossan, 2000). However, in summer 2000, the SBE approved the postponement until 2004 of the requirement that students pass the mathematics portion of the AIMS to earn a diploma. The Board also agreed to eliminate items covering trigonometry and calculus, subjects not generally covered by students until after their sophomore year, from the high school AIMS examination. Students graduating in 2002 would still be required to pass the reading and writing sections of the AIMS.

Faced with a second year of dismal test scores and continuing criticism of AIMS, particularly around issues of opportunity to learn, Superintendent Keegan and the SBE reconsidered their options once more. In November 2000, they announced they would indefinitely delay graduation requirements until they collected input from parents, educators, and the business community. WestEd, Arizona's regional educational laboratory, analyzed this public input and recommended in March 2001 that the state postpone the reading, writing, and mathematics tests as graduation requirements until 2005 and change the passing score on the mathematics assessment to a more moderate level.

In response to growing concerns from constituents and reflecting a change in membership, the state legislature became re-engaged in the high school graduation debate. The state Senate passed legislation in spring 2001 that would have pushed the high school graduation requirement back to 2004 and put the high school examination to a public vote if legislators found insufficient public support for it. The bill died in the House Education Committee, however, where the chair argued that the SBE might accept WestEd's recommendations for a delay (Scutari, 2001). The president of the SBE was reported as supporting a later deadline, conceding that many students "aren't sufficiently armed to pass this test" (Flannery, 2001).

In May 2001, the William E. Morris Institute for Justice, a public advocacy law firm based in Tucson, Arizona, filed a federal civil-rights complaint alleging that AIMS has a negative "disparate impact" on minority high school students in violation of Title VI of the 1964 Civil Rights Act. Analyses prepared for the Institute showed that 2000 pass rates for tenth-grade minority students were extremely low, both absolutely and as compared with the pass rates for White students. The Institute argued that the state's failure to take any substantive action to alleviate the adverse effects of AIMS, such as mandating remedial services or supporting research-based instructional programs in early grades, was even more problematic. Voters approved a $94.5 million increase in the state sales and use taxes in November 2000 that is earmarked for education, but only $1.5 million of this revenue will fund remedial efforts.

On August 27, 2001, the new Superintendent of Public Instruction, Jaime Molera, postponed the use of AIMS as a graduation requirement until 2006. The SBE, in May 2002, adopted an alternative method for assessing proficiency on state high school standards, the AIMS-Equivalent Demonstration, to provide students different ways of demonstrating achievement of the AIMS knowledge and skills.

CALIFORNIA

ASSESSMENT AND ACCOUNTABILITY POLICIES

California also has a long history of monitoring student performance through state assessments. The California Assessment Program, which began in 1972, used "matrix sampling" to provide school and district reports of student performance on basic skills content. Since then, the state assessment program has gone through a number of changes as policy makers sought to align testing with the state's evolving standards and curriculum frameworks and to create a system that would generate individual student scores. In 1997, the legislature enacted the Standardized Testing and Reporting Program (STAR) to measure student, school, and district performance in grades 2–11 on the state's new standards.

The California High School Exit Examination (CAHSEE), enacted in 1999, replaced local proficiency tests as a requirement for high school graduation. The CAHSEE is distinct from the STAR and the state's other high school assessment program, the Golden State Exams. Designed to measure student proficiency on the state's ninth- and tenth-grade standards in English/language arts and sixth- and ninth-grade standards in mathematics, the CAHSEE will become a high school graduation requirement effective with the class of 2006, a delay of 2 years. Under the original legislation, students could take the CAHSEE voluntarily in ninth grade, but had to take the test by tenth grade. Students who failed the examination had multiple opportunities to retake the test during eleventh and twelfth grades. The legislation establishing the CAHSEE also mandated an external evaluation of both the technical quality of the assessment and students' opportunity to learn the material covered by the test.

School accountability was limited primarily to public reporting until the passage of the Public Schools Accountability Act (PSAA) in 1999. The PSAA currently holds schools accountable for meeting annual growth targets based on their performance on the STAR. Over time, results of the CAHSEE will be incorporated into schools' accountability measures. The PSAA legislation also provides for a system of rewards to high-performing and improving schools, and additional resources to and, ultimately, sanctions for underperforming schools. Districts also must establish standards for promotion at pivotal grades. Results from the STAR must be considered in making promotion decisions.

CHANGES AND CHALLENGES TO THE HIGH SCHOOL ASSESSMENT

There was minimal opposition to the CAHSEE until the release of the 2002 results. Respondents noted that educators and the public generally view this test as a way of identifying and addressing the needs of the state's low-performing students and of promoting the alignment of curriculum and instruction in a decentralized education system. Policy makers, however, confronted issues related to the length and content of the test, cut scores, and implementation dates.

In December 2000, the SBE voted to shorten the high school assessment by reducing the number of items and removing some of the more difficult algebra questions. Field tests had shown that testing time could be reduced without compromising the reliability of the assessment. In addition, there was concern that some of the mathematics items measured content usually covered in algebra 2, a course that few tenth-grade students take. In winter 2001, the legislature grappled with two more controversial issues: how to treat the ninth-grade administration of the test (the first group of students to be tested), and whether to delay the requirement that students pass the CAHSEE to graduate from high school. The test developer and the external evaluator had raised concerns that allowing CAHSEE scores to count for ninth graders who voluntarily took the test in 2001 could jeopardize the establishment of valid and reliable cut scores because the state would not have a complete census of tenth-grade test takers. Educators and the external evaluator also raised concerns that schools had not provided students an opportunity to learn the material covered on the test. Proposals to make the ninth-grade administration a practice test for diagnostic purposes only and to delay the high school assessment were defeated in the legislature days before the first test administration in March 2001.

In June 2001, the SBE established passing scores for the CAHSEE using results of the ninth-grade administration—60% correct for English/language arts and 55% correct for mathematics. These scores were below the 70% score proposed by a panel of experts. Even with the lower passing scores, only 42% of the ninth graders taking the CAHSEE, and 23% of the Latino and African American test takers, passed both sections of the examination (Wise et al., 2002). The Disability Rights Advocates filed a suit claiming that the HSEE discriminates against students with learning disabilities because there is no alternative assessment, no procedure for requesting accommodations, and no process for appeals, and because the examination tests material that students with disabilities have not been taught. A federal judge subsequently ordered California to make test accommodations available to students with disabilities and to develop an alternative form of the test. High failure rates among tenth-grade test takers in 2002 sparked demonstrations by parents and advocacy organizations representing minority and low-income communities.

Legislation enacted in October 2001 gave the SBE authority to postpone the date of the high school graduation requirement if a second legislatively mandated study, due in May 2003, raised concerns about the technical adequacy of the CAHSEE or of students' opportunities to learn the tested material. The bill, AB 1609, also removed the option for ninth graders to take the test. When the second study projected that at least 20% of the class of 2004 would fail the CAHSEE, the SBE voted in July 2003 to postpone the consequences of the exam for 2 years.

MARYLAND

Assessment and Accountability Policies

The Maryland High School Functional Tests—assessments of basic skills in reading, writing, mathematics, and citizenship—have served as a high school graduation requirement since the 1970s. In the early 1990s, Maryland developed Learning Outcomes for grades K–8; the Maryland School Performance Assessment Program, to assess student performance on these outcomes; and a school-level accountability system based on both sets of state tests. The Maryland State Board of Education (MSBE) released Core Learning Goals for grades 9–12 in 1996, and one year later, approved the development of a new high school exit examination for the graduating class of 2004.

The High School Assessments is a series of end-of-course tests that will cover core academic areas in English, mathematics, science, and social studies. Twelve tests will be phased in over a period of years; students eventually must pass 10 of these exams to receive a diploma. Phase I of testing began with students entering grade 9 in fall 2001. These students will be required to take tests in English I, algebra, American government, and biology when they complete the appropriate courses. The state will set the cut score for passing these examinations in 2003. Assessment results for this and the subsequent ninth-grade class (classes of 2005 and 2006) will be reported on individual transcripts by the percentile in which the student placed compared with all others who took that particular exam. Results also will be used to analyze the progress that school systems and individual schools have made in preparing their students for the assessments.

Maryland public school students entering grade 9 in fall 2003 (class of 2007) must pass these four assessments to graduate from high school. A student who does not pass a test the first time will receive assistance from the local school system and may retake the test when local administrators agree the student is ready. Students also will take a geometry and a tenth-grade reading test to meet the requirements of the NCLB Act. The MSBE will decide when additional tests should be implemented for Phases II and III, including English II and III, earth/space science, chemistry, physics, U.S. history, and world history.

CHANGES AND CHALLENGES TO THE HIGH SCHOOL ASSESSMENT

Maryland has delayed implementation of its new high school graduation requirement twice, first from 2004 to 2005, and then from 2005 to 2007. The initial delay was an internal decision that reflected the difficulty of developing the new examinations as quickly as planned and concerns about how ready students were to pass the tests. The MSBE agreed to a year of "no-fault" testing in 2000–2001, and Superintendent Nancy Grasmick formed a committee of teachers, parents, secondary school principals, business people, and representatives from higher education to advise her on the implementation of the high school assessment.

In January 1998, the MSBE called for the development of a comprehensive K–12 program of assistance for students not succeeding in reading or mathematics or in one of the tested content areas. The plan, *Every Child Achieving: A Plan for Meeting the Needs of the Individual Learner*, recommends strategies "to prevent student failure through academic intervention, to strengthen teachers' skills and administrators' leadership by improving educator capacity, and to enhance learning experiences for very young children to ensure student readiness" (Maryland State Board of Education, 1999). It carries a $49 million price tag. When the legislature allocated only $12 million of this "safety net" program for the 2000–2001 school year, the MSBE delayed the diploma requirement a second time. Acting on recommendations from Dr. Grasmick, the MSBE voted to keep the testing program on schedule but made passage of the assessments a graduation requirement for the class of 2007. The legislature allocated a total of $19.5 million toward the intervention plan in 2001–2002. The next year, the legislature enacted a 6-year school funding bill that ultimately will give schools an additional $1.3 billion annually. The increased aid is targeted to the state's highest-need districts.

MASSACHUSETTS

ASSESSMENT AND ACCOUNTABILITY POLICIES

The Education Reform Act of 1993 created the framework for Massachusetts' assessment and accountability policies. This omnibus bill nearly doubled state aid to local school districts between 1993 and 2000 and raised all districts to a newly formulated foundation budget (Betts & Costrell, 2001). In addition, the legislation called for the development of state curriculum frameworks in seven core subjects, an aligned assessment program, and policies to hold districts, schools, and students accountable for teaching and learning the content of the frameworks. Students would have to demonstrate tenth-grade competency on the state assessment in the core subjects of English/language arts, mathematics, science, and social studies as one condition of receiving a high school diploma. A strong system of accountability was considered the *quid pro quo* for the major school finance reform.

The state developed curriculum frameworks during the mid- to late-1990s, and the first administration of the Massachusetts Comprehensive Assessment System (MCAS) took place in 1998. In 2002, students in grades 3, 4, 7, and 10 were tested in English/language arts, and students in grades 4, 6, 8, and 10 were tested in mathematics. Fifth- and eighth-grade students also took tests in science, technology, and history and social studies. In fall 1999, the SBE voted to apply the graduation requirement to the class of

2003, as scheduled, but initially in two content areas (English/language arts and mathematics), and to set the passing score at the bottom of the "needs improvement" performance standard. The SBE also gave students at least five opportunities to take the test—once in grade 10 and at least four times in grades 11 and 12.

The SBE adopted a comprehensive school and district accountability system at the same time. School performance goals, rewards, and sanctions are determined by both the absolute level of student performance and improvement during a rating cycle. State actions can include recognition, warnings, further review, technical assistance, and ultimately the removal of a school's principal. The first set of school performance ratings were issued in January 2001, just months before students in the class of 2003 took their tenth-grade MCAS tests. Nearly 25% of the state's schools (and 35% of its high schools) were identified as having "very" or "critically" low performance; most of these schools also failed to meet their improvement goals (Massachusetts Department of Education, 2001a).

CHANGES AND CHALLENGES TO THE HIGH SCHOOL ASSESSMENT

High failure rates on the MCAS have fueled opposition by civil-rights groups, the Massachusetts Teachers Association, and some suburban superintendents, parents, and students to the use of the test as a high school graduation requirement. In 2000, 34% of the state's tenth-grade students failed the English section, while 45% failed the mathematics section. Failure rates were considerably higher for African American and Hispanic students (Massachusetts Department of Education, 2000). Concerns also were raised about the impact of the MCAS on dropout rates and on special education, bilingual, and vocational education students. Supporters of accountability, including the business community, and some legislators and urban superintendents pressed the state to stay the course.

As proponents and opponents of the MCAS waged a costly public relations battle over the test, State Education Commissioner David Driscoll, Governor Jane Swift, and legislators put forth multiple proposals, ranging from replacing the MCAS with a new system of assessment to providing more exclusions or alternatives for students. In January 2001, the SBE approved policies regarding the retesting of students, including the use of a "focused" version of the MCAS. The shorter examination eliminates the more difficult questions used to measure higher levels of mastery, field-test items, and help with curriculum planning, but requires students to answer more questions to pass. Acting on the recommendations of a blue ribbon commission, the SBE also approved an MCAS appeal process in January 2002 that allows students who have scored close to the passing score to present alternative measures of their performance on the tested skills (Massachusetts Department of Education, 2002a).

In June 2001, the legislature's Joint Education Committee scheduled a hearing on 46 bills addressing the MCAS and the state's accountability system. The bills were hotly debated, but legislators took no action, preferring to review the 2001 test results before making policy changes. When significantly more tenth graders passed the MCAS in spring 2001, there was no impetus for the legislature to take action in the 2001–2002 session.

In September 2002, however, a lawsuit was filed in federal court on behalf of high school students who had failed the MCAS. Citing violations of the Fourteenth Amendment, Title VI of the Civil Rights Act, and provisions of the Massachusetts constitution, plaintiffs argued that students, particularly students of color, students with disabilities or limited English proficiency, and students attending vocational technical education schools, had been denied the opportunity to learn the tested curriculum. In addition, they charged that the state had failed to assist their schools, which had been identified as low performing by the state accountability system, and/or failed to hold schools accountable for providing timely and effective intervention.

PROBLEMS ACTING AS THE IMPETUS FOR CHANGE

Policy makers in the four study states have responded to four kinds of concerns about their HSEE policies: (1) high failure rates, (2) insufficient opportunities for students to learn the materials covered by the tests, (3) reliance on a single measure of high school students' performance, and (4) concerns about test properties. Policy makers are also sensitive to the threat of lawsuits and in some cases are looking at a recent decision in Texas, *G.I. Forum* v. *Texas Education Agency* (2000), for guidance on how to make their high school assessment policies defensible in court.

HIGH FAILURE RATES

The three study states that have administered their exit examinations and set cut scores all experienced high failure rates. Although students took the HSEEs under different conditions in each state, nearly half of Arizona and California students failed at least one section of their high school assessment. (Sophomores who took the MCAS in spring 2001 and ninth-grade students who took the CAHSEE in spring 2001 were the first classes to be affected by their state high school graduation requirements. Sophomores who took the MCAS in spring 2000 did not have to pass the assessment to graduate from high school. At the time they took the AIMS in 2000 and

2001, the English/language arts test was a graduation requirement for Arizona sophomores. Although Maryland had not yet set passing scores on its first phase of tests, it was estimated early in the test development process that only 50% of students would pass the assessments in the first administration.) Although student scores increased substantially in Massachusetts, 30% of tenth-grade students did not pass both sections of the test in either 2001 or 2002. Students performed better on the English/language arts than on the mathematics portions of their exams, however. This differential performance across subjects held for all racial/ethnic groups. (See Table 11.1.)

Some policy makers have argued that failure rates will drop over time, after high school students face the threat of not receiving their high school diploma. This did occur in Massachusetts, where failure rates dropped about 20 percentage points in 2001, across all racial/ethnic categories, for the first group of students to face the high school graduation requirement. In Arizona, however, the failure rates did not change significantly over time.

Minority failure rates remained exceedingly high across the three states, however, generally twice those of White students. The high and differential failure rates for minority students in Arizona became the basis of the civil-rights complaint filed by the William E. Morris Institute for Justice. The Institute argued that, when compared with those for White students, the pass rates for minorities fell well below the four-fifths (80%) standard for determining disparate impact applied in the Texas litigation. (In *G.I. Forum* v. *Texas Education Agency* [2000], the court used the U.S. Equal Employment Opportunity Commission's Uniform Guidelines on Employee Selection Procedures to determine whether the Texas high school exit examination had an adverse impact on minority students. Under these guidelines for employment testing, adverse impact is established when the passing rate for the minority group is less than 80% of the passing rate for the majority group [Phillips, 2000].) These low and disparate pass rates were found at grades 3, 5, and 8 as well. The Massachusetts lawsuit also argues that the MCAS has a differential and discriminatory impact on minority students, with 44% of the African American and 50% of the Hispanic members of the class of 2003 at risk of not graduating.

OPPORTUNITY TO LEARN

While some policy makers ascribe high failure rates to a lack of student motivation, others are concerned that high school students lack access to the content covered on the HSEEs. Court rulings on the constitutionality of high school graduation tests in Florida (*Debra P.* v. *Turlington*, 1981) and Texas (*G.I. Forum* v. *Texas Education Agency*, 2000) have identified criteria for determining whether high school students had sufficient opportunity

Table 11.1. Percent of Students Failing State High School Exit Examinations[1]

Test	AZ 2000	AZ 2001	AZ 2002	CA 2001	CA 2002	MA 2000	MA 2001	MA 2002
English/language arts								
All students	32	32	38	36	36	34	18	14
White students	19	18	20	18	22	27	12	9
African American students	46	46	52	50	50	60	40	33
Hispanic students	53	52	57	52	51	66	48	39
Mathematics								
All students	84	69[2]	68	56	52	45	25	25
White students	77	58	52	36	32	38	18	19
African American students	95	84	81	76	70	77	52	55
Hispanic students	95	86	86	75	67	79	58	58

Sources: Arizona Department of Education (2001a, 2001b, 2002a, 2002c); California Department of Education (2002); Lucas (2001); Massachusetts Department of Education (2000, 2001b, 2002b, 2002c); Wise et al. (2002).

Notes:

1. Percentages are for tenth-grade students taking the high school test that year (with the exception of California in 2001, which tested only ninth-grade students). In 2002, the cohort failure rates for the three states were: Arizona class of 2002: 12% of total students in reading, 54% in mathematics; California class of 2004: 52% of total, 72% of African American, and 70% of Hispanic students; Massachusetts class of 2003: 19% of total, 44% of African American, and 50% of Hispanic students.

2. Results on the 2000 and 2001 tenth-grade mathematics test are not comparable. The 2001 test includes only those concepts and performance objectives in the core high school curriculum, while the 2000 test includes a broader set of concepts.

to learn (OTL) the skills tested on a graduation test. These include adequate notice of the testing requirements for graduation, teaching the tested skills ("curricular validity"), multiple opportunities to take the test, and evidence of successful remediation efforts (Phillips, 2000). Debate over OTL in our study states focused on issues of curriculum and remediation.

One issue that policy makers face is whether the content covered by the HSEE is aligned with the state's standards. (See Baker and Linn, and Rothman, this volume.) High school examinations in three of the study states, Arizona, California, and Massachusetts, are designed to measure performance on tenth-grade standards. Arizona and California modified their mathematics examinations after determining that some questions required knowledge beyond that covered in algebra 1 and geometry, courses typically taught in the first 2 years of high school.

A more difficult issue is whether the content embodied in the state standards and assessments is taught in the state's schools. Formal and informal surveys of teachers and principals conducted in Arizona, California, and Maryland found that implementation of state standards was very uneven across schools and school districts. In California, for example, both high school principals and teachers reported a high awareness of state standards and efforts to align district and school curriculum with these standards. Fewer than half of the surveyed teachers, however, planned to modify their instruction or pay greater attention to content standards in preparation for the CAHSEE. Twenty percent of the teachers were unaware of *any* activities to help students prepare for the test (Wise et al., 2002). Educators were concerned about the low skill levels of students entering high school and estimated in spring 2000 (correctly, it appears) that half of their students were not prepared to pass the HSEE. They remain particularly concerned about the opportunities of students with disabilities and English-language learners to learn the tested materials (Wise et al., 2000, 2002).

About 40% of the educators responding to an Arizona Department of Education survey indicated they needed more time to align their curriculum, instruction, and instructional resources with the state standards (Koehler, Rabinowitz, Miyasaka, & McRobbie, 2001). Even the state conceded that "it appears that what is being taught to some students lags behind the expectations of the standards" (Arizona Department of Education, 2000). One observer reported that large numbers of Arizona teachers and administrators still see the standards and state test as external to what the schools are doing.

A third issue is whether students take the courses needed to pass the HSEE. Over half of California's high school students, and an undetermined number of Arizona high school students, had not taken algebra because their states did not require the course for high school graduation. It was not surprising, therefore, that students performed so poorly on the mathematics sections of the HSEEs. Policy makers in both California and Arizona subsequently have mandated that students take a mathematics course in which algebra is covered.

Finally, calls for change in all of the states have included arguments that more remediation is needed to get students ready for the test, especially in low-performing schools. In Maryland, the testing requirement year was pushed back by 2 years because the state budget did not include sufficient funding for a comprehensive intervention plan enacted by the State Board of Education in 1999. Only half of the principals surveyed in California reported plans to provide tutoring or other forms of remedial instruction to high school students who failed the CAHSEE (Wise et al., 2002). Respondents in Arizona and Massachusetts were also uncertain whether their states and districts will adequately fund and provide remedial services, although Massachusetts has allocated $40–$50 million a year for these programs.

MULTIPLE MEASURES

Testing opponents and representatives of special-needs students in the study states also questioned the use of one test as a requirement for high school graduation. Concerned about the "one-size-fits-all" nature of high school exit examinations, education groups in Arizona and Massachusetts have called for the use of multiple measures, including portfolios, grades, and local assessments to measure student performance against state standards. Policy maker assurances that students would have multiple opportunities to take the tests, or multiple testing formats, do not satisfy these critics, who view these definitions of "multiple measures" as too narrow.

TEST DEVELOPMENT

State assessments, and particularly high school graduation tests, should be valid and reliable and meet professional standards for test quality. In *G.I. Forum* v. *Texas Education Agency*, the court used the American Educational Research Association, American Psychological Association, and National Council on Measurement in Education *Standards for Educational and Psychological Testing* (1999) to evaluate the technical quality of both the test development process and the Texas high school examinations. Test development issues usually are addressed within state departments of education. In California, however, the short timeline for developing and field-testing the high school assessment raised concerns about the validity of data that would be used to set cut scores. As explained later in this chapter, this technical issue became embroiled in the politics of assessment.

MID-COURSE CORRECTIONS TO HIGH SCHOOL
EXIT EXAMINATIONS

Over the years, states have made a number of adjustments in their testing and accountability systems for high school students in response to technical issues, political opposition, and concern over high failure rates. Hess (2002) argues that these actions generally have included lowering the stakes, making the test easier, reducing the threshold required to pass, permitting some students to side-step the required assessment, and/or delaying the implementation of the examination.

To date, none of our four study states have abandoned their high school exit examinations. Arizona and California made their mathematics tests easier by removing items involving knowledge of algebra 2, trigonometry, and calculus, but officials in both states argued that this material generally is not taught until after tenth grade, the focus of their HSEEs. And, despite pressure from parents and advocacy groups, policy makers are holding the line on including all students in their HSEE requirements. The four study states provide test accommodations for special education students and have developed, or will develop, alternative assessments for students with severe disabilities, as required by federal law. Accommodations for English-language learners are less clear. Only Massachusetts offers its high school assessments in a foreign language (Spanish) to limited English proficient students. These students, however, must pass the English/language arts assessment in the English language. Policy makers in all four states also have withstood calls to issue multiple diplomas. Massachusetts recently created a state-endorsed "local certificate of attainment" for students who meet all of their class requirements but fail the MCAS.

Our states responded, instead, by reducing the cut scores on their high school assessments (at least temporarily), delaying implementation of the diploma requirement, and developing alternative performance measures. Two of the four states—California and Massachusetts—set the passing score for their HSEE at a level below what originally was intended or what policy makers had considered. Forced to use ninth-grade test scores as the basis of their decision, the California State Board of Education established passing scores for the CAHSEE that were 10–15 percentage points below those recommended by a panel of experts. The president of the SBE stated that "given the current situation [the lack of a tenth-grade census], our best course was to set the passing score as we did with the intention to move it up to a 70% passing score [the recommended score] for future classes of high school students" (California Department of Education, 2001a). Massachusetts set its passing score at the bottom rather than the top of the "needs improvement" standard, as some policy makers had proposed. Arizona is considering lowering the passing score on its mathematics examination. The fourth state, Maryland, had not gone through the cut score process yet.

Arizona, California, and Maryland have delayed the year in which students will be required to pass the high school exit examination in order to graduate. Policy makers in Massachusetts have left this option open. California's external evaluator initially recommended postponing full implementation of the CAHSEE requirement by 1 or 2 years to give schools more time to prepare students for the test (Wise et al., 2000), and the legislature subsequently granted the SBE the authority to defer the date of the graduation requirement past 2004 (California Department of Education, 2001b). When the second evaluation showed that many students still lacked opportunities to learn the tested material (Wise et al., 2003), the California SBE delayed implementation of the graduation requirement until 2006.

Finally, the Arizona State Board of Education enacted an alternative competency demonstration for students who cannot pass Arizona's high school graduation test. The state will develop several models of alternative assessments designed to provide students with another method to demonstrate their proficiency on the same standards tested by AIMS (Arizona Department of Education, 2002b). Massachusetts developed an appeals process that allows students who score within four points of the MCAS cut score to present alternative performance measures as proof that they have mastered the necessary tenth-grade skills. Nearly one-half of the students who failed the tenth-grade MCAS in spring 2001 scored between 216 and the passing score of 220 (Massachusetts Department of Education, 2001b). To be eligible for the appeal, students also must have taken the MCAS at least three times, maintained a 95% attendance rate, and participated in the tutoring or academic support services available at their school. Alternative measures include course grades, teacher recommendations, work samples, and scores on other standardized tests (Massachusetts Department of Education, 2002a).

POLITICAL ISSUES IN REDESIGNING ACCOUNTABILITY

The adjustments states are making in their use of assessments for high school graduation are highly consequential decisions. These decisions not only affect the life chances of thousands of students, but they also send strong signals about policy maker commitment to the entire standards-based reform agenda. If they weaken the requirements too much, by reducing rigor or delaying effective dates too far out into the future, policy makers may undermine the reform movement that they have worked hard to set in motion. On the other hand, if they ignore opposition and criticism, they risk provoking boycotts of the assessments and potentially more serious protests. They also, of course, risk harming students whose failure may reflect lack of opportunity to learn much more than their own academic limitations. Policy makers are trying to strike the right balance, sticking to their goal of ensuring that students meet standards by graduation, yet providing enough slack so that the system can adjust.

We do not know whether the four states examined in this chapter struck the "right" balance for their own political contexts. We don't know yet whether the mid-course corrections we have just described will turn out to be the last major adjustments or part of a series of continuing fixes and whether the eventual result will be the persistence of standards-based high school graduation criteria or their demise. We can, however, examine how these decisions were crafted politically and consider the political hazards that remain.

THE POLITICAL LINE -UP AROUND MID -COURSE CORRECTIONS

Decisions about high school exit exams are shaped primarily by five groups of actors: (1) top state leaders, (2) rank-and-file legislators, (3) education groups, (4) business leaders, and (5) the public. In all four states, *top leadership* across the branches of government has remained firmly behind the reform agenda and committed to adjusting but not abandoning the high school exit examination strategy. This is true even when the political parties differ. In Massachusetts, the Republican governor and appointed state board and chief state school officer have counted on the support of the Democratic legislative leaders—some of whom were among the original architects of education reform in 1993—as they have withstood opposition to the MCAS. Top leadership support is also apparent no matter which branch or policy maker takes the lead in recommending alterations or postponements. These decisions generally are made by state boards of education, but they can be pushed primarily by the chief state school officer, as in Maryland and now in Arizona, or by the governor, as in California and Massachusetts. Whoever takes the initiative, it appears that unity among top leadership is necessary to withstand life-threatening opposition to HSEEs.

If legislative leadership support were to weaken, HSEEs would be in considerably more peril. This relates to a second aspect of the political line-up, the fact that *rank-and-file legislators* are much more tentative about the examinations and the reform agenda and are introducing legislation calling for changes. Forty-six bills to change the design, administration, or implementation of the MCAS were introduced in the Massachusetts state legislature in 2000–2001. Arizona State Senator Jay Blanchard proposed legislation to remove the AIMS test as a high school graduation requirement unless there was a state referendum or some other way of determining broad public support for it. The measure passed the Senate but was killed by House education leadership. In California, the governor and legislative leaders supported legislation to delay the effective date for the HSEE so adequate cut scores could be set, but Senate Republicans managed to kill it. According to one Arizona respondent, legislatures are waking up to the outcry over HSEEs, having delegated much of the responsibility for assessment and accountability to state agencies. He said, "The legislature has abdicated its role in this process and now we realize that we have a problem." Without leadership holding firm, the legislative assault against HSEEs would be much more consequential.

Much of the legislative action is being pushed by *educator groups*. Teachers, principals, school boards, and administrators have joined together in a number of cases to press their claims that the HSEEs are premature, given the time it has taken to implement reforms, and that some kinds of students are disadvantaged by on-demand, timed paper and pencil tests. The Massachusetts Teachers Association (MTA) sponsored that state's Senate Bill 225 that would have scaled down the MCAS tests and limited their use to diagnostic purposes.

Education groups in Arizona produced a white paper calling for multiple assessments as a diploma requirement. They also have pressed for a very long phase-in time for the AIMS test to permit changes in instruction to take place in elementary grades, then middle and high school, before students are held accountable. According to representatives of these groups, they were blocked out of the decision-making process, and hence turned to the legislature, including legislators who are teachers. Some supporters of the HSEEs think that educator opposition is not just about opportunity to learn or other substantive concerns about appropriate assessment use. Instead they think educators are just ducking accountability. A business leader in Maryland, where teachers have not been vocal opponents, as discussed below, said, "There are some groups that do not want the assessment at all."

It is important to note that education organizational positions do not always reflect full consensus among membership. Policy makers in a number of these states say that rank-and-file members may have very different views than organizational leadership and that many individual teachers are enthusiastically implementing reforms. One important example of a schism among educators is the split between Massachusetts' urban superintendents and their suburban and rural counterparts. The urban leaders want the MCAS pressure to remain intact because they see changes in instruction and in student response occurring in response to the reforms; they worry that any delay in or watering down of the high school graduation requirement will undermine this progress.

Business leaders are generally as dedicated to reform as many education groups are opposed; their support of HSEEs has been critical to leadership's resolute stance. California Business for Education Excellence is closely in touch with the Governor's staff and State Board of Education and is working on an outreach campaign about the importance of standards-based reform. Similar activities have been undertaken by the Massachusetts Business Alliance for Education, Mass Insight Education, the Business for Better Schools Coalition, and other business leaders in Massachusetts. Some business groups supported advertising that counters the extensive MTA anti-MCAS campaign, provided information to the public, assisted school districts to implement reform, and worked with leadership to deal with anti-reform sentiment. The strength of their commitment is illustrated by one top business leader's statement that "there is an extremely important, in fact revolutionary, change that the state made in 1993 to give a good education to every child regardless of background, and that is going to take a major effort by everyone, and this is no time to give up on it." The Maryland Business Roundtable helped plan the implementation of the high school assessment and, like its counterparts in other states, has engaged in public outreach about standards-based reforms. Only in Arizona has business leadership been less than stalwart. Although top policy leadership thought business was still in its camp, the Greater Phoenix Chamber of Commerce, according to a legislator, "just backed away from endorsing the AIMS and is now saying that they are having trouble with it; they buckled because of the high number of juniors who have not passed yet."

The *public* is seen by political leadership as generally supportive of the reforms, although particular parent groups have been vocal opponents of HSEEs. Special education parents typically worry about the adequacy of accommodations, and suburban parents, such as those represented in the Coalition for Authentic Reform of Education in Massachusetts, worry about the narrowing of the curriculum and about potential black marks against their children who do so well on traditional measures. Policy makers frequently say that the parents of children that reforms are designed to benefit the most—low-income, minority students—are not the ones complaining so loudly. They tend to cite the general opinion polls as evidence that the public is on their side and see the organized parental groups and educator groups as nonrepresentative. For example, an Arizona poll found 82% of the public in favor of requiring passage of a standardized test before graduation. Lisa Graham Keegan, in announcing her resignation to head a Washington, DC-based institute, remarked that there is a "huge, huge disconnect" between education leaders and the general public (Kossan, 2001).

There may a split between parents and nonparents on HSEEs, however, that presents dilemmas for the reforms more generally. The general public is supportive of standards and accountability, while various parental groups—special education parents, suburban parents—are falling away. Urban parents may follow if high failure rates persist. The planned demonstrations in California are one example of this. Further, although generally supportive of HSEEs in national polls, 75% of parents either strongly agreed or somewhat agreed that "it's wrong to use the results of just one test to decide whether a student gets promoted or graduates" (Public Agenda, 2001). It seems unlikely that policy makers can ignore widespread parental disaffection, even though the rest of the public remains committed. However, it is hard to predict how the public opinion data will be interpreted by policy makers. Some Massachusetts MCAS supporters have taken heart in the fact that the decline in support for standards has plateaued—even that weak signal is seen as heartening.

THE MARYLAND AND CALIFORNIA DIFFERENCE

Maryland and California experienced a relatively moderate and polite debate around HSEEs, making these states an interesting contrast to Arizona and Massachusetts. Among our four states, the antipathy between educational and governmental leadership was strongest in Arizona and Massachusetts. Some of this is due to particular political histories. Lisa Graham Keegan antagonized teachers with her national leadership around a charter school/choice agenda and her abandonment of content standards that had been developed with educator involvement prior to her term. Former Massachusetts Board Chair, John Silber, was known for repeated attacks on teachers. The previous governor, Paul Celluci, proposed testing teachers in schools with high MCAS mathematics failures. Teacher groups challenged the policy without success in a Massachusetts court. In Maryland and California, on the other hand, the education groups felt more included in the process and were less likely to challenge the HSEE reform. In California, the Education Coalition, composed of the largest education groups, formed an assessment committee that has met with representatives of the Governor, State Board of Education, and State Department of Education. In Maryland, the state superintendent formed an advisory committee that included education groups. As a member of one of the associations represented said, "The better route to take was to work with the system to make it as good as it could be and to have an impact on it."

Governance structure also can be important. Maryland has a small education policy maker community, for example. With only 24 districts, it is easy to get everyone in the room and hash out the issues, and the Commissioner of Education meets monthly with all local superintendents. In addition, legislative powers are very limited. The legislature can only add to and not subtract from the Governor's budget and historically has delegated significant powers to the State Board of Education.

In both Maryland and California, popular leaders have emerged as champions of reform. The Maryland School Superintendent, Nancy Grasmick, has enormous personal authority, and in California a number of research brokers have tried to reach accommodations across reform supporters and opponents.

Another major factor setting Maryland and California apart is that the adjustments we examine in this chapter were made in advance of the setting of a cut score, during the test development phase. Unlike the Arizona and Massachusetts changes, which took place after initial testing and high, widely publicized failure rates, no one in Maryland and California yet knew how well—or poorly—students would do and the public was not yet energized about the results. In Maryland, the initial delay in the effective date of the graduation requirement was a technical decision, made in house by the State Board of Education because the end-of-course tests could not be completed in time. The second delay—and the decision to include HSEE scores on student transcripts until they would serve as a graduation requirement—was made after an estimate of high failures, but without any actual administration of the tests, which was not scheduled until fall 2001. In California, the Governor's decision to cut the length of the test was made before the first administration in spring 2001. California has and Maryland may go through more rounds of adjustments after students take their tests and cut scores are set. These later decisions may be more contentious, but if California's recent decision is an example, it also may be that very early flexibility and more deliberate decision making will head off the more polarized politics seen in Arizona and Massachusetts.

THEMES IN THE POLITICAL DEBATE

The politics of accountability redesign are characterized by several recurring themes that are evident in all four states. They generally relate to opportunity to learn, which as we have seen is a major point of contention between HSEE opponents and supporters. The debate over OTL focuses on: (1) whether students who need it get sufficient remediation and extra opportunities to learn, (2) the extent to which remediation and other aspects of providing adequate instruction are state or local responsibilities and whether the courts will find that they've met their responsibilities, and (3) the timeline for achieving OTL. In addition, in at least two of the states, information about OTL came from field-based research, which is playing an important role in decisions about adjustments to HSEEs. A final theme evident in these cases concerns the fairness of implementing stakes for students when systems holding adults accountable have not yet been firmly implemented in some of these states.

Large numbers of student failures or projected failures are raising policy makers' concerns about early intervention and remediation for low-performing students. Massachusetts has a statewide Academic Support Program that funds locally provided remediation (summer school, after school, and, more recently, intensified school day instruction), which is growing rapidly in size. The state invested $40 million a year between 2000 and 2002 for remedial help, plus another $10 million in 2001–2002 for juniors who did not pass the high school test. In response to an MSBE resolution, the Maryland State Department of Education developed a set of strategies for academic intervention, improving educator capacity, and ensuring student readiness. It was because the legislature did not fund important components of this program that the MSBE decided to delay the sanctions element of the HSEE. California students who are at risk of failing the HSEE, or of not being promoted, are entitled to unlimited hours of state-funded supplemental instruction. Governor Gray Davis also has invested millions of dollars in professional development institutes for teachers.

California, Massachusetts, and Maryland are examples of states accepting some responsibility for opportunity to learn. The definitions of state responsibility seem to run on a continuum. At one end is the view that states have a minimal role. They need only to provide general operating aid and the standards/assessment/accountability system, and it is up to districts to do the rest—to ensure that curriculum is aligned with standards, prepare teachers to teach the curriculum, and so on. In the middle range are conceptions of the state role that are slightly more directive. States should provide not only general aid, but state-funded remediation and professional development programs; the state provides targeted support, but the design and implementation of support strategies are up to the district. One step further toward state responsibility would be state-run programs, like California's extensive professional development institutes, in which the state takes direct responsibility for aspects of opportunity to learn. At the far end of the continuum is the existence of a state curriculum and efforts by the state to ensure that the curriculum is being enacted.

Policy makers are acutely aware of these distinctions and have varied views on what definition of a state role is sufficient. For example, top officials in the Maryland State Department of Education feel that the targeted intervention money is a *sine qua non* for state responsibility for OTL. Said one, "We do not feel in good conscience that, unless we get the money that we know is necessary to implement this academic intervention plan, we can tie the high-stakes assessment to graduation." In contrast, Massachusetts policy makers frequently referred to a "deal," in which the original 1993 reform significantly increased the state share of funding to districts and improved equity across districts at the same time as standards and accountability were being introduced. Districts were to get more money and, in return, they would be accountable for student learning. However, one business group leader acknowledged that money alone may not be enough. "There is state money and new programs but the state should probably be playing a bigger, more organized role to provide technical assistance and maybe get some new programs out there that run across districts." As in many other states, the Massachusetts State Department of Education has not kept pace in staff capacity with growth in expectations about the state role, so the desire for more assistance is hard to meet.

In each state, worries about litigation are forcing policy makers to think particularly hard about opportunity-to-learn questions. Some actions have already been filed, such as a California suit on behalf of learning-disabled students, an administrative claim under Title VI of the Civil Rights Act focusing on high minority failures on the Arizona assessment, and a federal lawsuit in Massachusetts on behalf of minority and special-needs students who failed that state's exam. Even where no suits have yet been filed, policy makers have been working with their Attorney General's office to prepare for action. Many are conscious of the *G.I. Forum* v. *Texas Education Agency* suit in which Texas successfully defended its graduation requirement based on multiple opportunities to take the graduation test and sufficient state funding. But Texas law also requires all public schools to teach the content of the state's curriculum (Phillips, 2000). It remains to be seen whether states with different definitions of their responsibility can withstand legal challenge.

Some who are concerned about opportunity to learn think that it is only fair to hold high school students accountable after they have been exposed to standards-based instruction for several years. Some educators in Massachusetts, for example, have suggested that a very long phase-in time, longer than the 7 years since the initial reform, is necessary to give students more exposure to reforms that have not yet been fully implemented. The state was slow to develop standards, and standards have since undergone revision, thereby not yet providing steady guidance to educators. In many districts, aligned curricula and opportunities for teachers to learn to improve their instruction are not yet in place. An outgoing state board member suggested that the MCAS should not be a graduation requirement until students who were subject to it from grade 1 reach grade 10 (Delattre, 2001). However, supporters of HSEEs think that students will not take the standards seriously unless there are consequences to assessment and that neither society nor the students themselves can continue to jeopardize the future through diplomas that offer no guarantee of learning. In their view, while the system may take years to adjust, schools need to find a way, through specially targeted interventions if necessary, to ensure that all students meet standards. The debate over how long it takes to provide opportunity to learn is an important one that we saw in all four states.

In order to learn whether there is sufficient opportunity to learn within their states, some of the policy makers we spoke to were turning to research and evaluation. In California, the legislatively authorized evaluations conducted by HumRRO (Wise et al., 2000, 2002, 2003) provided very specific data on the issue, examining programs and instruction in a sample of districts and informed the decision to delay the high school graduation requirement for two years. Arizona used WestEd, its federal regional educational laboratory, to analyze public input on how long educators and the public thought it would take to give students opportunities to learn the content tested on AIMS. On the other hand, very little research and evaluation have been commissioned in Massachusetts, where the state agency has been strapped for resources. In Maryland, the small number of districts makes it possible for policy makers to rely on direct testimony from educators and visits to the field about the presence or absence of aligned curriculum and other aspects of opportunities to learn. It is likely that the importance of the opportunity-to-learn issue will force states to get more information on the status of reform implementation. For most states with many districts, this will mean that they must commission studies. It is likely that research will play an increasing role in the continued debate over HSEEs.

A final theme is one that was more implicit than explicit in our interviews. In most states, accountability for adults is only in its infancy, whereas students are on the line in the very near future. In the states we have examined, very few schools have been sanctioned for poor performance. In Massachusetts, of 86 schools designated as "critically low," only 12 underwent the required in-depth reviews because of limited state capacity. In Maryland, 107 schools had been declared reconstitution eligible as of January 2002. Only four schools have been reconstituted by the state; three are being managed by a private vendor. California designated 3,244 schools as underperforming in 1999–2000, but has appropriated funds to assist only 1,270 of them.

Given this slow progress, it is not surprising that teachers see themselves as less accountable than others in the system. The Consortium for

Policy Research in Education conducted surveys of teachers in eight states that vary with respect to where stakes are placed (on schools versus students versus both) and the intensity or severity of the stakes. In each state, teachers believed that "schools" were held more accountable by states for student performance than they themselves were. In general, the same was true of their view of local district accountability; schools are on the line but they are less so (Elmore & Fuhrman, 2001; Goertz, 2001).

If adults are not taking the accountability system seriously enough to provide sufficient opportunity to learn, some might say it is not fair to hold students accountable (see Elmore, this volume). However, holding schools firmly accountable depends directly on state capacity, and when capacity is lacking, it is easier to delay or soften sanctions on schools without thinking about how that affects the accountability balance across adults and children.

CONCLUSIONS AND IMPLICATIONS

Our review of four states indicates that the "backlash" over HSEEs raises central questions about the purpose, design, and politics of student accountability systems. At issue in the controversies we have examined are the alignment between the assessment system and state standards, the severity of the stakes and the timing of their implementation, the definition and measurement of opportunity to learn, the definition of multiple measures, the balance of stakes across adult and student populations, and the extent to which state policy makers see themselves as accountable for well-designed systems and opportunity to learn. The contrasts among the states in the way adjustments to the HSEE systems were made suggest several implications for policy makers pondering high school graduation requirements.

One set of implications has to do with the process of designing accountability systems. Judging from the California and Maryland examples, reaching out to stakeholders, particularly educators and parents, early and often and including them in continuing design decisions can lead to a collaborative problem-solving approach. Open relations permit candid discussions about the state of readiness in the field.

Another set of implications has to do with opportunity to learn. Policy makers must identify and fund the types and amount of support and capacity building needed to provide students the opportunity to pass the tests. Policy makers also have to define what opportunity to learn means in their state. This is to some extent a legal question, and states certainly should keep an eye on developing litigation. But, more fundamentally, opportunity to learn is a question of fairness. It is not fair to deny students a diploma if they have not had a chance to learn the material assessed.

A final set of implications has to do with the extent to which states are accountable for the success of their own standards and accountability reforms. The HSEEs we have examined were all created by states, yet, as we have seen, policy makers differ considerably about the extent to which the state must actively fund and promote opportunity to learn. Culture, tradition, and politics influence decisions about the balance between state and local responsibility. However, in our view, both the courts and constituencies will appropriately press states to back up their assessment systems with sufficient funding and technical assistance, in the form of curriculum models, professional development, student remedial programs, and the like. We know that districts vary dramatically in their capacity to support instructional improvement (see, for example, Massell, 2000; Spillane & Thompson, 1997). "Demand-side" approaches, where states simply funnel money down to local districts, without efforts to help them use the money most productively or to set quality standards for providers from whom they might purchase assistance, are not likely to be sufficient.

Another aspect of state responsibility has to do with the extent to which the state enforces all aspects of its accountability system. As we have seen, school-level accountability often is held hostage to the absence of sufficient state department personnel or resources to adequately evaluate and/or provide remedies to failing schools. However, states seem ready to impose consequences on all students, even though the adults responsible for their education are not bearing the same degree of risk. The delay in school-level accountability may undermine the extent to which teachers attend to standards-based reforms and imperil opportunity to learn for students. And, the delay sends signals about the state's willingness to put itself on the line. States that are "failing" in their ability to help failing schools but enforcing HSEEs are risking making students bear the brunt of system failure.

REFERENCES

American Educational Research Association, American Psychological Association, & National Council on Measurement in Education. (1999). *Standards for educational and psychological testing*. Washington, DC: Authors.

Arizona Department of Education. (2000, November 28). *AIMS update*. Retrieved from www.ade.state.az.us/standards/AIMSUpdates/

Arizona Department of Education. (2001a, April 23). *AIMS 2000 results*. Retrieved from www.ade.state.az.us/standards/AIMS/Results/

Arizona Department of Education. (2001b, October). *AIMS: Analysis of spring 2001 results*. Retrieved from www.ade.state.az.us/standards/AIMS/Results/

Arizona Department of Education. (2002a, January). *Unpublished tabulations of the AIMS 2001 test scores*.

Arizona Department of Education. (2002b, May). AIMS–Equivalent Demonstration (AIMS-ED). Retrieved from www.ade.state.az.us/standards/aims/aimsed/

Arizona Department of Education. (2002c, August). *Arizona's instrument to measure standards (AIMS). Press release. Summary report for spring 2002 test administration.* Retrieved from www.ade.az.gov/standards/aims/results/2002 AIMSExecSum.pdf/

Arizona Department of Education. (2002d, October 15). New achievement profiles reveal most Arizona schools making progress. *Arizona Department of Education News.* Retrieved from: www.ade.state.az.us/services/pio/press-releases/2002/pr10–15-02.asp/

Betts, J. R., & Costrell, R. M. (2001). Incentives and equity under standards-based reform. In D. Ravitch (Ed.), *Brookings papers on education policy 2001* (pp. 9–74). Washington, DC: Brookings Institution.

California Department of Education. (2001a, June 7). State Board of Education releases high school exit examination results. *California Department of Education news release.* Retrieved from www.cde.ca.gov/statetests/hsee/

California Department of Education. (2001b, October 16). California high school exit examination (CAHSEE). *Assessment notes.* Retrieved from www.cde.ca.gov/statetests/

California Department of Education. (2002, September 30). Eastin releases spring 2002 California high school exit exam results. Attachments 1–4. *California Department of Education news release.* Retrieved from www.cde.ca.gov/news/releases2002/rel30.asp/

Debra P. v. Turlington, 644 F.2d 397, 6775 (5th Cir. 1981).

Delattre, E. (2001, March 1). Open letter to the Massachusetts State Board of Education. Boston: Boston University, School of Education.

Elmore, R. F., & Fuhrman S. H. (2001). Holding schools accountable: Is it working? *Phi Delta Kappan, 83*(1), 67–72.

Flannery, P. (2001, May 18). AIMS faces civil rights challenge. *The Arizona Republic.*

G.I. Forum v. Texas Education Agency, 887 F. Supp. 2d 667, 675 n. 7 (W.D. Tex. 2000).

Goertz, M. E. (2001). Standards-based accountability: Horse trade or horse whip? In S. H. Fuhrman (Ed.), *From the capitol to the classroom: Standards-based reform in the states* (pp. 39–59). Chicago: University of Chicago Press.

Hess, F. M. (2002). Reform, resistance, . . . retreat? The predictable policies of accountability in Virginia. In D. Ravitch (Ed.), *Brookings papers on education policy 2002* (pp. 69–122). Washington, DC: Brookings Institution Press.

Koehler, P., Rabinowitz, S., Miyasaka, J., & McRobbie, J. (2001). *AIMS as a high school graduation requirement. A report for the Arizona State Board of Education.* San Francisco: WestEd.

Kossan, P. (2000, November 27). By trying to do too much too quick, AIMS missed mark. *The Arizona Republic.*

Kossan, P. (2001, May 4). Keegan resigns as school chief. *The Arizona Republic.*

Lucas, G. (2001, June 7). "Abysmal" exit test results for ninth-graders. *San Francisco Chronicle.* Retrieved from www.sfgate.com.

Maryland State Board of Education. (1999). *Every child achieving: A plan for meeting the needs of the individual learner.* Baltimore: Author.

Massachusetts Department of Education. (2000, November). *Spring 2000 MCAS tests: Report of state results.* Malden: Author.

Massachusetts Department of Education. (2001a, January 9). *2000 school performance ratings issued for Massachusetts public schools.* Retrieved from www.doe.edu/ata/ratings00/

Massachusetts Department of Education. (2001b, October). *Spring 2001 MCAS tests: Report of state results.* Malden: Author.

Massachusetts Department of Education. (2002a, January 23). *MCAS appeals process unanimously approved.* Retrieved from www.doe.mass.edu/news/news.asp?id=488

Massachusetts Department of Education. (2002b, August). *Progress report on the class of 2003.* Malden: Author.

Massachusetts Department of Education. (2002c, August). *Spring 2002 MCAS tests: Summary of state results.* Malden: Author.

Massell, D. (2000). *The district role in building capacity: Four strategies* (CPRE Policy Brief RB-32). Philadelphia: Consortium for Policy Research in Education, University of Pennsylvania.

Phillips, S. E. (2000). G.I. Forum v. Texas Education Agency: Psychometric evidence. *Applied Measurement in Education, 13*(4), 343–385.

Public Agenda. (2001). *Reality check 2001.* Retrieved from www.publicagenda.org/specials/re2001/

Scutari, C. (2001, April 6). AIMS test not going to public vote. *The Arizona Republic.*

Spillane, J. P., & Thompson, C. L. (1997). Reconstructing conceptions of local capacity: The local education agency's capacity for ambitious instructional reform. *Educational Evaluation and Policy Analysis, 19*(2), 185–203.

Wise, L. L., Sipes, D. E., Harris, C. D., George, C. E., Ford, J. P., & Sun, S. (2002). *Independent evaluation of the California high school exit examination (CAHSEE): Analysis of the 2001 administration.* Alexandria, VA: Human Resources Research Organization.

Wise, L. L., Sipes, D. E., Harris, C. D., Collins, M. M., Hoffman, R. G., & Ford, J. P. (2000). *High school exit examination (HSEE): Supplemental year one evaluation report.* Alexandria, VA: Human Resources Research Organization.

Wise, L. L. et al. (2003). *Independent evaluation of the California High School Exit Examination (CAHSEE): AB 1609 study report.* Alexandria, VA: Human Resources Research Organization.

Chapter 12

Conclusion: The Problem of Stakes in Performance-Based Accountability Systems

Richard F. Elmore

PERFORMANCE-BASED ACCOUNTABILITY: A WORK IN PROGRESS

If nothing else, the chapters in this book demonstrate that performance-based accountability is much more a work in progress than a finished product. The current message of policy makers and advocates, fearing retrenchment on reforms to which they are attached, is "stay the course." But stay the course with what? As with any policy idea, performance-based accountability, at its best, is a skeletal design—a set of highly provisional ideas about what needs fixing in American education and how it should be fixed—which is played out in a complex institutional, political, and organizational arena. The test of this policy's success is not whether it survives "intact" in this arena, but whether it is robust enough, both in its initial design and in its myriad adaptations to specific problems and contexts, to influence behavior and values in a powerful way.

There is abundant evidence that this policy is more robust than any other in the field of education over at least the past 40 years. Performance-based accountability continues to dominate the policy agenda in states and localities as it has for the past decade-plus—a remarkable accomplishment in a political environment where reform agendas typically have shifted from year to year. With certain important exceptions, there has been a general increase in the clarity and utility of content standards over time, as well as an increase in the degree of alignment between tests and content standards (see Rothman, this volume).

There is also evidence that the fundamental message that content and performance standards should influence classroom practice has reached teachers in elementary and high schools (see Herman and Siskin, this volume), although not always in the form that policy makers intended. The idea of treating special education students and English-language learners as part of the same opportunity and accountability structure as other students is clearly embodied in policy at the federal and state levels, if not in practice at the local and school levels (Thurlow, this volume). There is a growing body of evidence that student performance, for African Americans and Whites, if not for Hispanics, is increasing, especially in strong reform states, while retention and progression are not adversely affected (Carnoy & Loeb, this volume). The recent reauthorization of the federal Title I program, No Child Left Behind, is an unprecedented use of federal money and authority to promote what has been, up to the present, primarily a state reform agenda, signaling an even longer-term commitment to performance-based accountability.

Another sign of whether performance-based accountability is a robust policy idea is whether policy makers are astute enough to recognize when it is necessary to make changes in policy design in response to new information about the policy's effects. As Fuhrman, Goertz, and Duffy (this volume) argue, there is abundant evidence that states at least are trying to manage the issue of stakes for students so as to maintain the political momentum of the reform while adjusting its specific provisions to the realities of implementation.

It is unlikely then that this reform will recede in the foreseeable future. If anything, political pressure for school performance will increase. This said, it is also clear that the reform's weaknesses and gaps will become increasingly apparent the further and deeper it extends into the complex institutional structure of public education. The issues here are both technical and organizational.

On the technical side, it is evident that what policy makers and the informed public *think* performance-based accountability is, differs considerably from what it *actually is*. In political discourse, it is common to hear both opponents and advocates speak as if test results were the metric of success in performance-based accountability. As Baker and Linn, and Herman (this volume) demonstrate, the idea of equating student learning with test performance is suspect, both in terms of the technical characteristics of tests and the incentive effects of testing on instruction. The key issue

here—probably regarded as excessively fussy and technical by reform advocates—is that no test, no matter how sound, can do more than *sample*
what students actually know in a given domain, and even at that, the conclusions one draws from test results about both student and school performance are subject to severe limits on reliability. Using tests as the exclusive
measure of performance for accountability purposes can distort conclusions
about what students actually know, by substituting knowledge in the sample for knowledge in the domain, and can influence instruction and school
organization in counterproductive ways by focusing attention on measures
of improvement that do not necessarily represent evidence of strong
learning.

The antidotes for these misuses of tests are obvious but difficult to
focus on in the rattling din of largely ill-informed debates about testing:
strong curriculum-embedded assessments of student learning that are immediately available to teachers as they engage in instruction; strong content
knowledge on the part of teachers and administrators so they can distinguish between the sample that the test measures and the domain that defines what students are expected to know; knowledgeable use of tests, with
a full awareness of their technical limits; multiple measures of instructional
quality and student performance, with no high-stakes decisions based on a
single measure; and, above all, adherence to clear principles of test use and
design for accountability systems of the type outlined by Baker and Linn
(this volume). Most of this advice is currently ignored, or attended to only
marginally, in the design and implementation of state accountability systems. A big part of the problem in the technical arena is that policy makers
and reform advocates often think they know more about testing than they
do, and as a consequence they think they are advocating for and implementing policies that are, in fact, quite different from what they think. Danger
lies here.

On the organizational side, it is clear that the complexities of improving
schools in the face of performance-based accountability are more apparent
to practitioners and researchers than they are to policy makers and reform
advocates. As both Herman and O'Day argue in this volume, the fundamental purpose of standards-based reform is not to improve test scores for students and schools, nor is it to get teachers to comply with external direc-
tives about what to teach—these are indicators of success, not success
itself. The purpose of standards-based accountability is to increase students'
access to academic content and to improve the quality of teaching and
learning in schools. Depending on the test and the initial performance of
students, it is possible, within limits, to increase test scores without significantly increasing either students' access to academic content or the quality
of teaching and learning. And the evidence accumulates that the schools

that most need improvements in access, teaching, and learning are often the ones that focus most on test scores and least on deeper improvements. This result is a classic example of what organizational sociologists call goal displacement: The challenging goal set by policy makers—in this case, improvement in access and learning—is displaced in favor of the easier, more feasible goal of teaching test items.

O'Day demonstrates that improving the academic culture of a school—particularly a low-performing school—is much less a problem of complying with the dictates of accountability policy than it is literally one of building an organization around a fundamentally new idea of itself, and this process is multilayered, extending from the individual, to the collegial group, to the school, to the system in which the school resides. Siskin (this volume) argues persuasively that this process of reconstructing schools is dramatically more complex for high schools than it is for elementary schools, and that the task is much more urgent for high schools because they are, by definition, the end of the line and the final reckoning for students.

While policy makers pay lip service to the problems of organizational capacity in schools and school systems responding to performance-based accountability, there is little evidence that states and localities have worked out the actual processes by which schools will become more coherent, instructionally focused organizations. The potential and actual disconnect between the testing side of performance-based accountability systems and the capacity-building side can only become more apparent—and more dangerous—as these systems work their way into schools and classrooms.

A central issue—if not *the* central issue—that joins these multiple concerns about the future of performance-based accountability, is stakes. At some point in the process of assessing students' and schools' performance, the assessing stops and the stakes fall. Accountability without stakes of some kind is a shadow game. In this concluding chapter, I will address the issue of stakes as an organizing theme in accountability policy.

THE PROBLEM OF STAKES: POLITICS, POLICY, AND PUBLIC ETHICS

Performance-based accountability systems operate on the theory that measuring performance, when coupled with rewards and sanctions—one version of what I will refer to here as stakes—will cause schools and the individuals who work in them, including students, teachers, and administrators, to work harder and perform at higher levels (for similar treatments of the theory of action behind standards-based accountability, see Fuhrman, Baker & Linn, Rothman, and Herman, this volume). The idea is appealingly simple: design an incentive structure that rewards students for engaging their energy in learning academic content at high levels, teachers for teaching a broad range of students more effectively, and schools for organizing themselves to manage instruction more effectively. This idea has achieved considerable social and political credibility with the spread of standards-based, or performance-based, accountability systems at the state and local levels. It recently has become the centerpiece of federal policy with the passage of the No Child Left Behind Act—the revised Title I of the Elementary and Secondary Education Act—which, among other things, requires states to engage in annual testing for individual students in grades 3–8. It sets in place rewards and sanctions based on state-prescribed formulas for annual increments in school performance. And it requires states to disaggregate student performance data by school, based on student demographics.

An important part of the working theory of these policies is that performance-based accountability is a necessary condition for large-scale improvements in student learning and school quality, and addressing the so-called "achievement gap" between poor, minority students and others. Absent a strong and coherent message, carried through the stakes these systems embody, schools will do what they want to do for students, or what they think it is possible to do, without necessarily paying attention to what they *might* be able to do if they were working at higher levels of effectiveness.

Another part of the working theory—less explicit than the former—is that students can be motivated to invest more in their own learning by being given direct feedback on their academic performance, benchmarked against statewide standards, and by bearing consequences, ranging from retention in grade to withholding diplomas, for failure to meet those standards.

Performance-based accountability systems are, to say the least, works in progress. Their designs are still schematic and, in many respects, underspecified. This reality is often lost in the highly charged political debate over the particularities of such systems. As noted above, it is difficult for policy advocates—or opponents, for that matter—to acknowledge that there are many things we do not know about the essential elements of accountability systems. Indeed, there are many things we can't possibly know except by experimenting and observing the results of these systems on the ground.

Nowhere is this question of what we don't know more apparent than in the issue of stakes. State policies require proficiency levels for grade promotion and graduation for students, for example, without any empirical evidence or any defensible theory about how much it is feasible to expect students to learn over a given period of time or what types of instruction have to be in place in order for students to meet expected rates of improvement (see Linn, this volume). Likewise, state policies set expected levels of improvement in schools without any evidence or theory about how schools actually respond to external pressure for student performance, and whether the ways in which they respond do or do not benefit students (see O'Day and Siskin, this volume). In addition, the tests on which stakes are based are fallible and limited measures; the statements they make about student and school performance carry margins of error for both students and schools, making clear judgments about performance difficult (see Baker & Linn, this volume). These limits of tests are overlooked routinely in current accountability policies.

State accountability policies are essentially political constructs; they represent consensus positions among key political actors about what it is reasonable and essential to expect students and educators to do about academic learning. These policies carry the authority of law. But they are also highly provisional social experiments. Most of the knowledge required to make them work more effectively—to meet the goals that policy makers want to accomplish and deliver the benefits that they promise to individuals—can be acquired only through observing how the policies actually work and developing more elaborate and complex understandings of how students and educators actually respond to the incentives they carry.

Acknowledging what we do and don't know about performance-based accountability carries an ethical, as well as a political, responsibility. If we actually don't understand the underlying parameters of a policy and therefore cannot predict their effects, is it ethical to use the policy to deliver life-altering consequences for individuals? We know, for example, with about as much certainty as it is possible to know anything in social science, that school attainment affects future income, and that attainment is related to cognitive skills that have value in the workplace (Murnane & Levy, 1993; Murnane, Willett, & Levy, 1995). The more years of schooling one acquires, the higher one's income. We also know that graduating from high school carries a substantial income premium, as does any participation in postsecondary education after high school. We know with some reasonable degree of certainty that retention in grade substantially increases the likelihood that one will fail to complete high school. Retention in grade once significantly increases the likelihood of dropping out; retention in grade twice makes it more likely than not that one will fail to complete high school.

Is it ethical, in these circumstances, to deny grade promotion and/or high school graduation to students based on policies that embody highly uncertain theories about the effect of incentives on the behavior of students and educators? In order to make a powerful ethical case for policies like this, one has to argue at least one of three positions: (1) the collective good that follows from the policy exceeds the sum of the individual costs entailed in the policy, and the collective good has been politically determined to be worth pursuing in its own right; (2) the individuals who are hurt by the policy are, in some sense, responsible for their own fate—they have, in effect, chosen the consequences they are bearing; or (3) those who are hurt by the policy, but not responsible for its consequences, can in some way be compensated by the winners for the damage they have borne.

Another, more slippery kind of ethical problem grows out of the question of whether organizations, or collectivities, actually can be held accountable for their impact on the life chances of individuals. A central premise of performance-based accountability policies is that they hold schools accountable for the performance of individual students. As we shall see in more detail later, the school as an organized entity can be a very elusive construction. Many schools in high-poverty neighborhoods, for example, have highly unstable student enrollments, high teacher turnover, and significant administrative turnover. These schools are the primary targets of the most punitive provisions of most accountability policies. Yet, in what sense are they "organizations," and in what sense can they be held collectively "accountable" for their impact on students? The central fact of their existence is that they have little or no binding capacity to act as organizations, and since many of the people who are present in the organization at time 1 are not present at time 2, it is questionable what or whom one is holding accountable for what. One possible answer is that it is not the school itself but the sponsoring organization—the school system—that is accountable. But, of course, the whole point of accountability for performance is that it is supposed to be located in the place where the work actually is performed, not in some distant place. What does it mean, then, to say that we hold a school accountable for its impact on students, when the membership of the organization is unstable and its very capacity to make binding choices as an organization is questionable? Can we discharge our public responsibility in any meaningful ethical way by charging manifestly incompetent, or incapacitated, organizations to be accountable for their impact on students when they are organizations in name only? Under what conditions does it become plausible to assume that school is actually a school for purposes of accountability?

Another problem arises out of the knowledge and competence of educators in schools. Is it ethical to hold individuals—in this case, educators—accountable for doing things they don't know how to do and can't be expected to do without considerable increase in their own knowledge and skill? It is plausible to assume that educators actually know how to substantially improve student performance, but that they are for some obscure reason withholding this knowledge because they have been insufficiently motivated or rewarded by the existing incentive structure?

The idea that teachers and administrators actually would refrain from doing something they know would contribute to student learning because they are insufficiently motivated or rewarded seems highly implausible. The more likely possibility, and the one that emerges from research on account-ability in this volume and in other places, is that educators literally do not know what to do. That is, they don't possess the knowledge and skill neces-sary to produce the kind of learning necessary to meet the requirements of performance-based accountability systems, and, more important, the account-ability systems themselves don't provide the knowledge and skill necessary to do the work. Whose responsibility is it to provide this knowledge and skill? Is it the responsibility of educators themselves to somehow find out what to do and then do it? Or is it a problem of collective responsibility? If it is collective, in whom does it reside? If it resides outside the school, who has the incentive to provide it and to raise the resources necessary to provide it? More important, can people in schools be held accountable for their effects on student learning if they haven't been provided with the opportunity to acquire the new knowledge and skill necessary to produce the performance that is expected of them?

There is a major ethical problem in the politics of stakes applied to students. When stakes are applied to educators—to teachers, administra-tors, and the organizations in which they work, as well as locally elected officials who are responsible for governing schools—they are applied to adult individuals who have the means to defend themselves politically against the consequences of the actions levied against them. They can, and do, engage in political action to shape and mitigate the impact of the poli-cies on them.

Students are, by virtue of their age and status, unable to act on their own interests with the same political force and authority as adults. They are represented in the debate on stakes, if they are represented at all, largely by adults, who claim to speak for students' interests, but who have their own individual and organizational interests that usually supersede the inter-ests of the students whom they claim to represent. The claim, "We're doing this for the students," usually means that there is a more or less bald appeal to some interest other than students following close behind. Insofar as stu-dents bear the consequences of performance-based accountability policies, then, they bear them as an indirectly represented party to the political de-bate that shapes the consequences for them.

It is not coincidental that policy makers speak of students largely as passive participants in accountability systems—people to whom account-ability provisions are addressed but who are seen as having no active role in determining the nature of these provisions—and that the politics of ac-countability are dominated by institutional interests—school systems, pro-fessional organizations, private-sector advocacy groups—who claim to speak both for their own interests and for the interests of students. In a pluralist democracy, which rewards the capacity to mobilize and voice political interests, being an unorganized and unrepresented interest is a serious liability. When other organized interests all claim to speak for someone, it is safe to say that none of them do. How do we exercise responsibility for the consequences of policies that fall on individuals who are unrepresented in the processes by which those policies are made and implemented?

Finally, it is important to acknowledge that performance-based accountability systems don't actually *create* stakes for students and educators; it is more accurate to say that they rearrange and redefine stakes. This is a political and ethical point that often is conveniently overlooked by vocal opponents of performance-based accountability systems. They often argue as if there were no stakes for students before the advent of formal accountability systems, which is, of course, manifestly untrue. Students who went to low-quality schools before formal accountability came into play got the same low-quality instruction the day before the systems went into effect as they got the day after, and they were adversely affected by that instruction—that is, there were "stakes" attached to being poorly educated. That these stakes were largely buried and invisible makes them no less real or consequential for the individuals involved. Students in low-quality schools pay a high price for being there. Likewise, educators working in low-quality or mediocre schools also could be said to bear the consequences of neglect—being chronically unsuccessful with students can hardly be said to be satisfying work. Accountability systems don't so much create stakes, then, as rearrange and redefine them, in some instances making the socially and politically sanctioned aims of schooling more explicit and locating responsibility more clearly in specific individuals. It is simply not accurate to say that this rearrangement and redefinition of stakes puts stakes where there were none before.

What is most notable about accountability policies, as they presently exist, is their avoidance of these issues in the details of their design and implementation. As states face the possibility of denying high school diplomas based on graduation exams, retaining students in grade based on proficiency tests, and closing failing schools, the problem of who is actually responsible for student failure has become deeply politicized. Opponents of "high-stakes" testing argue that performance-based accountability systems are inherently unfair to students and teachers, conveniently ignoring the fact that these systems exist because of the manifest failure of many schools to provide adequate learning for these same students in the past. Supporters of performance-based accountability systems respond to their critics by, on the one hand, arguing that it is important to stay the course with stakes in order to demonstrate the gravity of the problems facing schools and students, while on the other hand, publicly and privately exploring ways to reduce or alter the impact of stakes on students and schools (see Fuhrman, Goertz, & Duffy, this volume). Neither side of this debate seems comfortable publicly acknowledging that there may be much that we collectively don't know about how to design and implement accountability policies, that it is important to try to learn something about how these policies actually work, and that the level of uncertainty that surrounds the issue of stakes carries with it the ethical responsibility to be temperate in our actions.

THE THEORY AND PRACTICE OF STAKES : REASONING OUT FROM THE INSTRUCTIONAL CORE

Stated as a problem of policy design, the central issue is *on whom* stakes should fall and *with what consequences* in order to cause the level of *improvement* or *performance* that policy makers want. Stated as a problem of a theory of action, the central issue is the relationship between the allocation and intensity of stakes, on the one hand, and individual and organizational responses, on the other. That is, what kinds of stakes are likely to evoke what kinds of responses in which parties under what conditions?

The key gaps in existing accountability policies lie in the interstices of these questions. What behavior and resources are stakes supposed to mobilize? From whom? What is a good result? What are the preconditions that lead to a good result? And if these preconditions don't exist, how can they be mobilized?

Since the nominal purpose of accountability systems is to increase the quality of academic learning in schools and, hence, to increase student performance, it is hard to imagine a theory of how stakes work in schools that doesn't involve a theory of the instructional core and its relationship to the setting in which it sits. "Something" is supposed to happen as a result of schools and the individuals in them coming to terms with their performance and the stakes that are attached to it. What that "something" is, is largely unspecified in accountability systems.

Student, teacher, content

Many of us who work on issues of policy and its relationship to learning have been deeply influenced by David Hawkins's important formulation of the instructional core as the relationship between the "I" (the teacher), the "Thou" (the student), and the "It" (the content). Hawkins (1974) argues:

> No child . . . can gain competence and knowledge, or know [her]self as competent and as a knower, save through communication with others involved with

[her] in [her] enterprises. Without a Thou, there is no I evolving. Without an It there is no content for the context, no figure and no heat, but only an affair of mirrors confronting each other. (p. 52)

Becoming a competent learner, Hawkins continues, involves a gradual process of intentional emancipation of the student from the teacher as the mediator of content, accompanied by the development the knowledge, skill, and understanding necessary to become one's own teacher. This process depends heavily, Hawkins argues, on the capacity of educators, and eventually students, to make dispassionate and clear judgments about the extent and depth of their learning in the context of specific body of knowledge.

The child's overt involvement in a rather self-directed way, using the big muscles and not just the small ones, is most important to the teacher in providing an input of information wide in range and variety. . . . [T]he first act of teaching . . . the first goal, necessary to all others, is to encourage this kind of engrossment. The child comes alive for the teacher as well as the teacher for the child. They have a common theme for discussion, they are involved together in the world. . . . I remember being very impressed by the way some people, in an encounter with a young child would seem automatically to gain acceptance while other people, in apparently very friendly encounters with the same child, would produce real withdrawal and, if they persisted, fear and even terror. Such was the well-meaning adult who wanted to befriend the child—I and Thou—in vacuum. It's traumatic, and I think we all know what it feels like. I came to realize (I learned with a good teacher) that one of the very important factors in this kind of situation is that there be some third thing which is of interest to the child *and* to the adult, in which they can join in outward projection. Only this creates a possible stable bond of communication, of shared concern. (Hawkins, 1974, pp. 55, 57–58)

And, one might say, of common understanding. The purpose of stakes—of *any* incentive designed to affect academic performance—is to mobilize commitment, energy, and knowledge around the student's and teacher's mutual engagement in the content. To the degree that the student and teacher are in concert around this task, rather than in conflict, the level of engagement is likely to be high; to the degree that the student and teacher are in conflict, the level of engagement is likely to be low.

The level of engagement depends in turn on the degree of competence that the teacher and student bring to their work. Being a good teacher means making one's own learning—both as a fact and as a process—manifest in relation to a particular body of content; it means being on display, in some sense, as a learner and modeling this process for students. Being a good student means being a good apprentice to the learning that is manifest in the practice of the teacher, and, over time, assuming increasing control over that process oneself. The relationship of the student and teacher is disciplined by the presence of challenging content; mastery of content is, in a sense, the standard by which teacher and student judge whether the relationship is about learning, and the degree to which they are learning, as opposed to a personal relationship or a relationship with some other instrumental purpose.

The success of this triangular relationship depends on building a sense of efficacy or agency on the part of the teacher and student. People, in general, enjoy doing what they perceive themselves to be good at, and avoid doing that which they perceive themselves to be unsuccessful at. Low efficacy elicits low engagement; high efficacy elicits high engagement. A successful incentive structure, then, is one that draws the student and the teacher into situations in which they build efficacy and agency. As this happens, many of the rewards of academic work come from the work itself— the developing sense of efficacy and influence over the conditions of one's own learning—and fewer come from the external rewards and sanctions that accompany the work.

In this relationship, the teacher's sense of efficacy comes from the observed effects of her work with the student; that is, the teacher's agency is manifested in what the student produces by way of evidence of learning for the teacher in the moment. Immediate feedback from the student's learning is the most proximate source of motivation and indication of efficacy for the teacher. Getting this feedback requires: (1) that the teacher be competent enough in the content and pedagogy required to engage the student, (2) that the student be willing to engage the teacher at least to the extent that she provides some evidence of learning, and (3) that there is some common means for the teacher and student to understand the joint product of their work.

The student's sense of efficacy comes from a kind of willing suspension of disbelief in which the student agrees to engage the teacher around the content on the—often largely unmet—expectation that she will learn something that will have value, either intrinsically or in relation to some goal the student wants to reach. A good part of creating efficacy and agency in students consists of not just knowing how to teach but also understanding what it is that might have value to the student and making that value explicit in the relationship. When teachers say that some students are "easier" to teach than others, what they are observing is that some students come into the relationship equipped with a set of understandings that lead them to value certain things that the teacher regards as important—or at least they are compliant enough to suspend their disbelief in the lack of value. Some students—probably most students at risk of academic failure—come equipped with no such understandings and, possibly because of their previous academic experience, are unwilling to suspend their disbelief and may be actively resistant to what they regard as chronically unsuccessful teaching.

A student's academic competence—and therefore her ability to extract efficacy, agency, and value around learning with a given teacher—is a joint product of what the student knows and believes as a consequence of *prior* teaching, as well as the learning that grows out of *present* teaching. When judgments about the effectiveness of teaching are based on student performance at a single point in time, these judgments send very mixed signals to individual teachers and cloud the relationship between the student's learning and the teacher's sense of efficacy. What exactly is the teacher responsible for? The student's performance at a given moment? The learning that the teacher adds to the student's performance as a consequence of their interaction? Or some compound of the two? If the teacher is not responsible for the learning of the student that occurred, or didn't, before the student arrived in her classroom, who is? Holding prior teachers responsible for current levels of learning has value possibly for the present students of those teachers, but no value at all for the student in her present circumstances, since she can't recoup learning that failed to occur in the past.

At some point, the incentives that power the relationship between the teacher and the student lose their traction, failures become cumulative, and we have to invent organizational or collective incentives to minimize the likelihood that unsuccessful teachers will pass their failures on to others with impunity. We will come to this issue in a moment.

Reasoning out from the academic core allows us to think about stakes in terms of their capacity to mobilize and engage students and teachers in the common work of understanding content and in the larger task of passing the work of learning from the teacher to the student. As a general rule, incentives that draw the teacher and student together around the content are more likely to produce higher levels of academic learning than those that don't. Incentives that increase the level of competence of teachers as teachers (in the presence of content) and the level of competence of students as students (likewise) are more likely to produce higher levels of learning than those that don't. Incentives that reinforce the importance of academic content as the mediator of the relationship between students and teachers are more likely to result in higher levels of academic learning than those that don't. And incentives that focus on the learning that occurs between the teacher and student in the present, rather than those that hold the present teacher responsible for the student's past learning, are more likely to engage teachers.

Schools and school systems

It also seems evident that teachers and students who are incompetent at the work of learning have very strong incentives to displace responsibility, efficacy, and agency away from themselves and onto others. If the work of being a teacher and a student lacks meaning, if teachers and students lack the prerequisite knowledge and skill to engage one another in useful ways, and if the conditions of the work are such that it is not clear what the expectations are for what will be learned and how, then it makes sense for teachers and students to blame one another for failure, for teachers to blame previous teachers, and for educators in general to blame the communities and families from which students come. This is a world in which everyone except oneself is responsible for what happens. Low performance breeds low sense of efficacy, which in turn breeds low efficacy, and so on. How this changes is a subject we will return to shortly.

We get to the problem of organizations, as noted above, by confronting the problem that, other things being equal, ineffective teachers can easily pass their failures on to others, and the success of teachers and students at time 2 is heavily mediated by the success of the same students with other teachers at time 1. It is impossible, in other words, to solve the problem of increasing the performance of teachers and students in one classroom without also solving that problem in schools and school systems more generally.

American schools, on average, are notorious for being perilously close to organizations in name only. In the modal school, there is very little interaction among teachers around academic work. Most teachers think of their teaching practice as highly individual and idiosyncratic, and the data support the conclusion that there is more variation in instructional practice and student performance among classrooms in the United States than in any other industrialized country. Content is largely textbook-driven; textbooks emphasize topical coverage rather than understanding, continuity, and depth.

As students advance from elementary to secondary schools, they confront increasingly complex and unintegrated organizations. In many middle schools and most high schools, the subject-matter department is the dominant organizational unit above the classroom, for management purposes, not the school as a whole. Schools at this level are largely organizational fictions, at least in terms of the way they affect the actual work of teachers and students around content. In these organizations, adults function with relative autonomy in classrooms, with minimum oversight on curriculum from the departmental level, and virtually no influence on academic work from the school or system level. Students are the main source of continuity in these schools since they are the only members of the organization who are required to travel across internal boundaries in order to get their work done. Adults take little or no responsibility for the continuity and coherence of students' experience from one part of the organization to another. Learning, from the students' perspective, is a composite of discrete, often idiosyncratic, experiences accumulated into patterns that may or may not represent progress through a body of knowledge (see Siskin, this volume).

Local school districts, in their modal state, are similarly fictitious as organizations engaged in the propagation of learning. The leadership patterns and policy agendas of school districts are chronically unstable, reflecting the electoral cycles of local school boards and the weak incentives for retention of school superintendents. Systems tend to move restlessly from one policy and administrative initiative to another, with no direct connection to the academic core.

It is difficult to imagine an organizational form that is any *less* adapted to the demands of consistent, high-level engagement of students and teachers around content in the ways described above. Schools, in their modal form, are designed to buffer teachers from virtually any interference in the academic core; schools, and the people who work in them, have limited to no capacity either to influence or to improve instructional practice. Districts, which have nominal responsibility for the improvement of instruction, tend, if they have any capacity at all, to reinforce patterns of volunteerism, idiosyncrasy, and instability of goals in the way they deliver assistance to teachers and schools.

It is absolutely essential to understand that when policies lay down stakes on incoherent organizations, the stakes themselves do not cause the organizations to become more coherent and effective. The stakes are mediated and refracted by the organizations on which they fall. Stakes, if they work at all, do so by mobilizing resources, capacities, knowledge, and competencies that, by definition, are not present in the organizations and individuals whom they are intended to affect (see Herman, Siskin, and O'Day, this volume). If the schools had these assets in advance of the stakes, they presumably would not need the stakes to mobilize them. In this context, stakes make no sense as policy instruments unless they are joined in some systematic way with assistance that is designed to create the organizational assets that are required to respond to the stakes. In the absence of this kind of assistance, most schools and systems will respond within the constraints of their existing assets, which are, by definition, inadequate to respond to the task.

This view accords with the developing knowledge we have of how schools respond to external accountability systems that carry stakes of various kinds. These accountability systems produce a range of responses, rather than a single type of response common across all schools and school systems (see Siskin, this volume; also see Abelmann & Elmore, 1999). The best predictor of how a school will respond to the introduction of stakes at time 1 is its organizational culture and capacity at time 0; how a school looks at time 2, other things being equal, after the application of stakes at time 1, will be some incremental departure from how it looked at time 0. Hence, schools that have a weak instructional core in academic subjects, and low rates of student access and success in those subjects, tend to respond to new accountability requirements by "gaming" the system—teaching test items, rather than changing access, content, and pedagogy in academic subjects; by focusing on students who are at the margins of the performance levels in the accountability system, rather than the lowest-performing students or all students; and by encouraging certain students to be absent on test days. With increasing pressure, these schools might add academic content and remediation, but, other things being equal, don't tend to make large improvements in their core instructional capacity. Schools that have higher initial capacity in the instructional core—greater access to more-demanding academic content, more attention to success in those domains, clearer expectations for student academic performance, and so on—tend to respond to the external pressure of stakes, even moderate to low stakes, with organizational improvements that give increasing focus and coherence to their existing capacities. Hence, stakes work, if they work at all, by mobilizing and expanding capacities in high-capacity schools and creating potential demand for capacities outside the organization in low-capacity schools. In the latter case, if there are no capacities to bring to the organization, there is little reason to expect the organization to do anything other than make incremental adjustments to already unsuccessful practices.

At the individual and collective levels, stakes work by mobilizing capacities in the service of higher-quality instruction and performance. At the individual level, high-quality instruction requires high mutual engagement of teachers and students in content. To the degree that teachers and students bring the skills and knowledge necessary to be successful in this relationship, they are able to create learning that has mutual value, either intrinsic or instrumental. The stakes, and the external goal they represent, may be a way of focusing this knowledge and skill; they do not create knowledge and skill where none existed before. At the collective level, stakes are refracted through school organization before they reach teachers and students. American schools are modally not well constructed to focus external stakes into a productive relationship with the instructional core; in fact, they are mainly built to diffuse these influences. Hence, when stakes are applied across a number of schools, they produce a range of responses related to the schools' internal capacities around initial capacities of the organizations they affect.

DESIGNING ACCOUNTABILITY POLICIES

As noted earlier, the goal of accountability systems is improvement in access and learning, not simply reward and punishment for performance. Improvement can be measured, in part, by the assessments used in accountability systems, but these systems do not, in themselves, provide the capacities to improve. Improvement requires high levels of engagement among teachers and students around demanding content, and engagement increases with efficacy and agency. The resources that enable this engagement vary by teacher, by school, and by school system. Stakes for schools and students are effective in promoting improvement insofar as they enable and reinforce this engagement. Several design principles follow from this analysis.

The first is, in some sense, the most obvious and the most difficult to incorporate into existing state accountability policies. It is that individual and collective *stakes should be based on defensible, empirically based theories about what it is possible to accomplish on measured performance within a given period of time*. State accountability systems, and now federal policy, have set in place systems that allocate rewards and sanctions on the basis of schools' progress toward performance goals at rates that are arbitrarily defined, and in some cases probably educationally and psychometrically impossible. The evidence that supports these goals and rates of improvement, insofar as it exists at all, comes from the systems themselves, not from any external assessment, or benchmark, of what it is possible to achieve. Since the accountability systems are corruptible—indeed, there are strong incentives embedded in the accountability systems themselves to make rates of improvement look better than they actually are—they should not be the sole basis for determining what it is possible to achieve. Schools and the individuals in them should not be held accountable for producing results that are educationally or psychometrically impossible.

The kind of research that is necessary to establish external benchmarks for rates of improvement in accountability systems inevitably would raise the issue of the level of resources and capacity necessary to produce results. Having an external benchmark for rates of improvement, then, becomes a way of raising policy issues about capacity.

Demand for an empirically based benchmark for rates of improvement also would force states and localities to develop, in practice, a more specific working theory of how the accountability system is supposed to produce improvement in student learning. No accountability system currently has such a working theory at any level of specificity that is useful as a guide to action for school administrators and teachers. There are no direct connections, for example, between the assessments that are used to judge the performance of schools in accountability systems and the formative assessments that schools actually would need to have in place in order to judge whether they are making progress with students on a day-to-day, month-to-month basis between testing points. There are no ways of assessing the skill and knowledge requirements of teachers necessary to meet the expectations for teaching practice that will result in the learning that the accountability systems require, or the resources for professional development required to achieve these expectations. There is no clear understanding of how to make curriculum content and alignment decisions that actually support teachers and students in learning that is engaging and has value to them, while at the same time meeting the expectations for performance. Accountability systems are, at this point, policy constructs in search of a theory of action.

The second design principle stems from the accountability standards outlined by Baker and Linn (this volume)—that *stakes should be based on valid, reliable, and accurate information about student and school performance*. Empirically grounded theories of performance and improvement require measures of performance that are sensitive to instruction, that are broadly based enough to represent useful information about the content domains they sample, and that are used in ways that are appropriate to their technical characteristics. It seems reasonable to expect also that the tests should be aligned with clear and understandable content standards (Rothman, this volume), that these content standards should be connected to performance standards that are likewise clear and adaptable to differences among students (see Thurlow and Heubert, this volume), and that the performance measures should be verifiable against other measures (see Carnoy & Loeb, this volume). A central standard in the framework outlined by Baker and Linn is the idea that no decision that has a major impact on a student should be made on the basis of a single measure, nor should students be judged based on a single opportunity to demonstrate performance. A critical part of the theory of stakes is to engage students progressively in their own learning. This process requires accurate and fair assessments of students' knowledge and skill, but it also requires that the incentive structure reward students for persistence, effort, and engagement, not simply for a single performance. Accountability systems, and the stakes they entail, also should work to solidify the relationship between the teacher and the student in the presence of the content—encouraging sustained engagement and ownership of academic work by teachers and students, rather than single events.

The third design principle is that *students should not be held accountable for learning content they have not been taught.* As an ethical and political matter, students are both the clients and the unrepresented constituents of accountability systems. The institutional interests of teachers, administrators, and school systems are well represented in the politics of accountability. Insofar as there are stakes levied against these interests, they have ways of defending themselves politically. Students do not have ways of defending themselves, except by relying on other institutions and individuals who have conflicting interests, or, disastrously, by withdrawing from a system to which they have not consented. In a society where educational attainment is heavily related to future income, retention in grade, denial of diplomas, and dropping out have consequences that are extremely serious for students.

As a practical matter, it makes no sense whatsoever to levy consequences on students for failing to demonstrate knowledge or mastery of content they have not been taught. At present, there are no safeguards in any state accountability system or in federal policy that would establish whether students actually have received instruction in the content that is contained in the tests that they are expected to pass. If schools and school systems were required to specify when, where, and how students were to receive instruction in the content they are expected to master—not in general, as in curriculum guides and course titles, but the actual event in which the instruction took place and its effect on student learning at that time— the question of whether student failure is a consequence of the student's lack of engagement or the failure of the system would become clearer.

Under the current design of accountability systems, student stakes, where they exist, fall unambiguously on individual students, but stakes for educators are highly diffused throughout the organizational structures in which they work. Stakes seldom, if ever, fall with equal severity on individual adults, or on the organizations in which they work. So it is relatively easy for accountability systems, in the absence of countervailing pressures, to ratchet up stakes on students—the unrepresented constituency—and to allow stakes for institutions and educators to become increasingly diffuse. The discipline of having to account for the actual instruction students receive and its initial effects creates a countervailing pressure for schools to pay attention to whether they are actually discharging their responsibility for instruction. If it is impossible to establish whether students actually have been taught the content on which they are being tested, then it is the institutions that should be accountable for the failure rather than the students.

Requiring schools and school systems to account for what they teach, to whom, how, and when also focuses attention on the prerequisite knowledge necessary for students to meet performance standards and the issues of teacher knowledge and skill embedded in academic performance. Are students failing to meet performance standards because they have failed to attend school? Because they have been taught the content in a watered-down form that is not consistent with what they are expected to know? Because they cannot read at a high enough level to master the content? Because the teacher doesn't actually understand the content at a high enough level to meet the standards required of the student?

This principle presumably would require schools and school systems to develop much more individualized ways of understanding why students succeed and fail at academic work, and a much more detailed understanding of individual teachers' contributions to student learning. Most school systems currently have no way of following students' academic progress through the grade structure. Accountability systems operate at much too high a level of abstraction to make this possible; single test scores for individual students over time are neither very reliable nor very effective ways of diagnosing student learning. Tracking student performance over time requires formative assessments that are closer to the ground and more connected to the curriculum as it actually is taught.

The fourth principle is that *schools should be accountable for the value they add to student learning, not the effects of prior instruction; schools systems should be accountable for the cumulative learning of students over their career in the system*. Stakes, insofar as they fall on schools, should be assessed on the basis of what the school actually does or doesn't contribute to student learning, not on the basis of what the student has or hasn't learned in other schools. When a student enters ninth grade reading at the fifth-grade level, the school in which that student resides, and the teachers who engage that student, should be accountable for the increment in learning that occurs in their domain, against a reasonable standard of the progress that student should be able to make with high-quality instruction. The *system* is responsible for the fact that the student is reading at the fifth-grade level, and the system is therefore responsible for remediating the prior deficit that the student brings to ninth grade. To the degree that remediation occurs in the context of a specific school, then it should carry additional resources and these resources should carry additional accountability.

Exactly what it means for collectivities—such as schools and school systems—to be "accountable" for the value they add to student learning is, as we have seen, highly problematic. Collectivities have ways of diffusing stakes; the more pathological the organization, the more likely it is to deflect and diffuse the stakes that are leveled against it. Whereas stakes focused on individual students cannot be displaced, those focused on orga-nizations can be easily diffused. This problem is endemic to the design of accountability systems, but it can be mitigated by more specific and tar-geted reporting of performance data. School-level results should be re-ported, for example, by focusing on evidence of student growth as a conse-quence of instruction in that school. System-level results should focus on proportions of students failing to meet performance targets on a cohort basis, in the system as a whole, and proportions of students attending low-performing schools. The point is to focus on the type of data, their fre-quency, and the problems that schools and school systems should be ex-pected to do something about. Existing accountability systems, for the most part, send very confusing, and therefore relatively ineffective, signals about student performance—they do not differentiate between what a school adds to student performance and what that student brings to the school, they do not distinguish between what the school should be expected to do about student learning and what the system is responsible for, and they do not report information in ways that concentrate stakes on those who bear responsibility.

The fifth principle is *the reciprocity of accountability and capacity— for each increment in performance I require of you, I have an equal and reciprocal responsibility to provide you with the capacity to produce that performance*. Accountability systems do not produce performance; they mobilize incentives, engagement, agency, and capacity that produce perfor-mance. Accountability systems do not, for the most part, reflect any system-atic coordination of capacity and accountability, nor do they reflect any clear understanding of what capacities are required to meet expectations for performance and where the responsibility for enhancing those capaci-ties lies. A more specific and coherent theory of action for accountability systems would help. For example, in order to meet performance expecta-tions in a given content domain, teachers would have to reach a certain level of mastery of that content themselves, they would have to know how to engage students from a variety of starting points in that content, and they would require access to materials and formative assessments that would support their teaching, and the modeling of their own learning for students, in that content domain. Whose responsibility is it to ensure that these conditions are met? If it is the state that initiates the accountability requirement, then it is the state's responsibility to ensure that the capacities are in place to meet those requirements. But who actually provides the support that increases capacity, is a more complex question of comparative advantage. Districts have to have some presence, since they are the systems in which schools operate and they, as noted above, are responsible for performance problems that spill over school boundaries. Private providers might be more efficient in responding to demands for additional capacity, but they are unlikely to operate effectively in relation to accountability systems if they are not disciplined in some sense by state and local strategies. It is also not clear whether the knowledge and competence actually exist to provide the level of support to schools and teachers necessary to meet the demands of teaching required by performance standards. Are schools actually accountable for their own performance if they clearly can't provide the level of instruction necessary to meet standards, but no one, including the jurisdiction that initiates the accountability system, is able to provide them with support necessary to meet the expected level of instruction? To hammer on low-capacity, low-performing organizations, without providing investments in capacity, in effect encourages them to engage in practices that are not consistent with the goals of the accountability system.

Another difficult incentive problem lies in the domain of resources. There is substantial evidence now from school systems that have launched large-scale improvement processes that there are resources for investing in capacity at the school level that lie within the existing budgets of those organizations. To lay new resources on school systems, without requiring them to reallocate their own resources toward improvements in capacity, is to reinforce their own prior inefficiencies. So the principle of reciprocity also requires states—as the main agents of accountability—to orchestrate their own policies around capacity building, with the requirement that local school systems, and schools, should have to use their own resources first. The strategies for doing this are not well worked out.

The central fact of accountability systems as they presently exist is that they are political artifacts crafted out of relatively superficial and underspecified ideas to meet the demands of political action. They are not well-worked-out practical systems. They require substantial investments in developing working models of what it is possible to produce by way of performance on what sort of timeline, what capacities are required in order to produce these expectations, how those capacities will be provided, and what the impact of stakes, as they presently are constituted, will be on the actual improvement of instruction. These questions are central to the long-term success of performance-based accountability systems.

REFERENCES

Abelmann, C., & Elmore, R. F., with Even, J., Kenyon, S., & Marshall, J. (1999). *When accountability knocks, will anyone answer?* (CPRE Research Report No. RR-42). Philadelphia: Consortium for Policy Research in Education, University of Pennsylvania.

Hawkins, D. (1974). I, thou, and it. In *The informed visions: Essays on learning and human nature* (48–62). New York: Agathon Books.

Murnane, R., & Levy, F. (1993). Why today's high-school-educated males earn less than their fathers did: The problem and an assessment of responses. *Harvard Educational Review*, *63*(1), 1–19.

Murnane, R., Willett, J., & Levy, F. (1995). The growing importance of cognitive skills in wage determination. *The Review of Economics and Statistics*, 77(2), 251–266.

About the Contributors

Eva L. Baker is a Professor at the Graduate School of Education and Information Studies at the University of California–Los Angeles and Co-director of the National Center for Research on Evaluation, Standards, and Student Testing. She teaches courses in assessment policy, design, and technology. Her background was in curriculum development for young children, instructional technology, and teacher professional development, before she became interested in evaluation and assessment. Baker serves as the chair of the Board on Testing and Assessment of the National Research Council, and was a co-chair of the Joint Committee on the Revision of the *Standards for Educational and Psychological Testing* (published in 1999), sponsored by the American Educational Research Association, the American Psychological Association, and the National Council on Measurement in Education. Her current interests are the development of technology tools for assessing achievement and interpreting data, with work supported by the Office of Educational Research and Improvement and the Office of Naval Research.

Martin Carnoy is Professor of Education and Economics at Stanford University. He received his Ph.D. from the University of Chicago, Department of Economics. Before coming to Stanford in 1969, he was a Research Associate at the Brookings Institution. In 1984, he was the Democratic candidate for Congress in Silicon Valley. He has written on issues of economic policy, theories of political economy, the economics of education, and educational policy. He also has written extensively on educational financing issues, including the effect of vouchers on educational outcomes. Among his books are *The State and Political Theory* (1984); *Education and Work in the Democratic State* [with Henry Levin] (1985); *Faded Dreams: The Economics and Politics of Race in America* (1994); *Sustaining the New Economy: Work, Family and Community in the Information Age* (2000); and *All Else Equal: Are Private and Public Schools Different?* [with Luis Benveniste and Richard Rothstein] (2002).

Mark C. Duffy is a part-time consultant with the Consortium for Policy Research in Education (CPRE) at the University of Pennsylvania, as well as a full-time, stay-at-home dad. His research has focused on assessment and accountability policies across the United States. Duffy's publications with CPRE include the research report, *Assessment and Accountability Systems in the 50 States: 1999–2000*, and the chapter, "Resource Allocation in Reforming Schools and School Districts," in the book *School-Based Financing*. Duffy has a Master of Science degree in Public Policy from the Bloustein School at Rutgers, the State University of New Jersey.

Richard F. Elmore is the Gregory R. Anrig Professor of Educational Leadership at the Harvard University Graduate School of Education. He is also Co-Director of the Consortium for Policy Research in Education. Elmore's research focuses on the effects of federal, state, and local education policy on schools and classrooms. He is currently exploring how schools of different types and in different policy contexts develop a sense of accountability and a capacity to deliver high-quality instruction. He also has researched educational choice, school restructuring, and how changes in teaching and learning affect school organization. He teaches regularly in programs for public-sector executives.

Susan H. Fuhrman is Dean and the George and Diane Weiss Professor of Education at the Graduate School of Education, University of Pennsylvania. Fuhrman also serves as Chair of the management committee of the Consortium for Policy Research in Education. Fuhrman's research interests include state policy design, accountability, deregulation, and intergovernmental relationships. She also has conducted research on state education reform, state–local relationships, state differential treatment of districts, federalism in education, incentives and systemic reform, and legislatures and education policy. She is a member of the Board of Trustees of the Carnegie Foundation for the Advancement of Teaching, a member of the Council for Corporate and School Partnerships of the Coca-Cola Foundation, a member of the Board of Trustees of the Fund for New Jersey, and a member of the National Coalition on Asia and International Studies in the Schools.

Margaret E. Goertz is Professor of Education Policy in the Graduate School of Education at the University of Pennsylvania and a Co-Director of the Consortium for Policy Research in Education, where she specializes in the study of state and federal education finance and governance policy. Goertz has conducted extensive research on state education reform policies, state teacher testing policies, and state and federal programs for special-needs students. She recently concluded a 5-year study of standards-based reform in eight states and 23 districts in the United States, focusing on how teachers, schools, and school districts implement state standards and assessment and accountability policies. In addition, she recently conducted a study for the U.S. Department of Education of accountability policies in all 50 states and their interface with Title 1 policies. Goertz also has looked at how states, school districts, and schools are including students with disabilities in general education reforms and accountability systems. She has spoken and published extensively in the areas of state education reform. Her writings on standards-based reform and on state and local accountability have been published in *Phi Delta Kappan*, in the 100th yearbook of the National Society for the Study of Education, and by Teachers College Press.

Joan L. Herman is Co-Director of the National Center for Research on Evaluation, Standards, and Student Testing at the University of California–Los Angeles. Her research has explored the effects of testing on schools and the design of assessment systems to support school planning and instructional improvement. She is a frequent advisor to federal, state, and local agencies; a past-president of the California Educational Research Association; and current editor of *Educational Assessment*; and has held a variety of leadership positions in Division H of the American Educational Research Association and the National Organization of Research Centers.

Jay P. Heubert is an Associate Professor of Education at Teachers College, Columbia University, and Coordinator of the Education Leadership Program there. He is also an Adjunct Associate Professor at Columbia University's Law School. He teaches courses on law and education policy. He received his J.D. *cum laude* and his Ed.D. from Harvard University, where he taught from 1985 to 1998. He also served as chief counsel to the Pennsylvania Department of Education, a civil-rights lawyer at the U.S. Department of Justice, and a high school English teacher in rural North Carolina. In 1997–1998, he directed a congressionally mandated study of high-stakes testing for the National Academy of Sciences. A Carnegie Scholar (2000–2002), Heubert currently is conducting research exploring what is known about the effects of high-stakes testing on student achievement and retention, especially for students of color, immigrant students, and students with disabilities. In June 2001, he received the Harvard Graduate School of Education's Alumni Award for Outstanding Contribution to Education. He was co-editor of *High Stakes: Testing for Tracking, Promotion, and Graduation* (1999) and editor of *Law and School Reform: Six Strategies for Promoting Educational Equity* (1999).

Robert L. Linn is Distinguished Professor of Education at the University of Colorado at Boulder and Co-Director of the National Center for Research on Evaluation, Standards, and Student Testing. He is a member of the National Academy of Education. Linn has published over 200 journal articles and chapters in books dealing with a wide range of theoretical and applied issues in educational measurement and has received several awards for his contributions to the field, including the Educational Testing Service Award for Distinguished Service to Measurement, the E.L Thorndike Award, the E.F. Lindquist Award, the National Council on Measurement in Education Career Award, and the American Educational Research Association Award for Distinguished Contributions to Educational Research. He is the current (2002–2003) President of the American Educational Research Association.

Susanna Loeb is Assistant Professor of Education at Stanford University, specializing in the economics of education and the relationship between schools and federal, state, and local policies. She studies resource allocation, looking specifically at how the structure of state finance systems affects the level and distribution of funds to districts and how teachers' preferences affect the distribution of teaching quality across schools. She is particularly interested in issues of equity. She also studies poverty policies, including welfare reform and early-childhood education programs. Loeb received her Ph.D. in economics in 1998 from the University of Michigan, where she also received a Master in Public Policy degree.

Jennifer A. O'Day is currently a Principal Research Scientist at the American Institutes for Research. Since co-authoring two seminal papers on standards-based systemic reform in the early 1990s, O'Day has focused her research on school improvement, capacity building, and accountability in response to the standards movement. She is particularly interested in the equity implications of standards and accountability, and for the past six years has studied improvement efforts in low-performing urban schools targeted by state and local accountability systems. O'Day also has served on several national policy bodies, including the Pew Forum on Standards-Based Reform, the congressionally mandated Independent Review Panel for the National Assessment of Title I, and the Stanford Working Group on Federal Programs for Limited English Proficient Students. She has co-authored reports for the National Council on Educational Standards and Testing and the National Academy of Education, and has participated on technical advisory groups for national research and evaluation projects related to standards-based policies.

Robert Rothman is a nationally known education writer. He is a principal associate for the Annenberg Institute for School Reform and a consultant for various education organizations. Previously, Rothman was a Senior Project Associate for Achieve, Inc., and a study director for the Board on Testing and Assessment at the National Research Council, where he directed a study on standards-based assessment and accountability that produced the report *Testing, Teaching, and Learning: A Guide for States and School Districts*. Rothman was also the director of special projects for the National Center on Education and the Economy and a reporter and editor for *Education Week*. He is the author of *Measuring Up: Standards, Assessment, and School Reform* (1995) and numerous book chapters and articles on testing and education reform.

Leslie Santee Siskin, an expert on the American high school, is a sociologist of organizations and organizational change. Her research focuses on the structuring and restructuring of schools, on the sociocultural and political contexts of teachers' work, and, most recently, on issues of accountability, testing, and comprehensive school reform. In a series of books and articles, she has explored subject departments as sites where school structure, curriculum subjects, and teachers' lives intersect (realms of knowledge) and has raised the possibility of alternative configurations (subjects in question). She has taught at Hofstra and Harvard Universities and is currently a Research Scholar at the Institute for Social and Economic Research and Policy, Columbia University.

Martha L. Thurlow is Director of the National Center on Educational Outcomes. In this position, she addresses the implications of contemporary U.S. policy and practice for students with disabilities and English language learners, including national and statewide assessment policies and practices, standard-setting efforts, and graduation requirements. Thurlow has conducted research for the past 30 years in a variety of areas, including assessment and decision making, learning disabilities, early childhood education, dropout prevention, effective classroom instruction, and integration of students with disabilities in general education settings. Thurlow has published extensively on all of these topics. She was co-editor for 8 years of *Exceptional Children*, the research journal of the Council for Exceptional Children, and is associate editor of numerous journals.

Index